War and Peace wrestle desperately,
Fortune favouring first one and then the other.
May Peace – it is Europe's wish –
be victorious with splendid trophies!

Ambiguo pax et bellum
luctamine certant.
Pax, europa vovet,
laeta trophaea ferat!

THIRTY YEARS' WAR

THIRTY YEARS' WAR

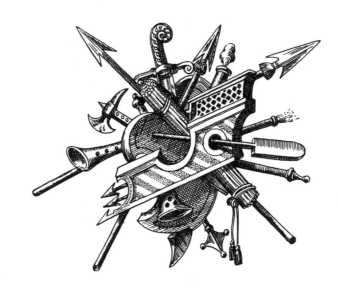

HERBERT LANGER

HIPPOCRENE BOOKS

NEW YORK, N.Y.

Translated from the German by C.S.V. Salt

Copyright © 1980 by Edition Leipzig
Design: Volker Küster
Produced by Druckerei Fortschritt Erfurt
ALL RIGHTS RESERVED
First Published in the United States 1980 by
HIPPOCRENE BOOKS, INC.
171 Madison Avenue
New York, N.Y. 10016
Library of Congress Catalog Card Number 79-90450
ISBN 0-88254-497-7

Printed in the German Democratic Republic

CONTENTS

INTRODUCTION

It is said that it was the English troops appearing on the Continental theatre of war in 1619/20 at the beginning of the Thirty Years' War who brought with them the custom of smoking the American tobacco plant which had already been known earlier in Spain and had been strictly prohibited in the Ottoman Empire. Despite mockery and learned tracts attacking it, the "drinking of tobacco" spread irresistibly throughout war-torn Central Europe and increasingly became the everyday habit of later generations. Almost unnoticed, however, in that eventful age, a transition took place from the older forms of printed material spreading the latest news to the regularly produced, printed newspaper. The Press, in the modern sense, had begun its career.

The art of war in Europe also changed in the course of these decades. The trend was in the direction of firearms and almost half the rank and file of a regiment were already musketeers. Some of the cavalry troops fought with short-barrelled guns or pistols and the artillery, becoming lighter and more manoeuvrable, was already a force to be reckoned with on the battlefield. The sting of gun-smoke obscured the scene for the combatants in action there. So that friend and foe could immediately be distinguished in the heat of battle, the first forms of uniform replaced the symbolic and coloured badges which were not easy to identify. And yet the greater the improvement in the methods of violent mass-destruction, the more powerful became the conscience and the accusing voice of the adversary.

It was in the middle of the Thirty Years' War (1618—1648) that a young Silesian poet wrote words of urgent warning. It is as if they were addressed to those alive today:

> "Eilt, dass ihr den Verstand zum Nutzen noch gebrauchet,
> Eh dann Europa ganz, das goldne Land, verrauchet!
> Ach, glaubt mir, einmal sich erretten von den Kriegen
> Ist mehr, als tausendmal unüberwindlich siegen."

Andreas Scultetus, from: Friedens Lob- und Krieges Leidgesang (1641)[1]

("Hasten, use your commonsense, Before the whole of Europe goes up in smoke, Believe me, avoiding wars is more Than a thousand victories.")

In their denunciation of every useless and senseless war of modern history, innumerable noble minds, artists and masters of the spoken and written word were still

You cannot take war across the countryside in a sack.

(17th century saying)

[1] Tränen des Vaterlandes. German Poetry from the 16th and 17th centuries. A Selection by Johannes R. Becher, Berlin, 1954, p. 229

to recall the fearful heritage of the 17th century as the omen, the first of the series of European wars, the historical model of all those that followed. From the description which has come down to us and which has been constantly supplemented by an infinite number of contemporary reports and even statistical evidence impossible to deny, the "Great War"— as it was called by the German author Gustav Freytag and later by Ricarda Huch—can be regarded as a star witness for the prosecution against war, as a political instrument of a special kind.

The list of battles fought during the war as such and in the wars associated with it are considerable when compared with subsequent European wars:

Bohemian-Palatinate Period (1618—1624)	8 battles:	Pilsen, Zablat, Prague I (White Hill), Wiesloch, Wimpfen, Höchst, Fleurus, Stadtlohn
Dutch-Danish Period (1625—1629)	4 battles:	Dessau Bridge, Lutter at the Barenberg, Stralsund, Wolgast
Swedish Period (1630—1635)	8 battles:	Frankfort on the Oder, Magdeburg, Werben, Breitenfeld I, Rain, Nuremberg, Lützen, Nördlingen I
Swedish-French Period (1635—1648)	13 battles:	Wittstock, Rheinfelden, Breisach, Breitenfeld II, Rocroi, Tuttlingen, Freiburg, Jankau, Mergentheim, Nördlingen II, Zusmarshausen, Prague II, Lens
Total	33 battles	

There are also estimates which put the figure at 80 major battles and sieges with a loss-rate of about 25 per cent.[1]

Military technology and the increase in hostilities led to a clear rise in firepower and destructive capability in the 17th century, the dawn of the manufacturing age. This is evident from the following estimate of the percentage of those killed in European wars:

12th c.—2.5 per cent	15th c.— 5.7 per cent	18th c.—14.6 per cent
13th c.—2.9 per cent	16th c.— 5.9 per cent	19th c.—16.3 per cent
14th c.—4.6 per cent	17th c.—15.7 per cent	20th c.—38.9 per cent

On account of the inaccuracy of the records available, only a rough estimate can be given of the total losses caused by the Thirty Years' War and its apocalyptic secondary manifestations—price increases, hunger, epidemics, diseases. About a quarter of the population were killed, i.e., some four to five millions. In the 1630's, the plague reaped its richest harvest, sweeping away more than half of the inhabitants in many parts of Germany. The losses in production materials and equipment, accommodation and cultural treasures can no longer be estimated, not even approximately. Imperial statesmen and diplomats reckoned that the Swedish soldiers destroyed or seriously damaged about 2,000 castles, 18,000 villages and 1,500 towns. A truly horrifying

[1] Eggenberger, D.: A Dictionary of Battles, London, 1971; Urlanis, B. Z.: Bilanz der Kriege, Berlin, 1965 (Russian edition Moscow, 1960)

result since this corresponded to about a third of all the houses in Germany. About half a century passed before the visible damage had been made good in town and countryside and in the landscape, too.[1] The worst losses were caused to domestic and farm buildings in rural areas and outside towns, to farming land—known as "war deserts" and to draught and slaughter animals. The total destruction of urban communities within fortified walls was not so frequent unless they were ravaged by fire, which was also a very common occurrence even in times of peace, of course. The sacking of towns resulted more from economic necessity than on account of military reasons and it developed as an uncontrolled privilege of the badly paid soldiery.

Great was the destruction caused by this long drawn out war, numerous were the sites designated as "deserted places" in the municipal tax-records and even more numerous were the devastated villages whose inhabitants were often obliged to flee

1 Mars, the God of War, begins his reign with fire and the torches of war. The guardians of peace are driven away and Justice departs from the world. Allegory of war. Copperplate engraving by Hendrick Goltzius, Moravská Gallery, Brno

[1] Handbuch der deutschen Wirtschafts- und Sozialgeschichte, ed. by H. Aubin and W. Zorn, vol. 1, Stuttgart, 1971

a dozen times at the approach of soldiers. Nevertheless, the picture of the complete devastation of the countryside conveyed by contemporary accounts which were often exaggerated and also influenced by the standards of our century is not an accurate one. Most buildings were constructed of wood, clay and straw and were thus more speedily replaced than those of stone. Reports of the depopulation of individual places at a certain time do not necessarily indicate an actual loss of life since the inhabitants might have returned at a later date or have settled down in the more peaceful parts of the vast realm. The forced appropriation of public or private funds did not always signify an economic loss but rather a redistribution in favour of the new owners. Trade links, fairs and branches of production vital for waging war suffered less than agriculture and its associated trades. Movable works of art, fine buildings, priceless libraries and archives were barbarically and senselessly destroyed on a scale impossible to estimate but many officers and generals were certainly aware of their value and took them away to safe places as *praeda militaris* or the booty of war.[1]

Deep marks were left by the terror and barbarity of the war in the consciousness and social behaviour of the broad masses of the people of Germany. This war seemed strange indeed to many of the authors of the time since the soldiery launched more raids and attacks against the peasants than the enemy on the field of battle. To be sure, the peasantry and the citizens of the towns did not allow themselves to be killed off without resistance and energetically defended themselves. Nevertheless, there remained the insistent question as to the why and wherefore of it in view of the numberless misdeeds of the apparently ever-present soldiers who fastened on to society like parasites. A punishment of Heaven or Hell of such severity and persistence surpassed the deeply rooted concept of human guilt and sin before God. The echo of despair to be heard everywhere, the questioning of the sense of earthly existence and the servility which was more common after the war than before are all signs that the self-confidence of broad masses of the population had suffered a serious setback.[2]

The view of the "national poverty" of Germany as presented by the bourgeois historians and poets should not make us lose sight of the destinies of other peoples during the Thirty Years' War. At this time, pictures such as the "European Theatre of War" or the "War Ballet" of the European potentates were all the rage and of the 50 wars from about 1600 listed in a news-sheet of 1650 the sections of the "Thirty Years' War" were noted only from the 32nd position onwards. Aleksander Brückner, the outstanding Polish linguistician and expert in literary and cultural history, considers that although Poland did not experience a Thirty Years' War the horrors of fifteen years of war (1649—1663) caused more damage to Poland's culture in half the time as compared with Germany.[3]

Although there can be no doubt that the Thirty Years' War was an especially bloody affair in the German-speaking area and in Bohemia, the events in Central Europe were entangled in a far-flung mesh of economic and political relations in Europe and overseas. Without Spanish silver from America, many a fleet would not have sailed, dozens of regiments would not have marched. Without the to and fro of the struggle for the *Dominium Maris*, the command of the Baltic, between Sweden, Poland and Russia, the course of the war at its climax is not to be understood. If the

[1] Franz, G.: Der dreissigjährige Krieg und das deutsche Volk. Untersuchungen zur Bevölkerungs- und Agrargeschichte, 4th edition Stuttgart, New York, 1979; Ergang, R.: The Myth of the all-destructive fury of the Thirty Years' War, Pocono Pines, 1956

[2] Poršnev, B. F.: Tridcatiletnjaja vojna i vstuplenie v nee Šcecii i Moskovskogo gosudarstva, Moscow, 1976, Chapter II

[3] Brückner, A.: Tysiąc lat kultury polskiej, vol. I, Paris, 1955

sultan had not been involved in an exhausting war with Persia—who knows whether the House of Hapsburg would have continued to survive.

There were two aspects to the war—the situation within Germany and that in Europe as a whole. Two groups of states emerged, even if this was sometimes only for a short period and clear only in outline: The Spanish-Hapsburg and the (essentially) Dutch-French sides. The former included the world-power of Spain with its Dutch and Italian possessions, the German Hapsburgs, the pope, Bavaria and some of the smaller German principalities; the second group, although at different times, consisted of the liberated Netherlands, England, France, Denmark, Sweden, Transylvania, Venice and the Protestant Union of Princes headed by the Palatinate. The first "camp" was intrinsically more stable but geographically more scattered, the second more cohesive but politically less stable.

In this complex and far-flung clash of interests, it was certainly a question of winning the "German civil war", which was a brawl between princes with religious overtones, for one side or the other. Nevertheless, something else was also involved which was incomparably more important: the consolidation of the first bourgeois republican state in the North of the Netherlands. After decades of war, the centre of feudal reaction—Spain—again took up the murderous struggle against the young Republic in 1621. The second historical contest which had to be settled was that between the outdated "imperial-universal" path of development and the "national state" approach, as embodied by France in particular. The German Reich, with its scattered territory, was an appropriate background for the staging of the European "War Ballet", it is true, but on this soil there were no questions of historic importance which had to be decided. Here princely power, already deeply rooted in social life—there the imperial dignity, here the Union—there the League, between them neutralist powers holding the balance—this was the situation along the fronts. In the contest between the living, it was difficult to say whether it was a question of religion or whether it was a matter of "region" and power; it remained the task of later scholars to draw a sober and clear dividing line. The "ecclesiastical element," meditated Goethe, "was the varnish with which passions and ambitions were coated to deceive oneself and others."[1] The contemporaries have left those that came later the idea and the concept of an uninterrupted "Thirty Years' War" (it could be said that it lasted even longer if considered from a different viewpoint) but they did not regard it as a typical "religious war", as it was subsequently portrayed by bourgeois historians. This is contradicted by basic facts in its course and especially by the collaboration, lasting some twenty years, of Catholic France with Protestant powers—the Netherlands and Sweden. Nevertheless, the great "Theatre of War" did not take place without religious disputes, slogans and motives. The state of development at this time did not yet offer any other view of the world for the masses than the religious one, nor for the ruling class nor even for the oppressed although it was precisely the Thirty Years' War and its forerunners which did much to discredit religion as a guide-line for living and governing.

One of the keenest minds of the time, the lyric poet Friedrich von Logau, found an apt comparison. He said that the "Great War" in its first half was like a lion still capable of great deeds; it subsequently changed into a goat defoliating everything

2 The dragon, assembled from military equipment and based on the shape of a cannon, is the largest of the imaginary figures in the etching "The Temptation of St. Anthony" (1635) by Jacques Callot.
Reproduction by Johann Wilhelm Baur. Art Collections Veste Coburg

[1] Goethes Gespräche. Gesamtausgabe. New edition by F. Frh. von Biedermann, 2nd vol., Leipzig, 1909, p. 156

11

and the "sweet custom" of making easy booty gained the upper hand.[1] In the words of the sensitive and poetic historian Ricarda Huch, the "Great War" was not like other wars but was a "disease on a shaken body which is allowed to continue because it cannot be combated".[2] This is the perception that the war resulted from an "out of phase" run of the world in a truly crisis-torn society which it, in turn, made worse. Since the national and social forces of progress in Central Europe were too weak, the only way out of this restless state was back into the old feudal society with its "forces of order"[3].

The Thirty Years' War has always held an irresistible attraction for authors, artists and musicians—whether in its heroic-tragic lion-form or in its nameless lamentation. The warlike clash of human passions contrasting with hard-headed calculating, splendour and misery, life and death alternating in quick succession, the collision of entire states and societies in the manner of gigantic battles—all this was and is still today a fascination for the creative imagination, providing an inexhaustible source of ideas for the arts, the lighter ones not excepted.

Schiller in 1786 admitted that his head became "quite hot" when reading the history of the Thirty Years' War. In 1796, after writing his "History of the Thirty Years' War" for the *Historical Calendar for Ladies* published by Göschen in Leipzig, he finally decided to give the Wallenstein theme a literary form. Schiller put his entire energy into the project and it became his greatest historical and classical drama.[4] Among the papers left behind at his death by Franz Grillparzer, the classical national poet of Austria, there was the manuscript of an historical state tragedy entitled "Ein Bruderzwist im Hause Habsburg" (A Brothers' Quarrel in the House of Hapsburg) and centred on the figure of the Emperor Rudolf II.[5] A few decades later, August Strindberg was working on a historical drama about Gustavus Adolphus with the sub-title of "The Thirty Years' War".[6] Brecht's "Mother Courage and Her Children", on the other hand, was not a historical drama, no more than the "Life of Galileo". It is essentially topical and, with the impact of its language and presentation, gives those who see it food for thought, forcing them to turn over in their minds the threatening question of the material nucleus of an exhausting war, such as that which again broke out in 1939 in a fearful form.

It was literally in the midst of the murderous events of the First World War that the highly individual novelist Alfred Döblin began to collect historical material and ideas for his Wallenstein epic. In his case, too, the historical event was only of a "material character"; Wallenstein, a "gigantic figure" and not at all in the manner of Schiller's "hero", represents the archetype of the successful winner of wars and the events which follow them. He resembles the modern industrial magnate, he is a "wild marauder who makes a profit from inflation."[8] It will be seen later that this analogy is not so very wide of the mark.

In addition to graphic art, it was also music which, in the course of the last three hundred years, found inspiration time and again in the subject of the Thirty Years' War. Weber's "Freischütz", a romantic folk-opera, is set in the period just after the end of the "Great War". The second hunter, Caspar, who had fought in the war, knows the sinister secret of casting magic bullets; however, he is subsequently struck

[1] Horn, F.: Die Poesie und Beredsamkeit der Deutschen von Luthers Zeit bis zur Gegenwart, 1st vol., Berlin, 1822, p. 211

[2] Huch, R.: Das Zeitalter der Glaubensspaltung, Berlin/Zurich, 1937, pp. 406/407

[3] With regard to the subject "crisis" of the century and comprehensive list of literature, see: M. Hroch/J. Petráň: 17. stoleti—krize feudální společnosti, Prague, 1976

[4] Hartmann, H.: Wallenstein. Geschichte und Dichtung, Berlin, 1969

[5] Grillparzer, F.: Werke, 1. Abt., vol. 6, Leipzig/Vienna, 1927

[6] Strindberg, A.: Strindbergs Werke. Deutsche Gesamtausgabe. Deutsche Historien, Munich, 1919

[7] Brecht, B.: Mutter Courage und ihre Kinder. Eine Chronik aus dem Dreissigjährigen Krieg, in: Versuche 9, Berlin, 1953

[8] Döblin, A.: Wallenstein. Novel, Berlin 1970, epilogue by M. Beyer

by the seventh one and dies. It was from one of the main events in the war, the tragedy of the Czech state and nation from 1620 onwards, that the painter and draftsman Mikuláš Aleš, who was influenced by the national neo-romanticism of the 19th century, took many of the subjects of his pictures. In the 1930's, Jaromír Weinberger created his musical Wallenstein tragedy. Richard Strauss wrote a "Festival Music in Living Scenes" from the Thirty Years' War, the premiere of which took place in 1892 in Weimar in the presence of the grand duke and duchess on their anniversary. The battle music of the first scene ("Bernhard von Weimar at the Battle of Lützen") was incorporated in the "Rosenkavalier" film of 1925 while the first and third scenes ("Encounter and Conclusion of Peace between William of Orange and Spinola") was played in fascist Germany (Magdeburg) in 1940 as "Battle and Victory Music". The expression of the contrast of the worlds of war and peace from the example of the end of the war in 1648 was the object of the composer in his one-act chamber opera "Day of Peace" which was performed for the first time in Munich in 1935. The scenario was written by Stefan Zweig. Karl Amadeus Hartmann, one of the outstanding symphonic composers of modern times and a man persecuted by the Nazis and driven into "inner emigration", wrote the cantata "Anno 48" from verses by Andreas Gryphius. It was only after the end of Fascism and of the Second World War that this moving work and the opera "The Youth of Simplicius Simplicissimus", completed in 1934, could be at last performed.

The exercise of organized military force to achieve political aims in class-society had developed into a fine art in the course of the millennia, even among the popular masses fighting for social progress. Even in the case of the Thirty Years' War, whose tendency and result on the soil of the Empire consisted in socio-cultural destruction, Man was unable to bring about this destruction without lending it the mark of craftsmanship and creative effort. Foundrymen lovingly ornamented bells and cannon alike with decorative figures; the soldier competed with the cavalier in matters of fashion; the most glorious feast for the eyes in this "visual age" was a military parade; nowhere but in the art of war was such direct practical encouragement given to mathematics and the natural sciences; alchemists even concerned themselves with the use of poisons in the field. Society had to pay a high price for this progress but without this price, which was paid not only by wars but also by oceans of misery and suffering in times of peace, mankind in class-divided society could not have advanced. War is the work of Man and can neither extirpate nor deny the legacy of Prometheus.

War, pest and famine are the three scourges of God

(17th century saying)

UNSTABLE RULE
AND APPROACHING WAR

THE GERMAN REICH:
CITIES, AUTHORITIES,
PEASANTS

3 A meticulously engraved view of some of the buildings of a Free City of the Empire: a square situated away from the busy city-centre and characterized by a well, gabled houses in Gothic or Renaissance style and a prestige building, the Braunfels as it was known, with an arcade, a delicate oriel and a representation of the Imperial eagle. At Frankfort on the Main. Copperplate engraving by Wenzel Hollar. Staatliche Graphische Sammlung, Munich

[1] Hoffmann, I.: Deutschland im Zeitalter des 30jährigen Krieges. Nach Berichten und Urteilen englischer Augenzeugen, Greifswald, 1937

[2] Bodin, J.: De la république, Paris, 1576; De republica, Paris, 1586, copy in Municipal Archives Stralsund

Complaining of the corrupt and accursed state of war, the well-known Frankfort publisher Mathäus Merian, in the preface to the great *Topographia Germaniae*, lauded his native land which had so many cities, castles, fortresses, monasteries, villages and hamlets and was favourably situated as scarcely any other country in Europe. The recollection of happier days of peace may have gilded much which had really been grey and contradictory. Yet even well-travelled and critical foreigners found enough to astonish them, reflecting the creative power of the people just as much as the fetters which were placed on them by a gradually but visibly declining social and ruling order.

The contemporary traveller noted, in particular, that the countenance of the countryside was marked by vast woods, some of which were difficult to penetrate; despite the many burdensome customs duties, rivers were still regarded as the cheapest and most convenient means of communication. They were also safer than the bottomless overland routes, through thick forests or across high passes, where all sorts of dangers and injustice lay in wait for the unwary.

Fertile districts included the meadow areas along the coast in the North, the "Börde" areas of Central Germany, Thuringia and the district of Weimar, large areas of Lower Bavaria and the densely populated Vogtland. In the view of the geographer Martin Zeiller, Lower Austria was inhabited by a sociable, hospitable people and possessed everything to nourish man in abundance. In the opinion of their visitors, however, it was the Rhenish Palatinate and Alsace which were the most beautiful and the merriest.

It is difficult to define the political spirit of the Central European realm which was officially known as the "Holy Roman Empire". A reliable English contemporary, who had travelled through it five times before the war chose the following simile: "The Empire at this day languisheth like a sparke lapped in ashes." Another observer was of the opinion that Germany is like a great river sluiced into sundry Channels which makes the main.[1] The great French political theorist Bodin stressed the loose diversity of state power while others saw the multiplicity of states precisely as a guarantee of "freedom"—like the *aurea libertas*, the "golden liberty" of the Polish-Lithuanian aristocracy. The war which was imminent was again to prove that the (princely) "German liberty" was the cause of the weakness of the Empire as such and was a basic evil of the social condition as a whole.[2]

However, the country was in no way poor when overtaken by the war. An adequate measure of basic material conditions ensured that the war, as it moved from one scene of action to another, would last for decades. In respect of density of population, the Empire occupied the fifth rank in Europe and sheltered one-fifth of all the inhabitants of the Continent. About 80 to 85 per cent of the population was engaged in agriculture. In areas such as Saxony with a high level of craft activity, this figure amounted to only 70 per cent and in the mining district of western Erzgebirge it was even as low as 50 per cent. What the traveller from abroad found the most remarkable was the fading "freedom" of numerous cities, a feature called into question by later historians. These fully merited their fame in the opinion of John Barclay, an author who was widely read for the time. In actual fact, even at the beginning of the 17th century, the signs of gradual decline, which were often enough the subject of complaint by those living there, were not immediately apparent to the visitor. It was much more frequently the case that the visitor's admiration was caught by the soaring spires of the great churches, the magnificence of the facades of the burgher houses, the long frontage of the newly built town-halls in such places as Augsburg, Nuremberg and Bremen and by the arsenals and warehouses with their tiny windows.

A noticeable stimulus and a powerful, bolder spirit was brought to the sluggish activities of trade and commerce which were threatened by the stagnation of the great business houses by foreigners who came in increasing numbers to seek political asylum, the chance of a business career and new contacts. The stubbornly preserved "freedom" of many provincial and Imperial cities gave them the opportunity they sought. Italian merchants and bankers kept an outstanding position in Upper Germany while to the areas to the north of the Main there came a lively stream of energetic Dutchmen, Englishmen and Frenchmen from the mid-16th century onwards.[1]

Of the inland economic centres of the Reich, Frankfort on the Main, the city where the emperors were elected and crowned, occupied an outstanding position. It was regarded by contemporaries as a "universal emporium literarum throughout Germany", since it was famed for printing, publishing and book fairs in particular. In 1608, the English globetrotter Thomas Coryat wrote that he had seen such an endless quantity of books in the Buchgasse that it had caught his admiration in the highest degree. This lane was "the very epitome of all the principle Libraries of Europe" and seemed bigger to him than St. Paul's Churchyard in London. The Parisian scholar Henry Estienne called it the "Athens of Frankfort", attracting the intellectual production of the whole of Europe, as early as 1574. However, about half of all the books were devoted to theological subjects. Nevertheless, works by famous scientists such as Kepler's *Harmonices mundi* (1619) or William Harvey's pioneer description of the circulation of the blood with the title *Exercitatio anatomica de motu cordis et sanguinis in animalibus* (1628) were also published here. It is known that in 1621 there were ten printers in business at Frankfort and that they operated 45 printing-presses. They supplied books and brochures to such publishers and booksellers as Aubry, Dambach, Kopf, Ruland and Schönwetter and others.[2]

It was here in Frankfort that an international business-world carried out its money transfers at the Exchange and it was on this aspect that business activities were increas-

4 The large numbers of boats regularly plying on the river led to the Frankfort Fairs held twice annually. The picture shows a craft being hauled upstream by horses. In the bows, behind the stock-anchor, two merchants are engaged in a lively discussion while the hired men on the cabin amidships concentrate their attention on the beer. The Market Boatman. Pamphlet (1596), after: Steinhausen, *Deutsche Kultur*

[1] Schilling, H.: Niederländische Exulanten im 16. Jahrhundert, ihre Stellung im Sozialgefüge und im religiösen Leben deutscher und englischer Städte, Gütersloh, 1972

[2] Lübbecke, F.: Fünfhundert Jahre Buch und Druck in Frankfurt am Main, Frankfurt on the Main, 1948; J. Benzing: Die Buchdrucker des 16. und 17. Jahrhunderts im deutschen Sprachgebiet, Wiesbaden, 1963

Die ſtadt Dantzig

A *Mons Episcopalis* .
B *Fluvius Raduna* .
C *Fossa Civitatis* .
D *Via Sælandiam versus* .
E *Hic Situla terrâ onerantur* .
F *Hic Situla exonerantur* .
G *Perticæ trochleatæ Funem Situlas onustas Vallum versus devehentem suſtentans* .
H *Perticæ funem vacuas Situlas Montem versus reducentem Suſtinentes* .

I *Templum S⁴ Trinitatis* .
K *Turris Templi Parochial* .
L *Carcer* .
M *Templum S⁴ Catharinæ* .
N *Templum FF: Carmelitar⁴* .
O *Templum et Hospitale S⁴ Eliſabethæ* .
P *Novum Cæmiterium* .

A *Der Biſchoffsberg* .
B *Die Radaune fluſ* .
C *Der Stadt Grabe* .
D *Der Weg nach Schotlant* .
E *Allhier Wirden die Eymer mit Erde gefullt* .
F *Allhier Wirdt die Erde auſ den Eymern auſgeworfen*
G *Starke Pfoſten mitt Windraden darauff die taw mitt vollen Eymern herab kommende ruhen thutt* .

H *Ein ſtarcker Pfoſten darauff die Tau mitt ledige Eymern herauff wieder gehend ruhen thut* .
I *Kirche zur H Dreyfaltigkeit ſonſten zu Grawmunchen genant* .
K *Thurn zur Pfarr Kirche* .
L *Der ſtock* .
M *S Catharinen Kirche* .
N *Der Weiſſen Munchen Kirche* .
O *S. Eliſabet Kirche und Hoſpital* .
P *Daſ Newe Kirch hoff* .

5 The reconstruction of the town fortifications of Danzig, in which earth was conveyed to the new bastions by a bucket chain spanning the Radaune, was considered to be an outstanding technical achievement. Copperplate engraving by Henryk Hondiusz (1644). Biblioteka Gdańska of the Polish Academy of Sciences, Gdańsk

[1] Die Reisen Philipp Hainhofers, in: Zeitschrift des Historischen Vereins für Schwaben und Neuburg 8/1881

ingly centred whereas Leipzig, the second great book-centre of the Empire, gradually assumed the role of a European trade fair. The vigorous business life, which had to adapt to the political situations and the fluctuations in power relations, also had unavoidable negative aspects—the merciless competition and the ruination of small workshops, proneness to crises, the widespread misery of the lower classes.

In addition to the old Imperial cities, whose economic life was certainly still capable of making an outstanding contribution but were nevertheless declining in power, a new and dynamic group of urban centres had long since appeared on the scene—residence-cities from which princely states were governed, where central authorities, a bureaucratic apparatus and a court society came into existence. The princely rulers regularly demanded taxes and gradually took over the independent rights of the small rulers and cities possessing Reich or semi-sovereign status. Of the many residence-cities of ecclesiastical princes, dukes and electors, it was especially Heidelberg, Munich, Salzburg, Prague and Dresden whose splendours made an impact on their visitors.

The Bavarian dukes, who—in the view of Hainhofer—often played with the idea of war and "constantly rounded off their land with enclosed or adjacent areas wherever they can", were especially active in forming collections and in the spheres of art and building so that the appearance of Munich would underline the princely right to determine the public and private life of its inhabitants.[1]

Contemporaries also confirm the growth of the political centre of the electors of Saxony—the city of Dresden. At first sight, it certainly made a warlike impression with its moats and ramparts, its thick walls and ashlar and the extended bastions with the menacing mouths of their great cannon. For the reconstruction of the fortifications of Dresden and other cities of the Electorate of Saxony according to the most modern Dutch principles, the elector appointed a master of this art, the topographer Wilhelm Dilich of Hesse who in 1640 published a notable textbook on the construction of fortresses, the *Peribologia*. About 300 mercenaries kept watch along the fortifications and at the gates and patrolled through the streets of Dresden. The chronicler notes 500 cannon in the arsenal and makes special mention of an "organ gun" whose 24 barrels could be fired simultaneously. On the five floors of the Dresden Armoury, there were weapons and equipment for thousands of men. A foundry and carpenter's workshop turned out large items of military equipment.[1]

In the ruling circles, especially in the cabinets of the principalities of Central and Upper Germany, it was feared—more than anything else—that a far-reaching peasants' rebellion could break out, as in the past. Individual incidents seemed to indicate that this really was imminent: in the provinces of Austria, in the ecclesiastical principality of Salzburg, in the Bavarian county of Haag, in the small territory of Rettenberg to the south of Kempten and in Breisgau, among the Sorb population of Upper Lusatia and in Silesia. Many relied on the communities and revived or newly established "alliances", organized specifically for this purpose, which they used to defend their interests against the increasingly harsher demands of the lords. The community associations gave the peasants the strength to defend themselves for years on end in many cases, helped those who were hesitant to stand on their own feet again and sometimes even used compulsion to influence those who did not want to join them for social reasons or because of their views.

The peasants' revolt, which shook both parts of Austria between 1595 and 1597, seemed highly dangerous for the survival of the feudal aristocracy.[2]

It had scarcely become "quiet" again in the Danube areas when in 1600 peasants, townsmen and salt-workers between Gmunden and Ischl and in the Salzkammergut district began to defend themselves, weapon in hand, against the brazen attempts of the Catholic authorities and priests to impose conversion by force. A mob of about a thousand rebels collected and the salt-workers in Hallstatt stopped work. This in turn meant that other groups of workers along the well-organized "salt route"—the boatbuilders and boatsmen on the River Traun and Lake Traun, the loaders for the larger ships, the lock-attendants at the Traun waterfall and the men working the ships on the Danube—could not work either.[3] At the request of the embarrassed Imperial lord of the district, the Archbishop of Salzburg agreed to act as an intermediary and invited the leaders to begin negotiations. In the meantime, a brave little group, "ordinary people" from the peasants and salt-workers, fought on against a superior enemy until the bitter end in February 1602.

Four years later, the Archbishop, who is described by the chronicle as having been very active in the building sphere, was obliged to stamp out the flickering flame of peasant resistance on his own estates. His commissioners appeared in Pinzgau with the intention of making a detailed inspection of the peasant holdings with a view to raising the tax assessments. The peasants lodged a protest but in vain. Relying on their own strength, they took an oath and assembled in Taxenbach and even in Zell, although the inhabitants there had called themselves "true servants of St. Rupert" (for the lord), since the Great Peasants' War of 1525/26. The citizens of the towns were persuaded to accompany the mercenaries to the mountains to force the peasants into submission and oblige them to pay higher taxes. Seven of the peasant leaders were captured;

In times of war, it is the peasants who suffer.
If it lasts long,
they have to slave their life out;
if it soon ends,
even the marrow is scraped from their bones.

Newmayr von Ramsla: Vom Krieg, 1641, Chapter III/17

[1] Zeiller, M.: Itinerarium Germaniae novantiquae, Strasbourg, 1632, p. 387ff.; Menzhausen, J.: Das Grüne Gewölbe, Leipzig, 1968

[2] Gruell, G.: Der Bauer im Lande ob der Enns am Ausgang des 16. Jahrhunderts, Vienna/Cologne, 1969; Eichmeyer, K./Feigl, H./ Litschel, W.: Weiss gilt die Seel und auch das Guet. Oberösterreichische Bauernaufstände und Bauernkriege im 16. und 17. Jahrhundert, Linz, 1976

[3] Beschreibung der eingespielten Salzstrasse: M. Merian: Topographia Provinciarum Austriacarum, Frankfort on the Main, 1716, pp. 9 and 81f.

6 Wooden bridges were built by human labour organized as teams to handle the heavy equipment—in this case a pile-driver raised by a pulley. As indicated by the tools and operations of the carpenters, building activities were based on human skills. From: Martin Hohberg, *Georgica curiosa aucta* II, Nuremberg, 1687

7 In many places, as at Ulm, the bleaching and washing operations in the production of linen were carried out on a large scale. A bucket-scoop mechanism, driven by waterpower, conveyed the water to the bleachingfield, which is intersected by trenches, where the bleachers poured it on to the lengths of linen spread on the ground. The wash-houses can be seen in the foreground. From: Martin Hohberg, *Georgica curiosa aucta* I

[1] Heinisch, R. R.: Salzburg im Dreissigjährigen Krieg, Thesis. Vienna, 1968; Wolf, A.: Geschichtliche Bilder aus Oesterreich, 1st vol. Vienna, 1878

two of them and the princely administrator of Zell, who had shown sympathy for the situation of the peasants, were decapitated.

In 1611, a new archbishop, Marx Sittich of the ancient family of the von Hohenems was installed in Salzburg with all pomp and circumstance. This and the reputation of this prince of the Church for harshness in religious affairs boded no good for the peasants of the region. Inspired by the successful work of "reformation" of the Hapsburgs in nearby Styria, the ostentatious prelate went to work in the same fashion, avoiding a head-on collision with the mass of his Protestant subjects and proceeding step by step and group by group, the whole action being planned like an *impresa* (campaign). It began in Pinzgau and Pongau. Sharp-eyed, barefoot Capuchin friars from Salzburg appeared in the villages and towns, had the administrators summon first the townsfolk, then the peasants and finally the miners and informed them that the archbishop ordered them either to become Catholic or to leave the area. Most of them initially remained true to the Lutheran "faith of their fathers", whereupon soldiers moved in to lend weight to the archbishop's ultimatum so that within a few years the area could indeed be regarded as Catholic again.[1]

Here, too, on the edge of the subsequent theatre of war, the princes believed they could indulge in pomp and circumstance and build splendid edifices but the unavoidable reverse side of the coin was the bitter misery of the ordinary people. "Oh God! Oh God! Have mercy! The Ziller Valley has become poor"—so sang the starving and ragged peasants in the mountains. Poll tax and other charges and military recruitment and duties were a heavy burden. Finally, in May 1645, it was the last straw:

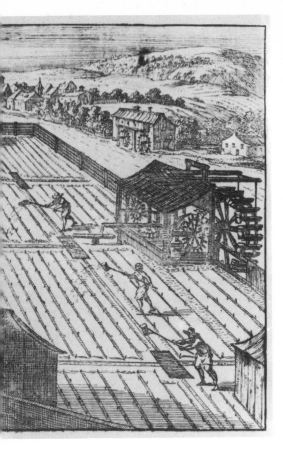

"Die Bauern und G'main ein ziemlich Heer" ("The peasants and the ordinary people, quite an army"), as the song went, stormed into the court-room in Fügen, threw out the princely officials, tore up the tax-lists and stripped the armouries. The "pacification" of the insurrection was remarkably mild and there were no sentences of death. The fear of the ruling personages was greater than their cruelty. A verse from the otherwise peaceful lament of the people of Zillertal about their situation must have made a threatening impression on their masters:[1]

> "Wenn oft einer hätt der Obrigkeit Gewalt,
> So möcht ich wohl sagen rund,
> So wär' er der allergrösste Hund,
> Zu dem Nehmen wär' er nicht faul,
> Er riss ain andern das Brod aus dem Maul.
> Darum will's gar langsam besser werden,
> Dieweil wir leben auf der Erden ..."

("Often when one had the power of authority, I say it plainly, He was the worst swine of all, He was not idle in taking, He snatched the bread from your mouth. That's why it must at last become better, As long as we live on the Earth ...")

However, it was not only the countryside but also many of the towns of the Empire which were shaken by serious social conflicts in the decades before the war and during

8 Operation of a glassworks with melting-furnace. The workers depicted here include glassblowers, furnacemen, finishers (foremen) and glass-porters. From: Martin Hohberg, *Georgica curiosa aucta* I

[1] Schmidt, L.: Historische Volkslieder aus Oesterreich vom 15. bis zum 19. Jahrhundert, Vienna, 1971, p. 63ff.; Steinitz, W.: Deutsche Volkslieder demokratischen Charakters aus sechs Jahrhunderten, vol. I, Berlin, 1955, p. 40f.

it and the parties engaged in it often exploited religious differences to further the contention between them. The uprising of citizens and journeymen in Frankfort on the Main of 1614, in the course of which, it is true, Jew's Lane was plundered but none of its inhabitants touched, was the most significant link in a long chain of municipal unrest directed against the impenetrable administrative intrigues of related patrician families. It was only with the assistance of the emperor and neighbouring princes and with draconic harshness that the insurrection in Frankfort, which was regarded as a potential precedent by the authorities, was suppressed. The house of the leader of the uprising, the baker and former soldier Vinzenz Fettmilch, was razed to the ground and a pillory erected in its place. This and the heads of the leaders, which were spiked on the bridge-tower and remained there till the following century, were a warning that "freedom" in the Free City was only for the small minority of the wealthy and the great landowners. Fettmilch's wish to be in the midst of the "action" when "the working people and craftsmen once more rise against the tyrants and blood-suckers in the Empire" was not fulfilled.[1] Among the ordinary people, however, numerous legends about the courageous rebels came into existence. Their deeds remained unforgotten and the probity of their leaders could not be disputed by even the worst of their enemies. When the city elders of Frankfort showed him the pillory with sinister pride, King Gustavus Adolphus remarked that this Fettmilch must have been a brave man to have caused the authorities so much trouble. Goethe called the executed leaders "sacrifices for a future better order".[2]

In Upper Germany, it was the small Free City of Donauwörth in particular that, as an exception, made a name for itself on account of the eventful clashes which took place within its walls. Situated not far from the strongholds of the expansive Catholic "salvation"—Bavaria and Austria, the Catholic community of Donauwörth had shrunk to some 16 families by about 1600. Their spiritual welfare was in the hands of the Benedictine monastery of the Holy Cross in the direct vicinity of the city. It was precisely there, however, that abbots and young monks were active who had been filled with religious zeal at the Jesuit college of Dillingen. Fired by the hatred of the few for the numerically superior Lutheran "heretics", they organized their followers in processions. With their Church banners fluttering freely in the wind instead of furled as prescribed by the regulations, they carried them across the territory of the city. The bishop of Augsburg, the emperor and the Imperial court counsellor defended their cause and encouraged this small group of Catholic priests to continue their processions. As a result, at the end of April 1606, another procession with challenging pomp wended its way across the city market to a village and back again. On this occasion, however, it was attacked by an angry crowd of townsfolk who cast down the banners and chased the participants through the dirty, narrow lanes back to the monastery. It is reported that the leader of the rebellious citizens, the goldsmith Schenk, said that he did not ask the emperor or the duke of Bavaria; the townsfolk should rather throw them in the Danube than discuss with them. As always in such cases, the town council endeavoured to meet the emperor half-way to prevent the ban of the Empire being pronounced, which was what had been threatened. However, the citizens' "Council of the Twenty", the aroused townsfolk and the guilds forced the town council

[1] Janssen, J.: Geschichte des deutschen Volkes, vol. 5, p. 664

[2] Goethes Werke, ed. by order of the Grand Duchess Sophie of Saxony, I. Abt., 26th vol., Weimar, 1889, p. 234f.

to hand over the town-key which signified, at least in part, the handing over of the authority of government to the townsfolk. The emperor immediately put the city under ban, on 12 November 1607, and ordered the duke of Bavaria to implement it. An army of 5,000 men marched in, the Lutheran preachers fled and the exercise of the Catholic faith and the authority of a new town-council was ensured. The duke of Bavaria charged the city for the costs which had been incurred and until they had been paid he kept the city as a pledge.[1]

The neighbouring Free Cities and the Protestant rulers were greatly dismayed at this development and the news spread in every direction of the unheard-of infringement of the Land Peace and religious liberty by the emperor and his allies. The Protestant princes of the Empire, who were likewise more concerned with "region" rather than "religion", used this happening as an excuse to conjure up the nightmare of a fatal "papist" conspiracy and finally to divide the Reichstag in Regensburg (1608). A contemporary wrote from there at the end of April that everything "was breaking down and in confusion and, in a word, moving towards war. God have mercy on us and the *gemeine Wesen*." An unmistakable sign that war was imminent was the founding in the same year of a military-political "Union" by the Protestant princes, in response to which the Catholic rulers set up the "League".

THE CLASHES AND QUARRELS
OF THE RULING PRINCES

In actual fact, "das gemeine Wesen"—a vague expression for the class-society of the time within the "Holy Roman Empire"—was displaying evident signs of disintegration which did not pass unnoticed and led to questions being asked. Would a new order result from the disorder, from the *dissolutio unitatis*? Could it be expected, as in Bodin's simile of the chicken and the egg, that life would emerge from a stage of "great stink", that society, shaken by all kinds of crises, would be renewed as had happened in England?

A pamphlet of 1618 with the title "Der heutigen Welt Lauff" (The Way of the Present World) obviously reflects a widely held view of the events in the Empire:[2]

> "Der Ein will diss, der Ander das,
> Daher entspringt gross Zanck und Hass,
> Ein jeder doch will haben recht,
> Das klagt leider manch armer Knecht,
> Der nicht zu reiten hat, zu Fuss
> Im Regen und Schnee lauffen muss,
> Der gemeine Mann thut leiden viel,
> Wenn nur das Leiden hät ein Ziel ..."

[1] Janssen, J.: Geschichte des deutschen Volkes, vol. 5, p. 292

[2] Wäscher, H.: Das deutsche illustrierte Flugblatt. Von den Anfängen bis zu den Befreiungskriegen, Dresden, 1955, p. 62

A Eiserne Pfannen darin das Haltz gesotten wird
B Eiserne Stangen so in mitten die Pfannen helt
C Rinnen darein das Haltzwasser geleut wird
D Wie man das Haltz in die Form geschlagt
E Brenntfeuer darvon sie sieden können
F Wasser Katz zum wasserschöpfen

9 The saltworks—as illustrated here by one
at Hallstatt at the foot of a salt-mine near
Gmunden in Upper Austria—with great salt-
pans and bucket-wheels for raising the brine,
consumed vast quantities of wood. The boiling-
house, in which ten or so workers were employed, can be regarded as a manufactory. After:
Mathäus Merian, *Topographia Germaniae*, Municipal Archives, Stralsund

("One will this, the other that, Thus there arise great quarrels and hate, Since everybody insists, he's right, This is the bitter complaint of many a poor wight, Who has not to ride but must walk on foot through rain and snow, The common man must suffer much, If only there was a purpose to this suffering ...")

The sigh of the author nevertheless seems to express the hope that the evil disorder at the expense of the ordinary people should not be so senseless. When was it ever possible to stamp out the last sparks of hope? The many actions fought by the peasants, the burning desire of Vinzenz Fettmilch for a world without "bloodsuckers and tyrants" and even the shaky freedom of the "Free Cities" are signs and evidence of this. Hesitant and isolated though these manifestations were and although they were more rebellious than revolutionary, they were a pointer to historical progress.

The driving forces and actions of the ruling feudal class took effect in quite the opposite direction. The "quarrels and hate" in which the princes and the emperor became increasingly entangled, concerned the question of ecclesiastical and secular land, especially because the hard-pressed Papal Church was evidently passing through a process of recovery from which the princes of the Reich—most of whom had appropriated Church territories—could expect nothing to their advantage. There was in 1582 the "War of Cologne" concerning the archbishopric of the same name, the quarrel about the "Strasbourg Foundation" of 1592/93 and the "Dispute of the Four Monasteries" in 1599—ominous signs of the tense contest between spiritual and temporal authorities.

The contradictions between them also became sharper with the attempts to gain control of trade-routes and trade-centres, ports, customs stations, busy coastal areas and natural resources since in comparison with the purely feudal powers these now became more important than hitherto. It was under new omens that the centuries-old dispute, which was considered to have already been settled, between princely "liberty" —i.e., particularist separatism—and the authority of the emperor since the latter, on the basis of an "Imperial policy" backed up by a vast area of patchwork territory, pursued the interests of the Hapsburg dynasty.

In their patrimonial dominions, however, the Hapsburgs saw themselves confronted with a growing opposition which was rapidly taking a definite shape and was capable of acting in a wily manner in depth, the social basis of this opposition being the rural and "castle" nobility. This "dualism" between the representative body of the estates and the ruler was a general phenomenon in Europe. It indicates that many of the members of the medium-rank and minor nobility, strengthened not least by their activities as entrepreneurs or through the gradual subordination of the peasants, were emerging as a feudal exploiter-stratum in rivalry with the leadership in the person of a single representative. Almost all the patrimonial dominions of the German Hapsburgs were characterized by the development of the opposition of the nobility, even though the rate at which this took place varied from one area to another. The nobles organized alliances among themselves and with powers hostile to the Hapsburgs, even coming to an arrangement with the sultan. In those areas where the doctrine of Luther appeared too mild, the rebellious aristocracy took up the sharper weapon of Calvinism to put forward demands, assemble its forces and obtain moral support by the postulated right of resistance to a "tyrannical" ruler. The movement also had intellectual and cultural pretensions which was reflected in constant representation, theoretical arguments, schools, libraries, printing-houses and an active body of preachers and teachers.

The never-ending small-scale war against the Turks, which after 1593 was again marked by great campaigns and battles, demanded men and money, especially the latter. New taxes were raised time and again which the subjects, in the face of bitter poverty, paid with the greatest ill-will. The representative bodies of the estates, however, reserved the right to approve taxes although the aristocracy as such was largely exempt from the obligation to pay taxes. As a consequence, the rivalry between the prince and the estates often took the form of a financial conflict.

The uncertain and straitened situation of the House of Hapsburg which was stubbornly dedicated to the cause of expansion were made worse by internal arguments which became known as the "brothers' quarrel". In the case of the bachelor Rudolf II, the head of the family with its many branches, there were increasing signs of mental disorder from the mid-1590's onward but the ruler did not cease to be active in the field of international politics, to wage wars or to conclude alliances. Yet, Rudolf, suffering from delusions of persecution, became less and less responsible for his decisions. At the Imperial court in Prague, a crowd of parasites, high officials and senior officers had gathered who sought profit from the disorder there. Mistrusting everybody, the emperor dismissed his best advisers until finally, about 1600, the "regiment of valets" developed from the voracious parvenus wandering around the Imperial quarters and it was these who made political decisions, audiences and statements of Imperial intent dependent on the size of the bribe. The mechanism of the supreme authorities of the Empire, which only worked reluctantly and with a great deal of friction at the best of times, came to a standstill. The hostile and energetic court of the Palatinate in Heidelberg was already toying with plans for winning other European potentates for the Imperial throne. This was why the family council of the Hapsburgs decided in 1606 that the emperor's brother, Archduke Mathias, should take over some of the authority of Rudolf. Mathias reached agreement with the leaders of the movement of the Estates in Hungary and concluded peace in Vienna in 1606 with Prince Stefan Bocskai, the leader of the great Hungarian-Transylvanian uprising, whose nucleus was composed of the Haiduks, free peasants practised in the use of weapons. The uprising had developed from a movement embracing all the estates and strata of society under the slogan of religious freedom and against the compulsion of Hapsburg recatholicization. Mathias was obliged to concede this freedom in the name of the emperor. There began the "Golden Age" of Transylvania, this being especially associated with the name of Bethlen Gábor who was elected prince in 1613. He became a popular ally for all the anti-Hapsburg forces. His marriage with the sister of King Gustavus Adolphus of Sweden underlined his good relations with one of the main powers in the anti-Hapsburg camp.

After the Peace of Zsitva-Torok (1606), the Turkish question became much less critical in the tangle of European conflicts although it remained an important issue and also constituted a potential nightmare of use for propaganda purposes.

The "brothers' quarrel" between Emperor Rudolf and Archduke Mathias continued to smoulder since the latter exploited the vigorous movement of the Estates in Hungary and the two parts of Austria which had joined forces in 1607 to exert pressure on Rudolf and ultimately to turn him off the throne. The two brothers recruited mercenaries, organized armies and threatened each other with war. The Bohemian Estates also had armed forces at their disposal. Rudolf begged them for help and in return had to concede to them freedom for all the Protestant confessions in the famous "Letter of Majesty" of 9 July 1609.

The *Passauer Kriegsvolk*, as they were called, were a motley collection of mercenaries recruited on behalf of the emperor by Archduke Leopold, bishop of Passau, who was about 30 years old. He was the nephew of Rudolf and an ambitious, adventurous man. This force was raised to take part in the dispute of the Jülich-Cleves succession in the theatre of war in Northwest Germany. To begin with, this military hydra with its twelve thousand heads—a savage and rapacious bunch for the most part—took all there was to take in the Danubian bishopric, fell upon Upper Austria at the end of 1610 and then, weighed down with plunder, moved towards Bohemia where there was the prospect of even greater booty. The Passau mercenaries did indeed capture that part of Prague known as the "Small Side" (Malá strana) and prepared to cross the Moldau and attack the New and the Old City. Troops of the Bohemian Estates thwarted this intention. The intermediary and pressure of the papal nuntius and Spanish envoy persuaded Rudolf to waive his claim to the throne and to dismiss the Passau troops. Mathias moved in as victor by the grace of the Estates, became King of Bohemia and was ultimately elected emperor in Frankfort on the Main. At the end of May 1611, when the crown of Wenceslas was placed upon his head, one celebration after another took place in Prague castle while in the New and Old Cities of Prague the serving of beer and wine was prohibited—counter to all the customs at such state events. Prague, which had long been known as the "restless city", was not to provide the spark for a new rebellion, at least not on this occasion.[1]

It was only in 1617 that the dynastic crisis within the House of Hapsburg was gradually overcome. Agreement was reached as to the successor of Emperor Mathias who was childless. The choice fell upon the implacable champion of the Catholic counter-reformation Archduke Ferdinand of Styria. The acquiescence of King Philip III of Spain, another candidate for the Imperial throne, was purchased with the "Oñate Agreement" secretly negotiated between Ferdinand and Philip on 20 March 1617 at Prague. Following this understanding, it also proved possible to elect Ferdinand as King of Bohemia who was crowned in June 1617 in Prague not without expressly assuring the Bohemian nobility of their privileges. The struggle for wealthy Bohemia, whose crown-lands also included Silesia and Lusatia and whose king was simultaneously one of the seven electors of the Empire, was necessarily a subject of great interest to a large number of European powers.

It was also from the much-contested Bohemia that the spark came which—to use Kepler's words—"set fire to the tinder". This spark was the abrupt deed of a radical group, members of the Bohemian Estates, which was intended, like the stroke of a sword, to sever the entangled knot of the contest between the Estates and the Imperial

[1] Janáček, J.: Pád Rudolfa II., Prague, 1973

ruler—the "defenestration of Prague" of 23 May 1618. Two ministers of the emperor, who resided in the Castle, were attacked after a violent quarrel with a group of conspirative noblemen and thrown from the window, together with an official of no importance at all. A miracle happened: all three survived the fall of some 17 metres and fled. It is even more surprising that the Catholic Church did not exploit this unique "case" to weave a new series of wonders. The subsequent rebellion of the Estates was obviously a great shock. When they had recovered, those most immediately concerned related that the Virgin Mary had wrapped them in her wondrous cloak as they fell so that they landed safely on the ground. The legend of the dung-heap on which they were supposed to have fallen is certainly more plausible but just as inaccurate as the explanation given to the astonished sultan—that they had landed on a great pile of paper, ample quantities of which were produced in the government offices at Prague. In reality, it was their thick clothing, the wearing of which was imperative in the chilly rooms of the castle even in May, which saved the three gentlemen, together with the fact that they landed on a sloping surface. An element of luck was also involved. This "defenestration", which followed the example of other such incidents elsewhere and was a not unusual Hussite custom, was intended to incite an uprising, in the further course of which the great example of the Revolution in the Netherlands, which likewise developed from a rebellion by the Estates, was to be followed.[1]

Not far away, there was also another area which might have provoked the great conflagration—Northwest Germany, the forefield of the great struggle between the Netherlands and Spain. It is true that the two powers had agreed on a twelve-year truce in 1609 but a treaty concluded between the free Netherlands, France and England in June of the same year was aimed at the consolidation of the young republic and against Spain. The latter, however, was still powerful enough to guarantee the continuation of a chain of friendly Catholic principalities in the Northwest of the Reich and concentrated its efforts on Cleves-Jülich in particular.

At the end of March 1609, the death of the mentally deranged Duke Johann Wilhelm of the duchies of Jülich, Cleves and Berg an the Lower Rhine marked the end of the ruling dynasty. Various princes claimed hereditary rights to the economically advanced and advantageously situated territories. Without consideration for any Imperial agreements, the Elector of Brandenburg and the Count Palatine of Neuburg speedily occupied the duchies. The troops of these "possessive princes"—so it was said by the people—were as destructive as the Turks on enemy territory.

However, for the Rhenish bishops, for the continuation of the war by Spain against the united Dutch provinces and for the emperor, the question of the new ownership of the duchies was a matter of crucial importance. The Archduke Leopold, who had been adopted by the emperor as a son, was consequently dispatched to Jülich and the two "possessive" princes requested to withdraw from the duchies. King Henry IV of France, who was allied with the Union and at the same time was encouraging the expansionist policy of the Duke of Savoy against Spanish Milan and that of the Republic of Venice against the Hapsburg territories of Styria and Carinthia, assembled troops for an invasion of the Empire. The plan was for a preventive action against the

[1] Petráň, J.: Staroměstská exekuce, Prague, 1971

10 Frontispiece of a book by Joseph Furttenbach the Elder, demonstrating the versatility
of the town councillor and architect of Ulm
with the aid of peaceful and warlike symbols.
Municipal Archives, Ulm, Schwörhaus

power of the Hapsburgs to be fought in a number of areas. The European war had already begun with the first actions being fought on the Lower Rhine when the guiding light of the undertaking, King Henry IV, was assassinated on 14 May 1610. The imminent conflagration continued to smoulder as a small-scale war between French, Dutch and Imperial troops along the reaches of the Lower Rhine until a compromise was negotiated in 1614, providing for the division of the disputed territories by Brandenburg and Palatinate-Neuburg.

In addition to the dispute of the Cleves-Jülich Succession, there was a series of other conflicts in European policy in which the Empire or parts of it were involved. These included the repulsion of the Turkish "foes of Christendom", the Kalmar War between Sweden and Denmark (1611—1613), the never ending hostilities between the principalities and republics of Northern Italy, in the midst of which or on whose frontiers various Hapsburg possessions were located. On almost all its frontiers, wars were waged which threatened to move across into the Empire. Alien powers sought and found allies, set up recruiting centres and marched their armies across Imperial territory.

PRICE–INCREASES, SUB-STANDARD COINAGES AND POPULAR UPRISINGS

A constantly recurrent topic in the daily conversation of working people and often associated with bad news of a political or military nature were the complaints about rising prices. These resulted not only from the fluctuations in yields and bread-prices but also from a long-term movement in prices of an insidious kind, a process for which the term "price-revolution" is used in research although it has not proved possible to fully explain the cause of this phenomenon. There was a continuing rise in the price of agricultural produce (especially cereals) in the hundred years between the early decades of the 16th and the beginning of the 17th centuries. To be sure, there was a rise in artisan products, too, since many of these were based on agrarian products, but the increase in price lagged behind the latter. Some of the consequences and concomitant phenomena of this shift in prices were higher profits for those owners of agricultural land who could freely dispose of their products and market them. These were the noble estate-owners who also began to acquire peasant land by the expropriation of the peasantry, as in the areas to the east of the Elbe.

Prosperous peasants with a fairly large economic and juridical area of activity benefited for decades from the continuing "agricultural boom". This agricultural "upper crust" was subjected to a torrent of strict official prescriptions, aimed at restricting undue expenditure on luxury clothing and excessive displays of wealth at weddings, baptisms, funerals and important festive days. There was a danger that the display of such prosperity would affect the strictly preserved divisions between the different strata of society. With the boom in agriculture, however, there was also the very real danger for the peasants that the aristocracy, who held the reins of power, would cut back the rights of the peasants by using the machinery of state, which was more highly developed in the downward direction, as an instrument for this.[1] The first to achieve their aim were the knights of Pomerania who, with the "Peasants' and shepherds' regulations" of 1618, classified and subordinated the peasants generally as *homines proprii glebae adscripti*—as serfs of practically slave-like status who were bound to the land. Far-sighted contemporaries had a foreboding of the evil consequences of such a drastic change. Balthasar Prütze, a member of the town council of Stralsund attacked such "barbaric and so to say Egyptian" practices which were justified by many jurists trained in Roman law who quoted learned arguments such as those of Professor Husanus of Rostock in his treatise *De propriis Hominibus*. Prütze warned of the consequences of such an enslavement of the peasants: "Freedom encourages acquisition, oppression makes slow hands."[2] He was to be proved correct.

The disadvantageous effects of the progressive rise in prices for agricultural products were felt especially by those workers and strata who were mainly paid in cash: miners, building craftsmen, domestic servants, messengers, servants, carters, boatmen, day-labourers and also teachers, parish-priests, municipal officials and scribes. In Göttingen and Meissen, wages in cash remained at practically the same level for the whole of the 16th century but the equivalent in rye for the same sum of cash fell by half between the end of the 15th and the end of the 16th centuries. In the Mansfeld copper belt, wages in 1600 were no longer sufficient to buy bread for the families of the miners. In 18 towns of the Electorate of Saxony, about 30 per cent of the population were affected by the fall in the real value of wages—a possible indication of the state of affairs in many areas of the Empire.

The general rise in prices, which, however, became less marked as one moved across Europe in a West-East direction, caused great unrest in many countries of Europe. It was explained by Jean Bodin, the French state theorist, by the fact that a constantly increasing supply of silver was coming from America—especially in the shape of the legendary Spanish "silver fleets" which were heavily guarded but nevertheless often captured. This flow, which reached a maximum in the last decade of the 16th century, did indeed cause a fall in the value of silver which, at the same time, was the most important metal for coinage; a gradual rise in prices was inevitable.

Working people were able to adapt to this creeping inflation for which the working masses in question could find no tangible cause. It was a different matter with the "coin clipper" inflation which coincided with the beginning of the "Great War". The broad masses were disturbed by the rebellions, military campaigns and battles and by the hither-and-thither in Bohemia, Upper Austria and Rhine-Palatinate but they were taken aback by the plunge in the value of the most current good coins which began after 1618, fell dramatically as from 1620 and was like a nightmare—sudden and paralyzing—between 1621 and 1623.[3]

Already at the turn of the century, when the danger of war was constantly increasing and with it the need for money of numerous governments in the Empire, some of the

[1] Mottek, H.: Wirtschaftsgeschichte Deutschlands. Ein Grundriss, vol. I, 5th edition, Berlin, 1973

[2] Prütze, B.: Ungefehrliche Reformation oder Regimentsordnung. Anno 1614, manuscript in Municipal Archives, Stralsund

[3] Opel, J. O.: Deutsche Finanznot beim Beginn des dreissigjährigen Krieges, in: Historische Zeitschrift 16/1866; Kulischer, J.: Allgemeine Wirtschaftsgeschichte des Mittelalters und der Neuzeit, 2nd vol., Berlin, 1954; Lütge, F.: Deutsche Sozial- und Wirtschaftsgeschichte. Ein Überblick, 2nd edition, Berlin (West)/Heidelberg/Göttingen, 1960; Mauersberg, H.: Wirtschafts- und Sozialgeschichte zentraleuropäischer Städte in neuerer Zeit, Göttingen, 1960; Redlich, F.: Die deutsche Inflation des frühen 17. Jahrhunderts in der zeitgenössischen Literatur. Die Kipper und Wipper, Cologne/Vienna, 1972

smaller rulers in the Upper Rhine area had violated the Imperial coinage regulations of 1559 by establishing on their own authority new mints in which coins were struck with scarcely half of the silver standard prescribed. They were known as *Heckenmünzen* (hedge coins). Their example was soon followed by Franconian counts and princes, in whose territories there were soon no other coins than the small denominations such as the six-batz and three-batz coins. The big thalers seem to have disappeared into thin air and their value rose unceasingly. In Strasbourg, one Imperial thaler was worth:

year		Kreuzer	year		Kreuzer
1600	—	76	1621	—	210
1618	—	96	1622	—	270
1619	—	100	1623	—	360—390
1620	—	140	1624	—	90

In 1618, there began a vigorous increase in the activities of the money-changers. Princes, minters and silver buyers competed with each other for possession of the noble metals. People flocked to the money-changers' booths on the market-places. The loud voices of the money-changers urged the public to come to their tables where the shiny new coins, issued with the approval of the authorities, glittered alluringly. The enterprising men behind the tables weighed good old money (which was not recognized as such by the ordinary people) in exchange for new coins and filled their sacks and boxes with the money they had enticed from the latter's purses.

The jangling and jingling at the money-changers' tables, observed on innumerable occasions, was dubbed *kippen* and *wippen* (clipping and weighing) in the vernacular, the cheating money-changers themselves being known as *Kipper* and *Wipper*. For one to two years they were a bourgeois trade, practised thousands of times, tolerated and encouraged by the feudal authorities but soon became suspect, then hated and ultimately justly punished by the people in many towns. The chronicle reports that in Strasbourg the "society of clippers and weighers", including female persons, had plied its trade in houses, streets and market-places.[1]

However, it was by no means the case that all the good old coins found their way to the money-changers' tables. Many people, especially in the villages, held on to their hard-earned gold and silver coins and mistrusted every innovation. As a result, smooth-tongued dealers began to travel around the countryside, calling on parish-priests, millers and peasants and exchanging old thalers, kreuzers and batzen of genuine silver for shiny new coins. The material with a high silver content wandered into the mints, sometimes via hardened middlemen. Metal was melted down and coins struck at a feverish rate there and then counted out into bags and boxes. It was like a fever— coins were bought, exchanged and sold everywhere. Town councillors, bailiffs, aldermen and even priests were caught by it. For those who worked quickly and were unscrupulous enough, this source of quick wealth was even surer than the lucky dips and lotteries at fairs and markets. Mints sprang up like mushrooms on a warm, wet day— in the Electorate of Saxony not only at Dresden but also now at Sangerhausen, Chemnitz, Leipzig, Zwickau, Annaberg, Eilenburg, Freyburg on the Unstrut and Naumburg. In Brunswick, there were already 17 mints in operation in 1620 but this figure

[1] Abel, W.: Massenarmut und Hungerkrisen im vorindustriellen Europa. Versuch einer Synopsis, Hamburg/Berlin (West), 1974, p. 42

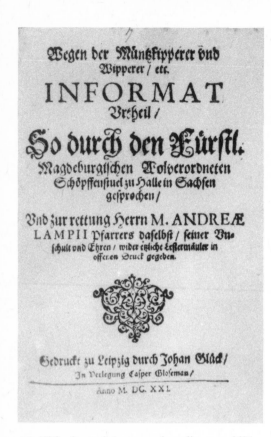

11 Title-sheet of the general verdict as published by the Jury-Court at Halle against the dishonest money-changers and coin-clippers (1621). Municipal Archives, Stralsund

rose to 40 within another three years. The spacious rooms of the monastery at Amelunxborn were transformed within a few months into a large workshop employing 300 to 400 workers.

A county squire (Junker) by the name of Hans Heinrich von Reizenstein in Lauenstein in Franconia used an entire forge for the striking of coins. The cautious and measured approach to business activities disappeared overnight and it was seldom indeed that the economic life of the Empire had known such feverish times. Inflation spread to great and small territories such as Brandenburg, the Electorate of Saxony, Anhalt, Brunswick, Magdeburg, Halberstadt, Mansfeld and the Thuringian and Franconian areas, Bavaria and Swabia being less affected. Worst-hit, however, were Bohemia, Moravia and Austria where the infamous coin-consortium directed hoodwinking operations on a large scale.

Unrest increased in the trading centres but the merchants and money-dealers were astute enough to establish dams against the flood. Since the merchants at fairs and large markets settled their mutual debts and obligations by bills of exchange made out to named persons and thus without transferring cash, this acted as a restraint on inflation. In addition, the town councils and the numerous depository and exchange banks and stock exchanges now coming into existence used fictitious currencies for clearing purposes, as in Hamburg and Ulm in 1619 and in Leipzig in 1635. The stratum of the bankers, who were international in orientation, proved capable of absorbing the shock of inflation; in the same way, in times of war, they demonstrated that they were flexible enough and sufficiently in demand not to be eliminated by the forces engaged in hostilities.

The striking of "long" coins in the innumerable mints, whether carried out legally or at night in remote places, gradually exhausted the supply of precious money. Why not then use copper which had long been a customary material for coins? As the chronicle of Sangerhausen reports, "Boilers, kettles, pipes, gutters and whatever was made of copper was removed, taken to the mints and turned into money ... If a church had an ancient copper font, it had to be taken to the mint and no saint could prevent it; it was sold by those who had been baptized in it."[1]

On occasion, "red foxes were given a white coat", i.e., copper coins were "silvered" in tartar but turned bright red again after only a week in circulation. The trickery became known and the entire business of recoining and exchange was exposed for what it was. Merchants became mistrustful when people at foreign markets refused to accept the "light" coins which bought less and less. In Strasbourg, children could even be seen playing in the streets with these coins. Rumours became certainty: the new money was worthless in actual fact. Everybody wanted to get rid of it quickly, it was used to pay debts and to establish foundations; hide-bound authorities were outmanoeuvred and cheated. Bakers, butchers and fishwives no longer took their wares to market, cobblers, tailors, potters, saddlers and ropemakers removed the goods on display and locked them up in their houses; peasants returned home with their grain and livestock and, in the end, "mischievously" kept back the whole of their field crops. Horror-struck, people saw that trade and exchange was coming to a standstill; how well-advised those were who had refused to sell anything of real value!

[1] Freytag, G.: Bilder aus der deutschen Vergangenheit, 2 vols., 1927, p. 266f.

In many places, bartering came back into fashion: commodities were exchanged for commodities. Yet there were too many who suffered, there was too much misery and poverty among those who were paid wages at fixed rates and even this was only in wretched substandard coins. Nevertheless, the price of bread continued to soar. In Memmingen, 12 bushels of corn cost about 20 gulden at the beginning of 1621, at the beginning of January 1622 still 21, in February 40 and in August 70 gulden. The start of the following year was not any better and by April the price had risen to 96 gulden. Finally, after the manipulations with the coinage had been overcome, it dropped in June to 24 and, after the harvest, to 14 gulden. The end of the inflation, which was one of the greatest catastrophes in the history of German coinage and money and was also rampant in England, France, Denmark and even the territories under Turkish rule, resulted not least from the fact that its product ultimately flowed into the pockets of the princely false-coiners—as taxes, customs duties and interest.

Nevertheless, they too had to pass through a period of fear and trepidation before their hasty but comprehensive coinage reforms took effect. These reforms did indeed stabilize the currency but the owners of "long" coins suffered losses of up to 90 per cent. A great storm of protest rolled over the "footpads, gallow-birds, pickpockets, leeches, villains, stinking usurers, hawkers and moneybags"—and other pungent terms expressing the anger of the people. Many of these expressions had been current in the vernacular since time immemorial and the occasional one was also a reference to usurious Jews ("money-Moses") who, once again in these hard times, served as scape-goats.

The poor people of the town of Bayreuth had already rebelled on 18 March 1621 since merchants and the town authorities refused to take the "bad" coins and the journeymen of the various crafts and trades demanded that the prices of bread and beer should be reduced. Money-changers' booths and mints were destroyed by the angry masses in many towns. Songs and verses reflecting this made the rounds such as: "Kipp die Wipp zum Tor hinaus, der Galgen ist dein Wechselhaus" ("Throw out the balance, the gallows are your counting-house"). In Halberstadt, the chapter of the cathedral had to call on armed servants in December 1621 to protect the houses of the mint-master Cyriacus von Lehr and other prosperous citizens from the attacks of the angry townsfolk. The chapter of the cathedral was obliged to expressly order the brewers to serve beer (since they had refused to take "light" money as payment).[1]

The conditions of extreme misery led to the uprising of the salt-workers and impoverished artisans in Halle. At the end of January 1622, a threatening crowd of starving people collected in the streets, their anger being directed against the bakers who were refusing to sell bread for "light" money. The intervention of the town guard seems to have prevented a real attack.

On the 12th and 13th of February, a crowd again collected and on this occasion also included soldiers, although the majority were salt-workers and journeymen. They plundered the houses and stocks of some "evil flayers and money-clippers" who are reported to have been bakers, needle-makers, carp-dealers and lucky-dip operators. It seems that the dissatisfied municipal soldiery could not be relied on either—the regional lord and administrator broke up the angry crowd by sending in horsemen, musketeers and pikemen who used cold steel to disperse the people. Some people were

12 Large was the number of coins minted by the many princes and Free Cities of the Empire, an impression of which is conveyed by the *New Müntzbuch* (1597), referring solely to the Electorate of Saxony. Municipal Archives, Stralsund

[1] Schrötter, F. von: Das Kippergeld in den Fürstentümern Brandenburg-Bayreuth und Ansbach 1620—1622, in: Zeitschrift f. bayrische Landesgeschichte 7/1934

injured and three men—a journeyman-carpenter, a former guildmaster and a confectioner (journeyman?)—were arrested and interrogated under torture. However, the verdicts—temporary expulsion from the town and an acquittal—were exceptionally mild. The court did not dare to name those who were really responsible.[1]

Magdeburg experienced violent days at the end of February 1622. The city council had leased the mint to a private person and it was from here, as from the princely mint at Wolmirstedt, that there flowed a ready stream of "light" coins. Two cobblers were engaged in the buying up of the old coins. In view of the increasing unrest, the council decided to confiscate their stocks of coins. Many hundreds of people must have taken part in the storming of the houses of other suspect-racketeers since, in the "calming of the mob" by armed forces, 16 inhabitants were killed and 200 injured. In Spandau, too, there were ominous "mutterings" from a "mob of scoundrels, big and small, like a swarm" and numerous houses, belonging to dishonest manipulators, were attacked. The councils of Leipzig and Dessau just managed to avoid the open expression of the wrath of the townsfolk and in Dessau the precaution was taken of disarming the citizens. The coin-clippers of the mining town of Freiberg did not escape their just punishment either—miners broke into their houses and plundered them.[2]

Concerning the uprising in Eisleben and Mansfeld, the chronicle reports that on the 6th, 7th and 8th of February the miners had rioted and "plundered the mints in the countryside and at Mansfeldt which make copper money and took everything". On the 8th of February, about a thousand miners gathered before the gates of the old quarter of Eisleben to punish the "coin-clippers and merchants". The mine-owners, in order to calm them, had to immediately advance them grain since the miners had neither wages nor bread enough to keep their families from starving.[3]

This violence was accompanied by a mighty flood of scornful, angry and sarcastic pamphlets, tracts, leaflets and sermons. Of the 40 tracts which survive, 13 have a popular content, 11 a religious one and 16 are of an economic, political and juridical tenor. The subjects of their attacks were the devilish "damned coin-clippers", the "desecrators of money, land and people", who were refused the sacraments and a Christian burial by zealous priests and the slaying and robbing of whom was said to be no sin. According to a decision published in 1621, the Consistory of the Electorate of Saxony at Wittenberg was not prepared to admit any unrepentant coin-clipper or money-changer to any religious ceremony at all. The authors of the pamphlets, who in general argued more lengthily against the evil, did not go so far as this even though they indicted the masters of the mints, the princes. Nevertheless, their tone was defiant, threatening and unmistakable. These are the words of a "teacher of coin-clippers and money-changers" in a song:[4]

[1] Neuss, E.: Entstehung und Entwicklung der Klasse der besitzlosen Lohnarbeiter in Halle. Eine Grundlegung, Halle, 1958

[2] Jessen, H.: Der Dreissigjährige Krieg in Augenzeugenberichten, Munich, 1971, p. 118

[3] Chronicon Islebiense. Eisleber Stadtchronik aus den Jahren 1520—1738, ed. by Rössler, H. and Sommer, E., Eisleben, 1822

[4] Scheible, I.: Die Fliegenden Blätter des XVI. und XVII. Jahrhunderts in sogenannten Einblatt-Drucken, Stuttgart, 1850, p. 176

"Viel Königen und Potentaten
Ist bei mir die Sach wohl gerathen,
Dass sie bekommen Gut und Geld,
Ja ganze Länder in der Welt,
Dess habens längst die Lehrenbrief,
Dort unten in der Höllen tief . . ."

13 Travellers on the highways of the period:
peasants, waggoners, soldiers and women.
Painting by Hendrick Avercamp. Historisches
Museum, Frankfort on the Main

14 The riverside scene includes some of the most important aspects of water utilization: water-mills, fishing-boats, barges and ferry-boats. Loading and unloading in the inland port at Mainz—as in all the larger ports—was handled by slewing-cranes powered by human muscles. At Mentz. Etching by Mathäus Merian. Staatliche Museen zu Berlin, Cabinet of Copperplate Engravings and Drawing Collection

15 Most bridges—like the small one in the background—were built of wood. The biggest stone bridge of the Empire, supported on 15 pillars, was across the Danube at Regensburg and was graced by three towers. To the right of the picture, there can be seen the typically mediaeval fortifications of the Free City with the smooth contours of its walls which were interrupted or reinforced by towers and gates. The cathedral stands in the centre of the city while busy watercraft, including timber rafts, may be seen on the river. From: Mathäus Merian, *Topographia Germaniae*, Municipal Archives, Stralsund

16 A ruined castle in the midst of an animated riverside scene—a sure sign that contemporaries were well aware of the changing course of history. Neuburg on the Rhine. Etching by Mathäus Merian. Staatliche Museen zu Berlin, Cabinet of Copperplate Engravings and Drawing Collection

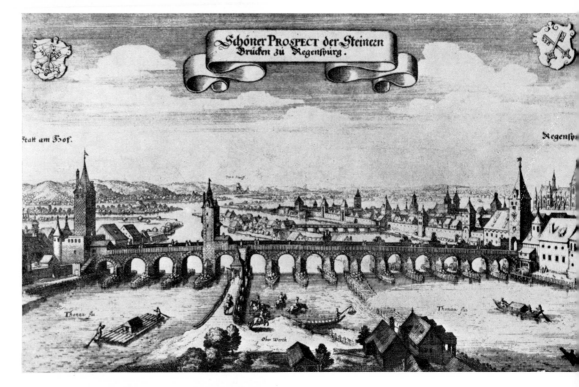

17 A Catholic service is being held here on St. Mary's Square in Munich, around St. Mary's Column, one of the principal symbols of the anti-Reformist cult of St. Mary. The monument was erected at the command of Maximilian, Elector of Bavaria, to commemorate the victory at the White Hill near Prague (1620). In the left foreground, singers and musicians are performing under the direction of a conductor wielding a baton. Copperplate engraving by Bartholomäus Kilian II. Staatliche Museen zu Berlin, Cabinet of Copperplate Engravings and Drawing Collection

18 Peasants brawling over a game of cards.
The great Flemish-Dutch painter, in a somewhat
grotesquely exaggerated form but without a
trace of contempt, shows peasants as they really
were in the poverty and coarseness of their
existence. Painting by Adriaen Brouwer. Staatliche Kunstsammlungen, Dresden, Gallery of
Paintings

19 This contemporary pamphlet shows peasants
with their implements and a boar-spear and,
on the left, a servant with a wooden toilet.
Detail of the satirical pamphlet "Dess Tilly
confect panquet" (1631). Museum für Geschichte der Stadt Leipzig

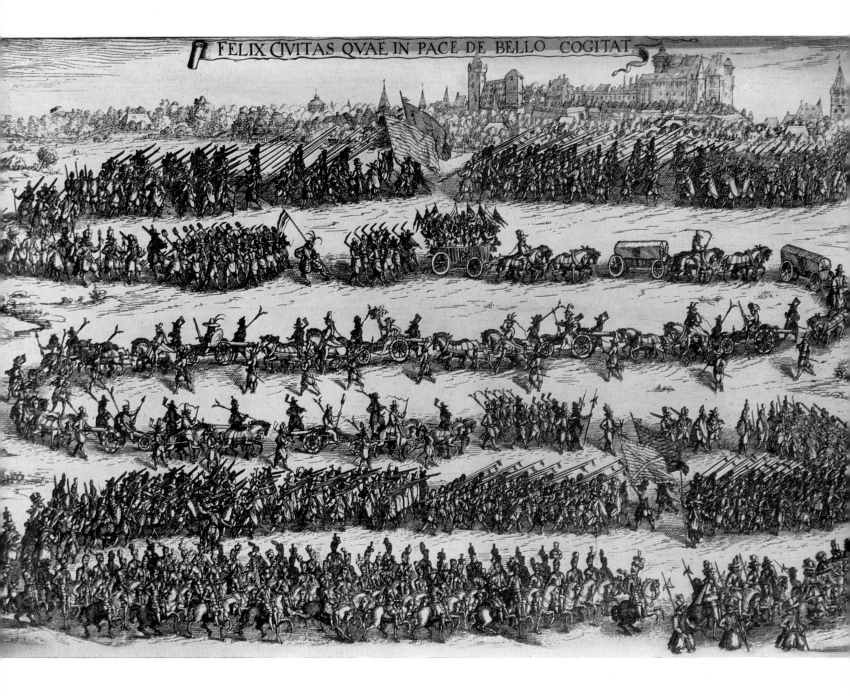

FELIX CIVITAS QVAE IN PACE DE BELLO COGITAT.

20 Nuremberg gunnery display: In a festive parade and to the sound of music, the house-holders demonstrate their fighting strength which is backed up by the manufacture of arms and trading in military equipment on a large scale. The artist, against the picturesque background of the Kaiserburg, depicts the following in a serpentine formation: about a thousand horsemen, musketeers, pikemen, artillerymen (constables), pioneers (the poorer citizens), flag-bearers, trumpeters, drummers and officers (with halberds). The impressive display is crowned by the slogan: Fortunate the city which is mindful of war in times of peace. Copperplate engraving (1614) by Peter Issel-burg. Národní Gallery, Prague

21 The open-air religious service was conducted according to Protestant rites in the St. Anne Collegium of Augsburg which had been set up on the centenary of the *Confessio Augustana* which had been laid down in writing at Augs-burg. According to the picture, far more than a thousand persons took part in it. Copperplate engraving by Raphael Custos (1648). Národní Gallery, Prague

22 In an atmosphere of stormy passions against the king as a "tyrant" and "friend of the heretics", Henry IV of France was stabbed to death in public by a Catholic fanatic called Ravaillac in Paris on 14 May 1610. This happened a few days before the king was due to journey to the Northern Army which was to invade the Empire in support of the Pro-testant princes. From: J. L. Gottfried's *Historische Chronik*

ANNO · COLLEGIVM NOVVM S·ANNÆ AVGVSTANVM · M·DC·XXXXVIII

EXECVTIO REBELLIVM FRANCOFVRTI A DMÆNVM,
XXVIII Febr. ANNO DN. cɔ.lɔ.CXVI.

DATE CÆSARI QVÆ SVNT CÆSARIS.

Zoll haus.

Rofszoll.

Der weg zum gericht.

Heir ist zu sehen wilcher
gestaldt ire kopf an de
bruckenthor zur Ewiger
gedechtnus seind auffgestect
worden, als Nemlich:

1. Fettmilchs.   2. Gerngross.
3. Schopp.   4. Ebalts.

Vahrhaffte abbildung der Echter Zu Franckfortt am Mayn, Vincentzen Fettmilchs Leckkuchen Beckers, Conraden Gerngross Schreiners, und Conraden Schoppen schneiders, welche vmb Jrer
Jn Anno 1612. erweckten vnd continuirten Rebellion zu fenglicher hafft genommen, und den 28. Febr. dises 1616. Jars, folgender massen anderen Zum abschäulichen exempel abgestrafft worde
Nemlichen seindt gemeltem Fettmilch die 2 finger hernach der kopf abgehawen, und sein corper geviertellt, die stuck uff die 4 strassen gehenckt, der kopff aber am bruckenthor auffgesteckt
entlich sein haus eingerissen worden, an dessen orts aine seullen zum ewigen gedechtnus auffgericht. Der gerngross, schopp und Georg Ebalit seindt geköpfft, undt Jrer drei kopffe zu a
Fettmilchs kopff gesteckt, die corper unter das hochgericht begraben. Ferner sandt Addolff Cantor, Herman Geiss, undt Steffen Wolff enthaupt, Jre Corper gleichweis unter das hoch
gericht gelegt, Weitters seindt 9 personen mitt rutten auss gesteuptt und ewig dess landts verwisen, Entlichen acht ander personen theils ewig, theils uff gewisse zeitt Inn
ellendt Ver Wisen Worden

23 The defeat of the radical townsfolk led to harsh punishment being inflicted on the leaders of the rebellion by the emperor, the princely rulers and the patricians of the Free Cities of the Empire. With a strong military escort as a precaution against another outbreak of public anger, Vinzenz Fettmilch and some of his comrades were executed on 28 February 1616 in the Horse Market of Frankfort. The executioner placed their heads on the Bridge Gate as a deterrent to all and sundry. A little more than five years later, a similar grim spectacle took place on the Altstädter Ring in Prague. Contemporary engraving

24 In 1617, the city council of Frankfort had a "column of shame" erected on the site of the demolished house of the "agitator" Fettmilch. Pamphlet (1617)

25 The angry artisans and craftsmen vented their wrath on the Jews who had the reputation of being shameless usurers. They were the scapegoats against which some of the popular energy was directed in the "Fettmilch Rebellion" of 1614 in Frankfort on the Main. The street known as the "Judengasse" (Jews' Lane) was plundered and its inhabitants, 1,380 in number, had to leave the city. Contemporary engraving. All three engravings are in the Historisches Museum, Frankfort on the Main.

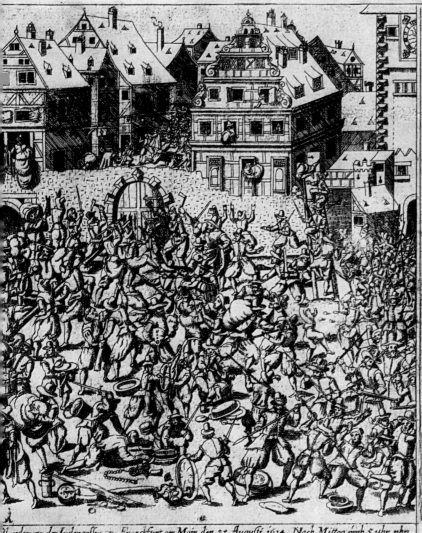

Plünderung der Iudengassen zu Franckfurt am Main den 22 Augusti 1614. Nach Mittag vmb 5 uhr von den Handtwercks gesellen angefangen, vnd die gantze Nacht durch Continuirt, da dann ein Burger vnd 7 Iuden gar todt bliben viel aber beiderseits beschedigt worden

Auszug der Iuden den 23 Augusti da man ihnen das Fischerfelds Pförtlein eröfnet, vnd sie vff dem Wasser hinauf vnd hinunder absahren lassen, da sindt ihrer 1380. Personen Iung vnd Alt, so zu der Pforten hinauß gangen, abgezehlet worden

26 The comet of 1618, drawn here on an exaggerated scale and generally interpreted as inauspicious, casts its ghostly light over the peacefully slumbering town of Heidelberg. From: Mathäus Merian, *Theatrum Europaeum* I

27 The "defenestration of Prague" of 23 May 1618—the abrupt deed intended by those responsible to initiate in the Bohemian areas a revolutionary transformation on the pattern of the Northern Netherlands—sparked off the war which, in a kind of chain reaction, spread across Europe. The picture captures that moment when, after an angry exchange of words, a group of radical members of the Bohemian Estates seizes the two Imperial governors, Jaroslav Martinic and Vilém Slavata, and the secretary Filip Fabricius (subsequently enobled by the emperor with the name "Von Hohenfall" ["of the great fall"]) and hurl them through the southwest window of the Green Room of the Bohemian Chancellery. Copperplate engraving from: Mathäus Merian, *Theatrum Europaeum* I

29 After the defeat of the uprising by the Bohemian Estates, there followed the punishment of the "rebels": twenty-four of them died bravely on the morning of 21 June 1621, dispatched by the sword of the executioner Jan Mydlář, an expert in his calling. Three of them ended on the gallows. The victors and judges, headed by Prince Charles of Liechtenstein, the Imperial governor, observe the executions, performed with Baroque pomp and circumstance, from the high tribune of the Altstädter Rathaus (the Town Hall of the Old Quarter). Contemporary pamphlet (detail). University Library, Greifswald

28 The heads of twelve of those executed were fixed to the bridge-tower in Prague and remained there for about ten years, apart from those that were brought down by the effects of the weather. Copperplate engraving (detail) from: Mathäus Merian, *Theatrum Europaeum* I

30 The Rector of Prague University, the Doctor of Medicine Jan Jesenský (Jessenius), suffered a particularly cruel fate. The executioner cut out his tongue and decapitated him. His body was quartered and the executioner's assistants placed the limbs on posts. Copperplate engraving (detail) from: Mathäus Merian, *Theatrum Europaeum* I

IVSTICIA

31 The aim of law and justice, which as an
allegorical figure in the foreground here carries
a balance and a sword as the symbols of
examination and punishment, was to provide a
deterrent for people. This was implemented by
corporal punishment or torture in public
(whipping, strappado, stretching on the rack—
left foreground—and the pouring of excrements down the delinquent's throat—
known as the "Swedish drink" in the Thirty
Years' War—and executions (burning at the
stake for witches, hanging, the wheel, de-
capitation). In the right foreground, a court
action is in progress, with the judge's bench, the
disputing parties, jurors and clerks. After Pieter
Brueghel's "Virtue" series, engraved by Philipp
Galle, the "Justice" sheet. Weimar Art Collections

32 Robbery was especially widespread before,
during and after the war and was not seldom
the expression of a negative protest against
feudal society. In this picture, the robber
Thomas Hans is being executed by one of the
cruelest techniques of killing—on the "wheel".
The executioners crushed the bones in the arms
and legs with a heavy cart-wheel, then the delinquent was bound to the wheel which was fixed
to a post. Copperplate engraving by Bartholomäus Kilian (1663). Národní Gallery, Prague

33 Public burning of witches. Etching by Jan
Luyken. Moravská Gallery, Brno

34 Biblical mystique in art: Saul and the witch
of Endor. Saul speaks with Samuel's ghost.
Copperplate engraving by Gabriel Ehinger after
Johann Heinrich Schönfeld. Art Collections
Veste Coburg

Viro Nobilissimo, Excellentissimoq, Domino DAVIDI THOMAN, JC.to Consiliario Reip. Au-
gustanæ Primario, Scholarchæ meritiss. &c. Artium Fautori, Aestimatorioq magno.

debiti cultûs gratia offert et dicat

35 The illustration in the pamphlet "Epitaphium oder des guten Geldes Grabschrift" depicts the main activities of the "coinage debasers": the melting down and striking of "Kippermünze" (substandard coins) and money-changing with coin-book and scales. From: Scheible, *Die Fliegenden Blätter*, No. 81

36 In the illustration on the leaflet "Eine neue Rätherschaft", a dishonest money-changer drives up the value of gold and silver coins. Those affected by this—an artisan, a merchant and an armed (!) peasant—in animated discussion. From: Scheible, *Die Fliegenden Blätter*, No. 83

("Many kings and potentates learnt the business well from me, So that they got property and money and even entire countries, They have long since got their indentures, Down there deep in Hell . . .")

An illustrated leaflet warns the coin-racketeers that they should not think that they will go unpunished because "great lords" also follow this dishonest trade. In a decision by the Jury Court of Halle concerning a case of coin-clipping, there is the following observation: "But it was rather the superiors who were those who undertook such coin-clipping and money-changing and dishonest trading in coins."

In a pamphlet in dialogue form entitled "Von letzten Teuffels Frucht/den Kippern und Wippern" ("Of the latest devil's brood/the coin-clippers and money-changers"), the "third speech of the coin-clipper" reads as follows:[1]

> "Was hast du dich und der Wipper Händel zu bekümmern/
> können doch Fürsten und Herren diese Leuthe von Kiphausen leiden/
> halten sie auch in allen Ehren/und für ihre liebe Getrewe . . ."

("Why be concerned about your quarrels with the money-changers/When princes and lords like these people from the money-clippers/they regard them highly/and for their loyal friends . . .")

There is a vigorous answer to this: "those who at the beginning changed Imperial coins without instructions and to their own advantage . . . and circulated sub-standard money . . . are to be regarded as nothing other than thieves, robbers and murderers, call them what one may." Could this be a reference to the princely coin-clippers, too? The people who heard these words delivered in the market-place and in the taverns certainly did not miss the allusion.

One author writes that since the price-increases and the reductions in the quality of the coins "may not and cannot take place without the permission of the authorities, it is easy to conclude who is the principal and basic cause of this evil".[2] The harshness of the situation was not felt at the princely courts since rulers purchased what they needed from their subjects at officially fixed prices.

> "Der Armen Seufftzen
> Uber die Ungerechtigkeit
> So uberhand nimpt diese Zeit,
> Durch ubermachtes Müntzn und Wippn,
> Die die Armen ins verderben kippn . . ."

("The poor sighed about the injustice, And so this time ran riot, Through coinage and money-changing, Which tip the poor into ruin") was a song which was heard in many places. It is said in a song about the "packmen and ropemen" who drove their pack-animals, loaded with goods, across the Alps and also across the Tauern Mountains that they did not like travelling through the land because food and fodder were far too expensive and in the end they would only become beggars.[3]

The ordinary people had seldom identified and condemned their principal foes.

[1] Municipal Archives Stralsund, 1621 or 1622

[2] Billich, C.: Unvorgreiffliches Bedencken, 1621, ibid.

[3] Historische Volkslieder und Zeitgedichte vom sechzehnten bis neunzehnten Jahrhundert, collected and explained by A. Hartmann, 1st vol., Munich, 1907, p. 153

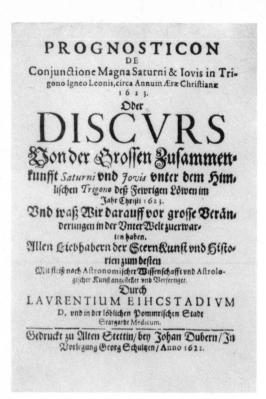

PROGNOSTICON
DE
Conjunctione Magna Saturni & Iovis in Trigono Igneo Leonis, circa Annum Æræ Christianæ
1 6 2 3.

Oder

DISCVRS
Von der Grossen Zusammen-
kunfft *Saturni* vnd *Jovis* vnter dem Him-
lischen *Trigono* deß Fewrigen Löwen im
Jahr Christi 1 6 2 3.
Vnd waß Wir darauff vor grosse Verän-
derungen in der Vnter Welt zuerwar-
ten haben.
Allen Liebhabern der Stern Kunst vnd Historien zum besten
Mit fleiß nach Astronomischer Wissenschafft vnd Astrolo-
gischer Kunst angestellet vnd Verfertiger.

Durch
LAVRENTIUM EIHCSTADIVM
D. vnd in der löblichen Pommrischen Stadt
Stargardt Medicum.

Gedruckt zu Alten Stettin / bey Johan Dubern / In
Vorlegung Georg Schulgen / Anno 1622.

37 In the astrological "Prognosticon" of
Lorenz Eichstad, the town physician of Stargard,
a portentous influence on terrestrial events is
attributed to the simultaneous presence of the
planets Saturn and Jupiter in the "third
celestial house" (1623). Municipal Archives,
Stralsund

[1] Janssen, J.: Geschichte des deutschen Volkes,
vol. 5, p. 669f.

FEAR,
EXPECTATIONS AND
UNSPOKEN HOPE

If the literature of the time is examined which concerns itself with the "way of the world", an attitude of expectation, apparent in a variety of forms and more or less clearly formulated, will be noted. At the beginning of the 17th century, a general rebellion by the people was what was feared by the emperor and the princes who were incapable of finding a political solution for the crisis in which they found themselves. They regarded the Netherlands as the driving force in this crisis and as setting an example. In a report of December 1614, a counsellor of Württemberg wrote that the Netherlands would find a large measure of support in the Empire in their efforts to expel the Catholic and non-Catholic princes and to establish a "democratic regime". As possible helpers and allies of the Netherlands, he named the Calvinists who had settled in the Empire following persecution in their native country and the middle classes—not so much the patriciate—of the Hanseatic and Imperial cities. He asserted that it was especially the middle classes who sought nothing more than "to set up a universal democracy". The united action of these municipal adversaries of the princes would encourage "the common mob and the country people" to take up arms (in the use of which the peasants "at many places are very well practised") and to move against the authorities. The author is of the opinion that it would be better not to fight against the Catholic princes than to have the Dutch States-General as allies.[1]

From the viewpoint of his own political crisis, much seemed worse to the writer of the letter than it really was but he nevertheless gives a clear description of those class-forces which could offer more or less determined resistance and be a danger to the princely upper class, the ruling part of the feudal class.

The practical policy of the uneasy princes and their advisers was usually bereft of any moral principles and was often enough the product of pure ignorance, greed and inability. At the time of the Thirty Years' War and in addition to religion, they made use of an already ancient means to give their actions a greater degree of certainty and the appearance of supernatural origin—astrology. No doubt about it whatsoever—people really did believe in the influence of distant constellations on terrestrial events and official science confirmed them in their erroneous belief. Astrologers and astronomers were respected members of the court. They determined the positions of the stars, prepared confusing and ambiguous prophecies and horoscopes and distributed them as pamphlets. It was in this manner that even Kepler, the court mathematician of the emperor and later of Wallenstein, was compelled to serve the mighty ones of the time.

Wallenstein ordered a horoscope from him via an intermediary in 1608, this subsequently being extended in 1625. The astronomer determined the constellation of the stars at the hour of his birth and wrote that the young man of noble family would

50

achieve an exalted position and great wealth. After all, was his constellation not the same as that of the mighty Grand Chancellor of Poland, Jan Zamojski, the "king-maker", and of Queen Elizabeth of England? Kepler did not hesitate, either to indicate the dark side, the price of such a predestinated career. His client would be considered a "lonely, underworld monster" respected by none but himself. For his subordinates he would be a hard task-master. Kepler predicted a very unfavourable situation for the beginning of 1634. Such a high degree of agreement with reality was no accident. The astronomer, familiar with the psychology and mentality of the Bohemian nobility, was a perceptive observer of terrestrial matters as well; and on Wallenstein the horoscope exercised a lasting influence, representing a kind of guide-line for his actions.[1]

38 This woodcut in a pamphlet shows some of the signs of the Zodiac which contemporaries asserted that they had seen (1627). From: Steinhausen, *Deutsche Kultur*

Kepler made the following remarks in 1618 about this particular way of earning a living: "This Astrologia is certainly a crazy daughter; but, dear God, what would her mother, the highly rational Astronomia, do if she did not have this crazy daughter? … And the Mathematicorum Salaria (earnings of the mathematicians) are so slight that the mother would certainly starve if the daughter did not earn anything." In his encyclopaedic *Piazza Universale* of the arts and crafts, Thomas Garzoni calls astronomy and astrology "two sisters who are worth keeping". The former, so he writes, is concerned with the theory of the heavens, with the movement and course of the planets and fixed stars, while the latter deals with practical matters: the deduction of statements for the future from the movement of the heavens and of the stars and the drawing of conclusions as to the character and career of man from his nativity. Garzoni regards this aspect as foolish and superstitious but he views the possibility of predicting the weather from the stars, determining the times for sowing and harvesting and detecting plagues in good time as tangible and useful.[2] This "Astrologia naturalis" was the most important element in the composition of calendars. It was a constant source of profit for authors and especially for publishers and was much in demand at the fairs in Frankfort and Leipzig.

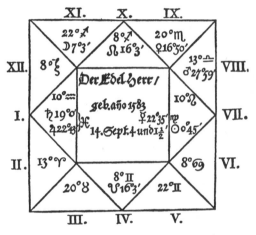

39 Kepler's first horoscope for Wallenstein (1608) with the twelve triangular "celestia houses" around the square of the nativity containing the date and hour of birth of the client. From: Steinhausen, *Deutsche Kultur*

Unusual celestial happenings such as comets, eclipses, parhelions and northern lights were considered to be omens of exceptional importance and the comet of November 1618 was interpreted by scholars and the uneducated alike as a highly significant *prodigium*, a warning of divine anger. David Herlitzius, the "Physikus" (municipal physician) of Stargard and court astrologer of Pomerania, immediately composed a *prodromus* (introduction) about the "tailed star". This comet appeared when Jupiter, the Sun, Venus, Mercury and the Moon were under the Earth (i. e., below the horizon) but the "evil and mischievous planets" Saturn and Mars were above. "Mars peregrinus", so it was said, had left the "eleventh house" of the heavens at this time, was four degrees in front of the tail of the Lion and threatened with many hostile, murderous attacks, false alliances and betrayals. Since the comet had flamed up in the constellation of the Scorpion, the "first heavenly house", it was asserted that pestilence, monster births, rain and floods, widespread death and a consequent rise in the price of fish and above all hate and dissatisfaction among the kings, rebellion, discord and war would inevitably follow. This was indeed the picture presented by the world and many had no doubt but that God intended to inflict punishment with the "rod of Heaven" and that this was certainly merited by mankind. The publication by Herlitzius was

[1] Janáček, J.: Valdštejnova smrt, Prague, 1970; Becker, W.: Das Horoskop Wallensteins von Johannes Kepler, Berlin-Steglitz, undated

[2] Thomae Garzoni Piazza Universale oder Allgemeiner Schauplatz aller Künst, Professionen und Handtwercken, Frankfort on the Main (Merian) 1641, copy in Municipal Archives Stralsund

40 Jakob Böhme, the "philosophizing cobbler" is regarded as the founder of modern philosophy in Germany. Portrait engraving by an unknown artist. Museum der Stadt Görlitz

answered by the physician and scholar Joachim Köppen of Magdeburg in a treatise which increased the nonsensical speculations still further. He saw Jupiter as the symbol for "gentlefolk" while Venus embodied "all the worldly lusts" and the star Boötes the "coarse Saxons" who were especially associated with the horse and cart. This abstruse work was actually published, together with a quantity of illustrated pamphlets and other tracts.

The interpretations of the comet presented the disasters and burdens inflicted on the common people as inevitable and at the same time paralyzed and unsettled them. The Duke of Pomerania, like other princes, ordered the priests in November 1618 to preach repentance from their pulpits so that the wrath of God, as indicated by the comet, would be averted. At the same time, however, the pulpit was the most important source of information and opinion.[1]

The crisis of society and government at the beginning of the 17th century, aggravated by uncompromising religious discordances, necessarily produced a variety of nonconformist ideas. One of the most widespread of these was the desire, expectation and argument for a "general reformation".

According to the much-read Englishman Fludd, who was well-informed about matters of astronomy, the nova of 1604 was an omen of the coming of a mighty potentate who would transform the existing conditions by "clementia et potentia,. arte et marte" (by clemency and power, by art and war). In 1614, an anonymous book was published in Kassel with the title of *Fama Fraternitatis*—one of a large number of the mysterious Rosicrucian treatises. It contains the doctrine of the sequence of the ages by the medieval mystic Joachim von Fiore, indicating in obscure words that the last age of the Earth and a new prophet, Elijah, were to be expected.[2] Apocalyptic ideas of a final catastrophe which would bring forth a new saviour were also disseminated by the great "teacher of the people"—Jan Amos Komenský (Comenius). These were the subject of renewed interest and became associated with such persons as Frederick V of the Palatinate or Gustavus Adolphus who, as the "Lion of the North", would destroy the "evil eagle" (the Hapsburgs) and the "Powers of the South", the "wicked dragon of the West" (papacy, Empire and Spain). A charcoal burner of Styria, who refused to retract even under torture, prophesied great misfortune for Emperor Ferdinand II.[3]

In 1614, two preachers greatly disturbed the authorities of the Electorate of Saxony. They originally came from Thuringia and found interested listeners in various cities, including Leipzig and Dresden. One of them, Ezechiel Meth, asserted that he was "the great prince Michael", that Lutheran baptism and Communion were nothing but sorcery, that there was no resurrection from the dead and no eternal soul. Man could participate in the joys of eternal life even during his lifetime. In the eyes of the clergy, who acknowledged the authority of the temporal institutions, this was blasphemous heresy of the worst kind and the prophets were expelled from the country.[4]

The Austrian exile and schoolteacher Paul Matth, to whom the "great light" appeared one night in 1622 as a divine sign of a new life in spiritualized piousness, did not use such sharp words but was likewise persecuted by his former co-religionists. He was obliged to leave his family, leaving Linz for Regensburg and moving on from

[1] Bülow, G. von: Der Komet von 1618, in: Baltische Studien 35/1885

[2] Peukert, W.-E.: Die Rosenkreutzer. Zur Geschichte einer Reformation, Jena, 1928; Yates, F. A.: Aufklärung im Zeichen des Rosenkreuzes, Stuttgart, 1975

[3] Haase, P.: Das Problem des Chiliasmus und der Dreissigjährige Krieg, Thesis. Leipzig, 1933; Egelhaaf, G.: Gustav Adolf und Deutschland. 1630—1632, Halle, 1901

[4] Vogel, J. J.: Leipzigisches Geschicht-Buch/ Oder Annales ..., Leipzig, 1714, p. 353; Janssen, J.: Geschichte des deutschen Volkes, vol. 6, p. 432

there to Nuremberg where various sects and prophets were active. When his adversaries vigorously opposed him here, too, he withdrew to "the midst of the woods", ploughed the soil and grew his own food as a hermit. Matth was against the practise of confession and the celebration of Communion and stood for freedom of conscience. He was a representative of those who sought God, not because they expected the imminent end of a sinful world and its renewal but because he believed that the realm of God was to be found in the human heart. Silence and hope until the "star of the East" appears—that was his maxim.[1]

Among all the hope and fear that abounded, there flared up once more and now for the last time the idea of the coming of an emperor who—from a position of low rank in society—would become master of the whole of Europe. Holzhauser, the prophet of this emperor, took his vision of a great universal monarchy from the writings of the mystic Joachim von Fiore, to whom reference has already been made.

Even after the war, as reflected in Grimmelshausen's *Simplizissimus*, solitude was regarded as the way out of a corrupted world by some people while others put their hope in a comprehensive reform of the socio-political conditions. This hope was set in the realm of dreams in which the emperor was replaced by a "German hero", who would appoint a college of wise men. The hero and the parliament of wise men would have no need of soldiers to implement the "general reformation" so long desired by the common people.[2]

Not so easy to classify as the solitary prophets who sometimes caught the attention of princes and generals were the religious sects which were found throughout the Empire. These groups, which subscribed to a variety of beliefs and principles, were not characterized by any socio-revolutionary spirit. Mysticism of many shades and hues dominated their ideas, God lived within them or was to be seen in every aspect of Nature and they dissociated themselves from any outward appearance of ecclesiastical organization. Although they totally rejected all kinds of force and despised religious wrangles, they were held to be a provocation and danger by the official church since the "sectarians" for the most part did not attend church ceremonies, met in private dwellings and evolved their own simple forms of piety.

It was with particular energy that the authorities searched for the writings of Caspar Schwenckfeld and of the vicar Valentin Weigel from Zschopau since they opposed Luther's "truth of the Scriptures" and his doctrine of the sacraments with their subjective "truth by revelation". Their teachings were readily accepted by a large part of the population in Silesia since the small-scale political structure, the economic prosperity, the many travellers passing through the area and the considerable tolerance in religious matters favoured sectarianism of a private and personal type.

The founder of modern German philosophy, Jakob Böhme, also belongs to the tradition of mysticism, individual faith and pantheism (the doctrine that equates God with Nature) associated with Paracelsus and Sebastian Franck. Born in the village of Alt-Seidenberg in Upper Lusatia, Böhme learned the shoemaker's trade and settled in 1599 in Görlitz, the place where most of his works were produced. After years of meditation in which he grappled with and absorbed the teachings of the

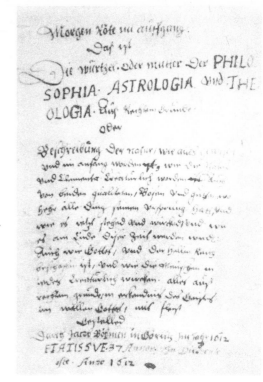

41 Title-page of the original manuscript of *Aurora* by Jakob Böhme (1612). Museum der Stadt Görlitz

[1] Soden: Kriegs- und Sittengeschichte der Reichsstadt Nürnberg, vol. 3, p. 154ff.; Dülmen, R. van: Schwärmer und Separatisten in Nürnberg (1618—1648), in: Archiv f. Kulturgeschichte 1/1973

[2] Der abenteuerliche Simplicissimus, IIIrd Book, 4th chapter

42 Jan Amos Komenský (Comenius), called the "teacher of nations", when he was sixty years old. Etching by Wenzel Hollar in England. Moravská Gallery, Brno

[1] Böhme, J.: Aurora oder Morgenröte im Aufgang. Edited and with an introduction by G. Bartsch, Leipzig, 1974

[2] Geschichte der Erziehung, 11th edition, Berlin, 1973

[3] Böck, G.: Thomas Campanella: politisches Interesse und politische Spekulation, Tübingen, 1974; Andreae, Johann Valentin: Christianopolis, 1619. Original text and translation from D. S. Georgi, introduction by R. van Dülmen, Stuttgart, 1972

above authors, he wrote his *Morgenröte im Aufgang*, subsequently entitled *Aurora*. It was circulated as a manuscript and a large number of additional tracts followed it in the next few years. It was only the goodwill of some noble patrons that saved him from worse persecution than the ban on writing imposed by the orthodox clergy. With a Lutheran turn of phrase, often obscure in word and content, Böhme taught that Nature (= God) embodies the power of eternal birth and that this world of Nature is not at rest but contains "nothing but a rough, bitter fiery and noisily burning tearing and raging", "a rebellious being" and "a sheer fury". What a clear acknowledgment this is of the unity and diversity of the world, of the inner momentum resulting from contradictions. His choice of words is admittedly emotional and incorrect but extremely productive. Nor does the strange language obscure his shining faith in mankind (and not the God of the time): "And Man is everything." Böhme's writings were taken to the Netherlands and to England where they were printed, distributed, read and passionately discussed. Their spirit passed into the confusing ferment of the intellectual life of these dynamic, revolutionary countries. In Germany, Böhme's ideas became associated with the great Pietist movement of ethical and intellectual revival.[1]

It almost seems as if the world torn by war with its profound class-contradictions was imbued with a desire for better people and a happy world in a much more intense manner than would otherwise have been the case and that the intellectual quest for ways and for remote ideals became even more insistent. Many placed their entire hopes in sciences and their ennobling and educational influence. Johann Heinrich Alsted taught philosophy and theology at Herborn. He was untiring in his search for knowledge, published works of an encyclopaedic character and provided a stimulus for various branches of knowledge, including pedagogics, one of the outstanding representatives of which was active at this time—Jan Amos Komenský. Profoundly convinced of the ability of man to absorb education to an unlimited degree, the latter wrote numerous books on practical pedagogics, including textbooks and manuals and—inspired by the aim of renewing all things in life—began work on a mighty "pansophy", the treasury of all knowledge. Komenský was not only the pupil of Alsted at Herborn but also the enthusiastic follower of the scholar David Pareus of Heidelberg who, at the university and in his home, the "Pareanum", imbued his students from many countries with his idea of the reconciliation of the Evangelist religious community. Komenský subscribed to this and proposed that a *collegium lucis* of enlightened men should be established. As with his teacher Alsted, his rational irenic theology was mingled with obscure chiliasm, the desire for a "realm of God".[2]

Komenský was also familiar with the writings of the restless and much-travelled vicar Johann Valentin Andreae of Württemberg who was the author of a social utopia, the fourth of its kind in Germany. This was published at Strasbourg in 1619 under the title *Rei publicae Christianopolitanae descriptio* and was the—less clear—Christian-German counterpart to the utopia *Civitas solis* (The Sun-State) by the Italian Tomaso Campanella, a work which was well-known later on[3]. Andreae drew up a plan for an ideal city, organized along Christian and communistic lines, in which human activities were arranged in concentric circles: outside the walls, areas were allotted for the cultivation of land and the raising of livestock, for mills and bakeries, for the slaughter-house, public kitchens, laundries and warehouses and places for work in which fire was used; within the city, provision was made for the workshops of the artisans, the communal residential quarters, gardens and open areas. In the centre of the city, there was to be a four-storey building as the residence of the "triumvirate" who were to govern in a wise and comradely manner. The upper floors of this building were to contain the heart of the community—the scientific, technical and educational facilities: library, archives, printing-shop, laboratories, pharmacy, an anatomical and physical "theatre", schools with residential accommodation, lecture rooms and hospitals and a law cabinet. In the courtyard, there was to be a church and a council assembly hall. Andreae believed that the ethical driving force of human society was not the striving for profit but work and the desire for the prosperity of the community, Christian love and education of a high standard. The bold dreamer regarded the essential nature of religion not as the obedience of man cursed by original sin but in bliss and the moral renewal of the human race.

Wolfgang Ratke (Ratichius) toyed with a project concerning the reform of practical education. Following his studies in Hamburg, Rostock and Holland (1603—1610), he started work in Frankfort on the Main on a draft for the renewal of the educational system and of the social and cultural conditions. On 7 May 1612, he submitted a memorandum to the assembly meeting there for the election of the emperor. This contained proposals for the rapid learning of the ancient languages, the cultivation of the German mother-tongue and the convenient introduction and peaceful main-tenance of "a harmonious government and, at last, also a harmonious religion ..." However, the princes did not react.[1]

Ratke could not escape the harsh and restless destiny of a proponent of such bold and noble ideas. Where, with fervent zeal, he began to make changes in lessons and schools, his enemies from the ranks of the theologians in the royal and municipal authorities, who dominated everything of an intellectual nature, lost little time in throwing doubt and suspicion on his efforts. They asserted that Ratke prevented the children from reading the Bible, that he was an heretic and an adversary of the ruling class and that he was a member of the much-reviled sect of the Rosicrucians. The illustrious humanist remained steadfast and remained convinced of the correctness and practicability of his ideas until his death.

The various learned and linguistic societies of the time were also inspired by the desire to provide a progressive stimulus through education and the cultivation of the language. Joachim Jungius, a follower of Ratke's, founded in Rostock a "Collegium philosophicum"—the first association of scholars in Germany. It was intended to serve the "investigation of truth from reason and experience". In 1617, at the suggestion of Prince Louis of Anhalt-Köthen who took an interest in literary matters, there was founded at Weimar the first of the German "language societies"—the "Fruchtbrin-gende Gesellschaft" (the "fructuous society"). The principal model on which these societies were based was the "Academia della Crusca" at Florence, the aim of which was to separate the bran (crusca) from the pure flour in the (Italian) language. The "Academia" did indeed publish a Vocabularium (dictionary) of the Italian lan-

43 Johann Valentin Andreae, a vicar of Württemberg and the author of the utopian *Christianopolis*. Copperplate engraving by Wolfgang Kilian (1648). Moravská Gallery, Brno

[1] Die neue Lehrart. Pädagogische Schriften Wolfgang Ratkes. Introduction by G. Hohen-dorf, Berlin, 1957; Alt, R.: Bilderatlas zur Schul-und Erziehungsgeschichte, vol. 1, Berlin, 1966

guage in the year 1612. Prince Louis became a member of the Florentine academy in 1600.[1]

In the course of its existence, the German "Fruchtbringende Gesellschaft" had a total of almost 900 members. According to its statutes, those with intellectual ambitions from all classes and creeds were eligible for membership. But the aristocratic element predominated, the result of this being that symbolism and the ceremonies of the association became more important than the actual academic and poetic work with the German language after 1650. Although this cultivation of the language was the principal merit of the society and especially of its middle-class members Christian Queintz and Justus Schottel, symbols and names nevertheless indicate that its aims were wider than this. The "fructuous" occasionally called itself the "Christenburg" or the "Collegium solis" as well, these names being inspired by the illustrious utopias of Andreae and Campanella. The later symbol of the society, the palm, became the symbol of renewal in general. In the course of the war, other language societies came into being, the most important of these being the "Deutschgesinnte Genossenschaft" and the "Pegnitz-Schäfer" in Nuremberg. The two latter societies had an almost exclusively middle-class membership while the "Orden" of Nuremberg even admitted women. To be sure, the numbers of those united in these societies were not large but it was here that the striving for progress in the bourgeois sense, for the enrichment of that which was not only an intrinsic part of the people but also owed its existence to the people—the language—took shape. This was logically the front line in the resistance to the sterile imitation of alien tongues at court and to shallow popular literature of the "charming" type. On the other hand, as translators, they provided access to the great works of Dutch, French, Spanish and Italian literature. In contrast to the rapacious wars of the ruling circles, they cherished the concept of a peaceful and fertile encounter between people and nations.

WITCH-HUNTING

At the same time as learned men increased their humane efforts to lessen barren religious hatred and to make the world a more moral place through education and culture, much of Germany was overtaken by a fearful wave of socio-psychic persecution—witch-hunting—for which no really satisfying explanation has yet been offered. It was probably associated with acute social contradictions but can by no means be directly or solely inferred from these since otherwise man-hunts such as these would regularly occur at times of extreme crisis. This, however, it not the case.

The persecution of witches in Europe dates back to the 15th century but it was only about the middle of the 16th century that it developed into an epidemic affecting many countries which reached a climax at the beginning and after the middle of the

[1] Otto, K. F.: Die Sprachgesellschaften des 17. Jahrhunderts, Stuttgart, 1972; Geschichte der deutschen Literatur, vol. 5. From 1600 to 1700, Berlin 1963; Bulling, K.: Bibliographie der Fruchtbringenden Gesellschaft, Berlin/Weimar, 1965

17th century. In Central and Northern Germany, this climax came at the end of the 1620's. It was at this time, too, that pogroms of the Jews again occurred in a series of cities, including Frankfort on the Main, Worms and Jena, the confusion in the coinage adding tinder to the general situation.

On the order of the King of Spain, about 300,000 Moriscos (Moorish Arabs who had embraced Christianity) were classified as "infidels" and expelled from Castile, Valencia, Catalonia and Aragon between 1609 and 1611. In Germany, too, but on a lesser scale, there also began the forced emigration of "exiles" who were driven from their native land for religious reasons.

These inhuman practises in the exercise of government created an atmosphere of terror, suspicion and persecution. The fear of any other force at all was likewise accentuated as soon as a name could be given to it—the vengeance of God, the Devil—and of the "witches" in intimate contact with him. Every religion of Western Europe has proclaimed that their existence is possible and certain. Ancient superstitions, which continued to survive in lonely mountainous areas in particular, kept the belief in the existence of witches alive in the public imagination.[1]

This belief only turned into hysteria after the existence of witches had been described in terms of incredible madness and horror, the product of crazy, pedantic intellects and sick imaginations as recorded in innumerable, weighty volumes on "demonology", in pamphlets and in illustrated leaflets. Fanatical sermons, special trials, the posing of leading questions by judges, "confessions" obtained under torture and "evidence" by blood-thirsty witnesses filled with hatred continued to add more and more gruesome details. In these conditions, it was almost impossible to find reasonable counter-arguments or to offer a defence since the scene was dominated by the basest feelings and a state of terror which in actual fact were tolerated and cultivated by learned circles in close touch with the official authorities.

If often happened that the seeking and persecution of witches assumed epidemic proportions and that nobody—regardless of his or her religion—was safe from denunciation in such an atmosphere of panic. Most of the victims were elderly women who were accused of trafficking with the Devil. Judges and torturers forced them to confess that they had ridden through the air to the witches' sabbath and had met Satan for a disgusting nocturnal sex orgy on such mountains as the Brocken, the Huy at Halberstadt, the Fichtelberg, the Zobten or the Heuberg, for example. Details of the satanic meal, the witches' dance and the sex orgies were the subject of abstruse and scholarly disputes in which not only ascetic monks took part but also crowned heads (James I of England).

The leading lights of science, critical minds and world-famous scientists—such as Grotius, Galileo, Descartes, Bacon or Kepler remained silent on the subject. It was only thanks to his position as Imperial mathematician that the latter was able to save his mother, Katherina, who had been accused of witchcraft, from being burnt at the stake. In 1580, Bodin published a learned work in which he demanded the death at the stake not only for witches but also for those who did not believe in their existence.[2]

After a century of practice, witch-hunting was given the official blessing of the Church in its most exalted form already at the end of the 15th century. In December

[1] Trevor-Roper, H. R.: Der europäische Hexenwahn des 16. und 17. Jahrhunderts, in: Religion, Reformation und sozialer Umbruch. Die Krisis des 17. Jahrhunderts, Frankfort on the Main/Munich/Berlin (West), 1970 (from the English edition of 1967); also comprehensive list of older literature: Soldan-Heppe, N. Paulus, G. Hansen, H. C. Lea, L. Thorndike et al.; Baschwitz, K.: Hexen und Hexenprozesse. Die Geschichte eines Massenwahns und seiner Bekämpfung, Munich, 1966

[2] Bodin, J.: De la démonologie des sorciers, Paris, 1580

44 On the instructions of the Bishop of Bamberg, a new "Malefizhaus" (malefaction) was built in 1627 for the holding of trials against witches. Copperplate engraving by Mathäus Merian the Elder, Güstrow Museum

1484, Innocent VIII issued the papal bull *Summis desiderantes affectibus*, appointing two Dominican scholars—Heinrich Institor and Jakob Spranger—to liquidate the witches tracked down in Germany. In 1486, the two inquisitors published the first great encyclopaedia of demonology, the *Malleus Maleficarum* or the "Witches' Hammer". By 1669, it had been reprinted about 30 times. The Catholic clergy had acquired sufficient experience in persecution in the course of its pursuit of "heretics". This now proved useful in the organized and subtle identification of another alien group of outsiders—women who were said to be "witches".[1]

The great *Practica nova imperialis rerum criminalium* (1635) by Benedict Carpzov, a jurist and court counsellor of Leipzig and a European authority in matters of penal law, was known as the "Lutheran witches' hammer" He also referred to a number of Catholic authors to prove that all those who confessed—including those who only believed that they had been present at a witches' sabbath—must be executed since the will was said to be part of faith. By his verdicts at Leipzig, he sent hundreds of witches to their death at the stake and sophisticated the techniques of torture. He attended Communion every week and is said to have read the Bible 53 times.

In Germany, Johann von Schöneburg, archbishop of Trier, and Julius Echter von Mespelbrunn, the Lord Bishop of Würzburg, set examples of witch-hunting on a massed scale, following preliminary exercises in such Lutheran principalities as Brandenburg, Württemberg and Baden. The archbishop, a militant advocate of the counter-reformation, persecuted and expelled first the Protestants and after this the Jews. Then it was the turn of the witches: 368 were burnt in 22 villages in seven years. The victims included also very old people and children and even personages in high positions, such as the supreme judge (who was too mild), were not safe. The executioner strutted around in public, displaying the gold and silver earned from the death of his innocent victims.

The Lord Abbot of Fulda, Balthasar von Dernbach, who had returned to his territory in 1602, employed witch-hunting as an instrument for the forcible recatholicization of the area. His reign of terror was maintained by a *Malefizmeister* (master of malefaction) and a "travelling inquisition", which had a predilection for rich villages. Within three years, 250 alleged witches had been put to death. Dernbach's Protestant contemporary, Duke Heinrich Julius of Brunswick, a prince well-acquainted with foreign languages, interested in law and science and an art-lover who himself wrote dramas, was one of the most zealous witch-hunters. It is reported that at the time that he governed the place of execution resembled a wood—so numerous were the blackened stakes to which the unfortunate women had been bound when they met their death.

The mania, for which the spiritual and temporal princes were largely responsible, reached a climax in Germany in the 1620's. The growing power of the Catholic emperor was reflected in the Edict of Restitution of 1629 which provided a new stimulus in the Reich for the zealous continuation of religious persecution.

It was in Würzburg once again, under the pontificate of Philipp Adolf von Ehrenberg, that rabid witch-hunting took toll of 900 people, including even priests and children. Fuchs von Dornheim, his neighbour at Bamberg who was known as the "Witches' Bishop", had a "house of malefaction" specially built for the barbarous court-proceed-

[1] Grigulevič, I. R.: Istorija inkvizicii, Moscow, 1970; German: Ketzer—Hexen—Inquisitoren, 2 vols., Berlin, 1976; Hauben, P. J.: The Spanish Inquisition, New York/London/Toronto, 1969

ings. In his brief period of office, 600 people died a ghastly death by fire. One of those burnt at the stake was the lenient Episcopal Chancellor who confessed under torture that he had seen five burgomasters and councillors of Bamberg at the witches' sabbath —all of these subsequently being executed. One of these, under sadistic torture, had named another 27 people and had confessed to being in league with the Devil. In a letter to his daughter while he was held prisoner, he wrote that all this was untrue and mere invention. The mania of witch-hunting raged in like manner in Baden, in the Bishopric of Eichstätt, in Coblenz (part of the territory of Trier), in Ingolstadt in Bavaria, at the residence of the Elector-Archbishop of Cologne at Bonn and in Alsace. No witches or scarcely any were burnt in the Duchy of Cleves, in the Palatinate, in Nassau or in the majority of the Imperial cities, though people lived in fear here, too.

It is true that suspicion and the death penalty occasionally struck at members of the prosperous strata and the upper classes but the great majority of the victims came from the mass of the working people or impoverished groups. Most of those executed were elderly women, on whom a life of hard work and worry had left its marks. Outwardly visible infirmities, particular physical features (warts, birthmarks, sties) or deformities, ugliness, inability to weep or the alleged "evil eye" were regarded as practically incontrovertible evidence. Accusations were frequently motivated by greed since the possessions of the victim were shared out by the informer, judge, executioner and the authorities. However, it was seldom indeed that denunciations were made against members of the leading circles since ruling power and social standing acted as effective barriers against this.

The first doubts concerning the persecution of witches and its juridical and ethical basis appeared only a century after the publication of the "Witches' Hammer", during the first great wave of executions by fire. How much courage was needed for this is illustrated by the fate of the first public critic, Johann Weyer (or Wier). Born in Brabant, he was one of the outstanding physicians of his time.[1] He detested and fought against Spanish rule in the Netherlands. With the tolerant Duke of Jülich-Cleves-Berg as his patron, he believed himself safe enough to write his work *De praestigiis daemonum* at Hambach Castle. This was published in 1563, six editions and some supplements following in the next 20 years—an indication of the topicality of the subject discussed. Nevertheless, Weyer's book had hardly any practical effect within his lifetime. Witch-hunting and the fear of the Devil were too deeply rooted and his adversaries were too numerous. They called Weyer an heretical follower of Waldus and Wycliffe and his book was burnt at the University of Marburg. Duke Alba of Spain demanded Weyer's extradition and he met with the opposition of French Calvinists and of Bodin who called him a godless person and an accomplice of Satan. To be sure, Weyer had not denied the existence of witches but he wrote that all the actions said to have been committed by those "miserable old women" were deceptions of the senses, emanating from devils or diseases. The humanist scholar himself only just managed to escape a cruel death. His arguments were quoted by all the subsequent opponents of witch-hunting.

Of these, a special place is merited by Friedrich Spee, a scholarly Jesuit and the author of tender poems. The influential Order had compelled the Catholic theologian

Witch-burning in Lohr

Before and after the year 1628, they took sharp action here against the sorcerers, demons and witches, of whom very many were burnt, including also boys of 11, 10, 9 and 8 years.

From: Topographia Franconiae (Merian), 1655

[1] Geschichte der Medizin, ed. by A. Mette and I. Winter, Berlin, 1968, p. 187

Cornelis Loos to retract his criticism of the persecution of witches. Nervertheless, the subsequent excesses in the grotesque campaign against witches in the first decades of the 17th century caused a crisis in the Jesuit Order and an increasing number of warning voices were to be heard, including that of Adam Tanner, a prominent Jesuit of Ingolstadt. In 1627, at the bidding of his superior and after successful teaching and pastoral work in Cologne and Paderborn, Friedrich Spee was sent to Würzburg, following a request by Philipp Adolf von Ehrenberg, the bishop to whom reference has already been made, for a father-confessor for the witches sentenced to death. Spee accompanied no less than 200 to their place of execution—and considered that not a single one of them was guilty. The bishop's judges regarded the sympathetic and pious man with growing distrust and he eventually had to go.

Spee later wrote that what he had experienced in Würzburg could not easily be expressed in words. Nevertheless, his troubled conscience led him in 1631 to compose the most eloquent protest against the persecution of witches, his *Cautio criminalis, seu de Processibus contra Sagas ...*". This was initially circulated as an anonymous handwritten manuscript since Spee had to fear the possible consequences but a well-meaning friend took it to Rinteln where it was published anonymously in the same year by a courageous university printer, Petrus Lucius.[1] Spee considered that the princes would never eradicate evil in this manner and that the whole of Germany was smoking with the fires that were obscuring the light. Everything told by the "witch-doctors" was based on confessions obtained by torture; torture filled Germany and other countries with witches of unimaginable cruelty. Spee did not deny their existence but he cast doubt on the value of confessions which were regarded as the most important evidence for a verdict of guilty and the subsequent sentence. This scepticism also convinced a friend of the Jesuit priest who held the same view. This was Philipp von Schönborn, the later Bishop of Würzburg and Archbishop of Mainz and he ultimately prohibited the persecution of witches in his principalities. In other countries and territories, however, the terror and hysteria emanating from the judiciary authorities continued to rage and, towards the end of the century, again increased to a horrifying extent, even reaching as far as the New England colonies in America. The mania then died down and ultimately disappeared everywhere.

It was the scholar Christian Thomasius of Halle who, in his sensational dissertation of November 1701, called for the ending of trials of witches since witchcraft was an imaginary offence. In his treatise, Thomasius writes that it is the great French philosopher and mathematician René Descartes (Cartesius) who deserves the credit, with his bold idea of the universality of the (mechanical) laws of Nature, for the gradual disappearance of demonology—"scholastic eccentricity" says Thomasius—from many of the universities.[2]

The mediaeval religious concept of the world, in which evil spirits and demons —Satan, his helpers and allies—were an important part, disintegrated to an ever increasing extent but a very high price had to be paid for this progress in terms of human suffering. The witch-hunting mania of the 16th and 17th centuries and the struggle against it are impressive evidence that certain elements of this view of the world were capable of releasing a raging force of destruction.

[1] German translation published as "Gewissens-Buch" 1647 in Bremen; numerous new editions, among others: Cautio criminalis, Weimar, 1939; Excerpts in: Friedrich Spee: Lied und Leid, Berlin, 1961

[2] Thomasius, C.: Über die Hexenprozesse. Revised and edited by P. Lieberwirth, Weimar, 1967

GLORY AND MISERY
OF THE FREE MERCENARIES

"THE SOLDIER ALONE
IS A FREE MAN?"

Like scarcely any other in history, the picture of the Thirty Years' War is marked by a strange type of soldier. The mass-character and the negative perfection of this type of warrior were so fascinating that they provided an inexhaustible source of inspiration for poetry and art. Schiller's "Wallenstein" is probably that work of literature in which the essential features of the soldier of the Thirty Years' War are presented in their "classic" form in the shape of individual figures and as a "mass-hero". While working on the "Demetrius" fragment, Schiller intended to write a tavern scene in which the "great latitude for adventurers and fortune-hunters" was to be depicted from the Polish example.[1] The stage image of the soldier of the Thirty Years' War was enriched significantly by the accusation made by Brecht in "Mother Courage and Her Children".

While the soldiers in "Wallenstein's Camp" have the glittering but deceptive illusion that they are the "master of the devastated world", the progressive desolation of this world is not without effect on the soldiers and the canteen-woman who is profiting from this war. In the regiments of the Duke of Friedland, the soldiers hated by the oppressed working classes and estates take full advantage of freedom, this rare and precious thing; the career and travels of Mother Courage take her to the extremes of human misery. The whim of Fortune is the central concept, the purpose of life of Wallenstein's horsemen. Brecht's drama follows the logic characteristic of a predatory war waged by the exploiting class. Schiller, using material from original sources, also presented this with historical fidelity.

For most of the eyewitnesses of the Thirty Years' War, soldiers were the incarnation of every vice and devilish characteristic, behind which their masters and paymasters (many of whom failed to keep their promises), the crowned heads, the authorities and the war-profiteers frequently concealed their historical guilt. It was with a sure hand, however, that Schiller traced the social relevance of the parasitic existence of soldiers in feudal society. Since this consisted exclusively of "masters and servants", human liberty prospered as an artificial manifestation outside this social order but not without being a threat to it at the same time.

The exclusive freedom of the soldiery was necessarily a phantom concept since—as extolled by Holck's musketeer in "Wallenstein"—it boldly sweeps aside the ordinary people, destroys their work and that of the peasants and morally corrupts them. The mercenary, unrestricted by any bonds of law and order, can feel free only because killing is his trade and because a violent end is the aim which he is set. "He who can

War is my homeland,
My armour is my house,
And fighting is my life.

Soldiers' saying, 16th century

[1] Schiller: Sämtliche Werke, 21st vol., Berlin, 1948, p. 203

Wenzel Hollar sculp.

Abrah Hogenberg exc.

45 Young cavalier. Etching by Wenzel Hollar.
Moravská Gallery, Brno

look Death in the face, the soldier alone, is a free man." Reaching for fictional freedom at the price of their own life—this is the image used by Schiller to reveal the tragedy of the free mercenaries of the 17th century in their extreme form, the analogies of whom with robbers were obvious and whose dividing lines were never far removed from beggarly poverty on a mass scale.

The place of the soldier serving for money in late feudal society was defined by clearly formulated social and juridical statements. These standards had emerged in the course of the centuries and followed the classic pattern of the Roman legionary which, for its part, had continued in the Italy of the late Middle Ages.

The fighting capabilities of regional men-at-arms of peasant or plebeian origin had been demonstrated at the end of the 15th century in the struggle of the Swiss against the knightly armies of Duke Charles the Bold of Burgundy in particular. This experience and the increasing spread of commodity-money relations enabled German princes, too, to recruit soldiers "from the land"—lansquenets. They were no less brave than the Swiss but their discipline was regarded as doubtful. The Emperors Maximilian I and Charles V made use of them in numerous wars. In the course of the 16th century, two groups emerged, these being known as the "Upper German" and the "Lower (or North) German" soldiery. Free peasants were no longer numerous in Upper Germany, so these men were recruited from bourgeois and plebeian circles.

In the Imperial decrees and appointments of the second half of the 16th century, they were referred to as *Fussknechte* or *Knechte*, which was the term for an unmarried young man (not a serf). In this period there was also a gradual change to the "free soldier"—a mercenary who undertook military service for anyone who needed him.[1]

The "troops", as the mercenaries were now known, became increasingly more numerous and the definition of their place in late feudal society again became a matter of ever greater urgency. From his knowledge of writings on military theory and from his own extensive experience in the wars with the Turks, the Imperial counsellor and commander Lazarus von Schwendi had compiled his "Reutter-Bestallung" as early as 1570. This work on the conditions of mercenary service consisted of no less than 294 articles on the exercise of military service, discipline and on the legal status of hired mercenaries. The universal nature of the problem was underlined by the resolutions of the Reichstag at Speyer in the same year: a "Reichsreuterbestallung" and articles for the infantry provided the basis for a new martial law. From the turn of the century onwards, "war regulations" appeared in rapid succession.[2]

The best-known German military theorists at the time of the Thirty Years' War, Johann Jacobi von Wallhausen, who prepared manuals for the first German military academy (in existence from 1616 to 1619) of Prince John the Elder of Nassau-Siegen, and Johann Newmayr von Ramsla, in the service of the Dukes of Saxe-Weimar, set exacting standards for the military profession. In his *Art of War on Foot*, Wallhausen lists those qualities which once made a soldier and which should now characterize him once again. He was to have "God in his heart", i.e., be pious, and abhor all vices, sins and "devilish arts". "Disciplina militaris" had to be regarded as the "respectaculum" of virtues and "brotherliness" among the soldiers was to be encouraged. These moral standards were supplemented by Wallhausen with the demand for physical

[1] Möller, H.-M.: Das Regiment der Landsknechte, Wiesbaden, 1975

[2] Team of authors (headed by G. Förster): Kurzer Abriss der Militärgeschichte. Von den Anfängen der Geschichte des deutschen Volkes bis 1945, Berlin, 1974; Delbrück, H.: Geschichte der Kriegskunst im Rahmen der politischen Geschichte, 4th part: Neuzeit, Berlin, 1920; Razin, E. Istorija vojennogo iskusstva, vol. 3, Moscow, 1960

In war, there is no law and order, It is the same for man and master.

17th century saying

and professional excellence—always be alert and have the "foe in view" and the "gun in hand". Expertise in weapons and "drill" had to be completed by a certain measure of basic knowledge of mathematics and fortifications.[1]

The specific nature of his "work" made it necessary for the active soldier to clothe himself in an appropriate manner. Hans Conrad Lavater of Zurich recommended good shoes and stockings, two thick shirts, outer clothing of leather if possible and a voluminous, thick coat plus a felt hat for protection from rain and cold. Items of clothing should not have much fur or many seams to prevent vermin from gathering. This was an attempt to avoid epidemics since it frequently happened that spotted fever decimated entire armies, rendering them incapable of combat.[2]

It was suggested that clothing should be of light colours, corresponding to the field insignia of the general—obviously an attempt to promote morale and vocational pride. It was usually the case that a profusion of colours predominated. The trimmings and the generous cut of military clothing underlined the carefree nature of a soldier's life and the gap between this and the monotonous existence of the working masses, between this and the starving, God-fearing sinner.

Clothing mostly consisted of garments which happened to be in fashion at the time and were the customary apparel of the townsmen and peasants. Stockings were tied with a ribbon below the knee and the generously cut breeches, also tied with a ribbon, were worn long. The soft Walloon cavalry collar was turned over the doublet and leather buff and the sleeves were also edged with lace. Over his sleeved jacket, the soldier wore a long, loose cloak which was dashingly thrown over the arm and shoulder. The wearing of a splendid suit of brightly coloured clothes in the manner of noble gentlemen was, at the same time, the outward expression of the intention to lead a possibly short but merry life. Music, dancing, gambling, cursing and coarse, obscene jests were a part of this. Many a young lad was probably attracted to the "drums" solely by the splendid sight of a noisy group of brightly arrayed soldiers. As it was, the generous cut associated with the dashing soldiery, which was closer to French informality than the stiffness and pomposity of Spain, had an influence on civilian fashions. Prosperous offspring of the middle class, young noblemen and officials exaggerated this informality to such an extent that a caricature of military dress was the result. Those whose loose clothing, decorated everywhere with ribbons, flapped around their bodies were known as dandies. They wore floppy, broadrimmed hats, decorated with a long, curved and brightly coloured feather. The tops of their boots were turned over and hung down in soft folds. Giant spurs of glittering metal gave a ring to their step, echoing the clatter of their light swords. The practical and comfortable clothing of the soldiery was adapted to the drawing-room and for strolling through the town.[3]

A man or youth capable of bearing arms changed, above all, his social position when he volunteered to join the "colours". Once again following the example of ancient Rome, Newmayr lists the "privileges and rights of soldiers". As a rule, the mercenary possessed no landed estates and his property largely consisted of the personal things that he took with him, booty gained in war, his pay and gifts. However, he did not loose his right of inheritance and even enjoyed a priority in claims to estates. In

[1] Wallhausen, J. J. von: Kriegskunst zu Fuss, Oppenheim (Th. de Bry), 1615, copy in Biblioteka Gdańska

[2] Lavater, H. C.: Kriegs-Büchlein: Das ist /Grundtliche Anleitung zum Kriegswesen, Zurich edition (J. J. Bodmer), 1651, copy ibid

[3] Thiel, E.: Geschichte des Kostüms, Berlin, 1963; Kybalová, L./Herbenová, O./Lamarová, M.: Das grosse Bilderlexikon der Mode, Prague, 1969

preceding page:

46 Picture of a man in armour (young commander) with red armband—a sign of identity in battle. Painting by Anthonis van Dyck. Staatliche Kunstsammlungen Dresden, Gallery of Paintings

47 Young man mounting a horse. A masterly impression of an everyday scene. Drawing in red chalk by Jacopo Chimenti, known as Empoli. Weimar Art Collection

48 General of the Thirty Years' War—in attire of fashionable elegance. His professional requisites seem hardly more than decorative accessories. Painting by Wybrand the Elder Simonsz de Geest. Staatliche Museen, Meiningen

S. Della inu. 80 fec.   Cum Piuil. Regis

51 Polish cavalrymen with maces. Etching by Stefano della Bella. Staatliche Graphische Sammlung, Munich

52 Column of soldiers with baggage-train. The "military worm" passes through the countryside in loose order.

53 A soldier's wife by a gun on a deserted battlefield.

54 Peaceful camp-scene in a fortress equipped with heavy guns. Etching by Stefano della Bella. From: *Varii Capricii Militarii*. Moravská Gallery, Brno

preceding double-page:
49 In front of the sutler's tent. Genre scene of an essentially idyllic nature. Painting by Philips Wouwerman. Kunsthalle Hamburg

50 Officer writing a letter. The basic impression of self-confidence, underlined by ornate and imaginative dress and a proud posture, is to be noted time and again in portraits of officers. Painting by Gerard Terborch. Staatliche Kunstsammlungen Dresden, Gallery of Paintings

55 Guardroom with soldiers playing cards. Painting by Jakob Duck. Museum of Graphic Art, Budapest

56 Imperial musketeers in position with an officer giving them instructions. Drummers and pikemen can be seen in the background. Sketch in oil by an unknown artist on a page of an Italian ledger. Heeresgeschichtliches Museum, Vienna

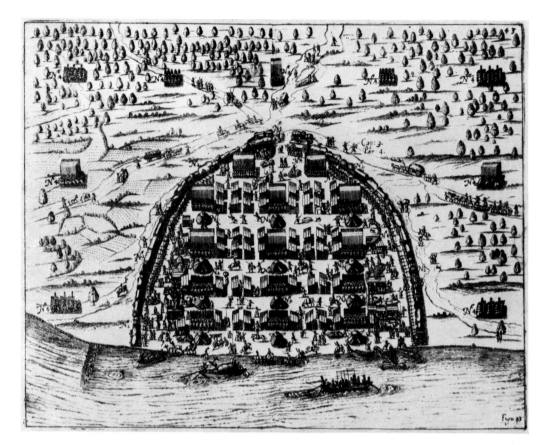

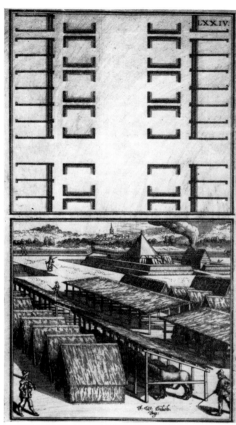

57 Fortified camp along a river-
bank in the shape of a barricade
of waggons. After: J. J. von Wallhausen, Kriegskunst zu Pferd (1634).
Biblioteka Gdańska

58 Lightly built quarters for soldiers
and horses in a fortified
camp with the commander's tent
in the background. After: J. W.
Dilich, Peribologia, Frankfort on
the Main, 1640. Copy in Municipal
Archives, Stralsund

59 Imperial troops under General
Tilly bombard the strongly fortified
camp of the main Swedish army
under Gustavus Adolphus at
Werben on the Elbe (1631). The
camp area is protected by the
river which can be crossed by two
pontoon-bridges. On the other
side, the town fortifications form a
compact part of the extended
earthen rampart which was
erected within two weeks. From:
Mathäus Merian, *Theatrum
Europaeum* III

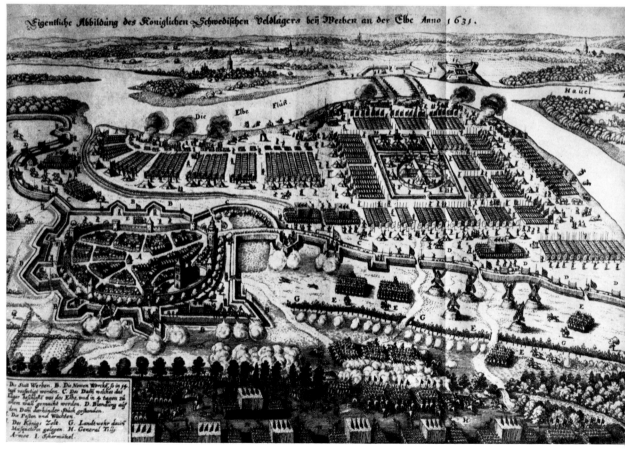

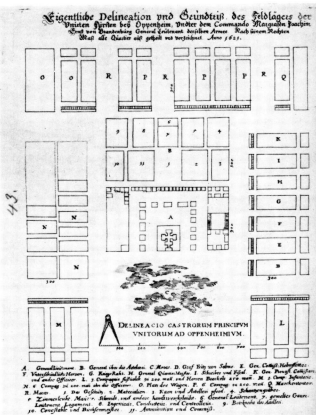

60 A mobile smithy for the fitting
of horseshoes was an essential part of
armies on the march, especially for
cavalry forces. Model from J. Carl's
collection "Das kleine Zeughaus".
Germanisches Nationalmuseum,
Nuremberg

61 Plan of the field-camp of the
Union army under Margrave Joachim
Ernst of Brandenburg at Oppenheim
(1621) with an extensive "camp-state"
(A, D—K) and artillery (B, 1—11).
Güstrow Museum

62 Weatherproof tents with splendid
linings provided luxury and comforts
for officers in the field. Model from
J. Carl's collection "Das kleine Zeughaus". Germanisches Nationalmuseum
Nuremberg

63 This camp-scene shows some of the many
types of soldiers: a group playing dice, braggarts,
veterans, daredevils, sinister outsiders, layabouts
and, in the right foreground, a musketeer
in search of fleas. Painting by Sebastian Vrancx.
Kunsthalle Hamburg

64—69 A fork-musket of 18 to 22 mm calibre
was 135 cm long and weighed about 5 kg.
With a powder-charge of 36 to 38 g and a lead
ball of a good 40 g, it had a maximum range of
1,200 m but the impact on fairly soft materials
was only effective up to 220 m although the
missile could penetrate the armour in use at
the time at a range of a good hundred metres.
Selected phases in the loading and discharge
procedure with short muskets and fork-muskets
with matchlock:
Insertion of the powder-charge in the barrel;
in the case of the fork-musket from prepared
leather or wood receptacles which were quiet
in use and were carried on a bandolier; the
short muskets were charged from the powder-
horn, after which the ball was rammed down.
Pouring of the priming-powder on the pan
which was connected by a duct to the powder-
charge in the barrel;
The glowing slow-match (twisted hemp,
saturated in sugar of lead solution) is clamped
between the lips of the match-holder and the
right hand shields the priming-pan from wind
and rain and stray sparks;
Release of the match-holder by the trigger,
bringing the glowing end of the match into
contact with the fine-grain powder in the pan.
For close-combat, the musketeer was equipped
with a side-arm.

70/71 Pikeman on the march and in combat.
In battle, his was mainly a defensive function,
the pikeman opposing the attacking cavalry
with a closed barrier of inclined spears, braced
with the foot. All illustrations after: Jacob de
Gheyn, Waffenhandlung. Museum für Deutsche
Geschichte, Berlin

72 Wooded landscape with a hold-up by a
group of marauders who had been waiting in
ambush. Painting by Jacques Fouquier. Kunsthalle Hamburg

73 Cavalry engagement. The picture shows
that phase of the battle in which, following the
clash of the formations involved, fighting
continued in a number of man-to-man or group
combats. Painting by Palamedesz. Historisches
Museum, Frankfort on the Main

74 Raid on a military camp. Next to the figure
of a horseman in the centre, there is, character-
istically enough, a woman with a child. Painting by Jacob Weyer. Kunsthalle Hamburg

75 Everyday scene in a military camp: argument over false dice with an officer or provost trying to settle it, brawls, duels. Etching by Hans Ulrich Franck. Germanisches National-museum, Nuremberg

76 Soldiers and whores in a tavern. Etching
by Hans Ulrich Franck. Staatliche Graphische
Sammlung, Munich

77 A gipsy halt (*c.* 1621). On the left, in the
foreground, there is a group of card-playing
soldiers who are obviously accompanying the
wandering gipsies. In the midst of the busy
goings-on of the camp, a woman, leaning
against a tree, is giving birth to a child. Etching
by Jacques Callot. From: *Das gesamte Werk*,
hand-drawings

78 Soldiers brawling over the division of the spoils. Painting by W. C. Duyster. Staatliche Kunstsammlungen Dresden, Gallery of Paintings

79 Peg-leg—the pictorial representation of the old saying: young soldier—old beggar. Etching by Jacques Callot from the Beggar Series. From: *Das gesamte Werk*, hand-drawings

80 Troop of soldiers on the rampage. "They do not stand guard, they occupy no emplacements, they launch no attacks nor do they have enough to eat!" (Grimmelshausen: *Simplicissimus* IV/13). Etching by Johann Hulsmann. Staatliche Graphische Sammlung, Munich

81 The battlefield: the corpses of men and beasts. At the side of the horse, there can be seen a plunderer of the battlefield, laden with booty. Etching by Karel Dujardin. Moravská Gallery, Brno

following page:
82 The Guard at the Gate. For the first time
in Dutch genre painting and from the example of
military life, there are suggestions of sadness and
desolation here, presenting in touching manner
the solitude of a man bound by close links to
his environment. Painting by Carel Fabritius
(1654). Staatliches Museum, Schwerin

accordance with the strict delimitation between professions in the structure of feudal society, soldiers were not permitted to pursue "civilian occupations" (trade and commerce); agricultural work was despised and this was why the mercenaries refused to take part in the construction of fieldworks. This and the driving of carts was the work of peasants. Soldiers were free from taxes and feudal duties of any kind and were not required to pay customs duties. In contrast to the humble population, they were also permitted to hunt—"an allegory of war"—but not in the forests of the local potentate.[1] The wearing and use of weapons were in keeping with his professional status; since this right was denied to the mass of the peasant population or was only permitted by the ruling class in times of emergency for a limited period, the use of weapons conferred a certain social status, as was also the case among the townsfolk.

The soldier on active service lost the rights he had according to the customary regional or municipal law and was not subject to the jurisdiction of the civil authorities. His conduct was judged according to the exceptionally severe *jus militaris* as codified in the "articles" and "orders" and which could only be pronounced by military courts and military judges (auditors). Verdicts were carried out by provosts specially appointed for the purpose and their men who were part of the staff of a military formation. The military delinquent was put in irons, unlike the townsmen and peasants who were placed in the stocks or put in prison. As an "honorable person", he could not be hanged on a common country gallows or at a common place of execution; trees or a "garrison gallows" had to be used for the purpose. In the towns, these gallows could not be set up outside but had to be erected on the market square.

However, being a soldier in the "Great War" also meant being on the same level as many members of the nobility. Numerous hidalgos served as ordinary soldiers in the ranks of the well-practised Spanish infantry which had emerged in the course of the Reconquista. Noblemen also served as minor and medium-rank commanders in French, Dutch, Bohemian, Polish and German cavalry units. Even after the war had begun, a marked degree of social prestige was still associated with the military profession and especially with the cavalry. The trade of war, although regarded with disgust and despised by peasants, the craftsmen of the guilds and merchants, also offered hard-working men, who often had no future prospects at all, the chance—slight though this was—of improving their position through their own efforts. The craving for adventure, a feeling which existed even among the oppressed classes and of which there is ample evidence, drove journeymen, wage-labourers, young peasants and students to the recruiting tables. Official bans on recruitment had little effect. The status of free birth had long since ceased to be a condition for acceptance as a recruit.

The longer the war lasted, the more rapid the spread of pauperization among working people. It is known that not only miners and salt-workers but also peasants were in such dire straits that they joined the "military" just to keep body and soul together. In Upper and Lower Austria, it was frequently the prospect of forced conversion to Catholicism that had the same effect. It is reported in a newspaper of the time that "in these places (April 1633) the drums are being vigorously beaten to recruit soldiers and many come on account of the good money, the journeymen going to war in large numbers. The peasants of the little district of Ob der Enns do not want to be reformed

Like the dyer's nag,
the townsman, slow and stupid,
goes round only in circles.
The soldier can become anything,
since war is now the slogan
on Earth.

Schiller: Wallensteins Lager 7

[1] Newmayr von Ramsla, J.: Handbüchlein darinn/Das gantze Kriegswesen kürtzlich gewiesen wirdt, Leipzig (J. Grosse Erben), 1631, p. 137ff., copy in Biblioteca Gdańska

83 Army on the march. The baggage-train with carts, spare horses, cattle, drovers, women and other camp-followers can be clearly identified. Etching by Stefano della Bella. Moravská Gallery, Brno

[1] Jessen, H.: Der Dreissigjährige Krieg in Augenzeugenberichten, Munich, 1971, p. 335
[2] Chaboche, R.: Les soldats français de la guerre de Trente Ans, in: Revue d'Histoire Moderne et Contemporaine 1/1973

(i.e., forcibly converted to Catholicism) and are going to war in large numbers, there being nine to ten thousand of them in Friedland's army."[1] Flight to the regiments of Wallenstein in particular, who was indifferent to denominational differences, seemed an obvious alternative. It was normally very difficult to persuade peasants to leave their fields, homestead and hearth. Calculations made from the lists in the famous "Hôtel des Invalides" in Paris showed that—with peasants accounting for 90 per cent of the entire population—52 per cent of former mercenaries in the 17th century came from the towns. It was only when the fury of war repeatedly spread over flat country areas that the number of peasants joining the army rose to more than 60 per cent. To begin with, it was obviously a rare event that peasants flocked to the colours in large numbers.[2]

On the other hand, people who had lost their original place in society for one reason or another, criminals and work-shy characters on the make from a variety of countries began to collect in ever increasing numbers. The areas providing most recruits for the armies proved to be Upper Germany with its many towns and innumerable small farms, the Alps and the mountainous areas of Central Germany, the Swiss cantons, the Italian principalities and republics and France, England, Ireland and Scotland.

The internationalization of mercenary forces began as early as the 16th century. Emperor Maximilian I had once banned the German lansquenets from serving foreign rulers but this had long since been forgotten. The "free soldier" offered his services to anyone who wanted them and could pay him. Gustav Freytag aptly remarks that practically every army was a "pattern-card of different nationalities" and that the typical mercenary of the Thirty Years' War had no real national links at all. An exception to this was the Swedish army during the first phase of its operations on Imperial soil. Up to about the Battle of Breitenfeld in September 1631, Swedes and Finns accounted for half of the rank and file and almost all the officers, after which this "national nucleus" significantly declined in importance. When their pay was irregular or failed to materialize at all, mercenaries frequently considered their oath of loyalty and obedience as no longer binding. With few exceptions—such as Elector Maximilian of Bavaria, Tilly and Gustavus Adolphus—nobody required a mercenary to be a member of any particular religious faith. If he changed sides of his volition, this was considered a violation of his oath and punishable but it became increasingly pointless to putt him on trial for this. The relations between a soldier under oath and his commander or the owner of his regiment were practically reduced to a bare business arrangement. The qualities of the recruit became less important—what mattered was money.

The political crisis of the Swedish command in the Reich after the death of Gustavus Adolphus resulted mainly from its inability to obtain sufficient supplies for its armies. The fact that money had become the cardinal point of the soldier's trade involved a fatal risk for the mercenary in particular since, apart from his labour-power, he had very little else. He was "left unpaid and sacrificed by the sword and hunger" by the generals, his "employers" and unscrupulous and greedy officers. In the last third of the war, there was an increasing number of those cases of which Gustav Freytag writes: "The devastation of the countryside took a fearful revenge on the armies themselves, the spectre of famine, the harbinger of the plague, stalked through the camps ..."

Although not exactly of a high poetic standard, the *Soldaten Lehrbrieff* ("Soldier's Indentures"), as printed in *Philander*, aptly characterizes the fate of the soldier:[1]

> "... Du musst Gott und dem Vatterland
> Zu Schutz und Ehren thun Beystand
> Und dich offt ducken, hucken, schmiegen,
> Offt wenig schlaffen, übel liegen,
> Offt hungern, dursten, schwitzen, frieren,
> Bald was gewinnen, bald verliehren
> Und allenthalb dess Unfals dein
> Und deines Glücks gewertig sein."

("You must help God and Fatherland, For protection and honour, And often duck, hump your load and crawl, Often sleep but little, lie uncomfortably, Often hunger, thirst, sweat and shiver, And everywhere to be ready for your fate or fortune.")

Of three captive soldiers

At Düring they were executed
All three at the same time
In the open market,
because of duty,
no man should destroy it.
May God take them to the hall
of Heaven.

From: L. Erk: Deutscher Liederhort, No. 12 c (Verse 11, 1632)

[1] Moscherosch, H. M.: Gesichte Philanders von Sittewald, ed. by F. Bobertag, Berlin/ Stuttgart, 1961, 6. Gesicht: Soldatenleben

Every Colonel,
Adjutant or Captain
knows well that no doctors,
learned men or other God-fearing
people come to him,
but a mob of bad boys from
all sorts
of nations and strange people who
have left wife and
babe, food and everything to
follow the war.

From: Adam Junghans von der Olnitz's
Kriegsordnung 2nd part

The newly recruited journeyman or peasant now found himself in a completely new milieu. Together with the "old sweats", cynical, cunning and loquacious as they were, he aspired to the rare and transient state of happiness and fortune. It was a life of extremes; brief moments of pleasure and deceiving brilliance often changing abruptly to hopeless, wretched poverty which, however, seldom excited any sympathy.

The organization of such a collection of "military material" as a functioning military formation was in the hands of the highest state authorities—the emperor, princes and cities. They appointed a colonel or captain by giving him an officer's commission and the authority to form a regiment or troop. The *Bestallungsbrief* ("letter of appointment") laid down the number of soldiers and units, their pay and the place of assembly while the *Artikelsbrief* ("document of articles") specified the legal procedure and the juridical and social relations within the unit. The holder of the commission usually advanced the money needed for the recruitment and organization of the unit so that the commander-in-chief was in his debt. This also represented a guarantee for the latter, however, since the creditor would hesitate to refuse his services to his exalted debtor.

The commission for the recruitment of a military formation, in order to make an impression on those concerned, was frequently couched in solemn and terse language. In a commission issued by King Christian IV of Denmark in 1625, it was a question of recruiting a foot-troop, i.e., a company of 200 men, of "good, manly, able and experienced German soldiers". The captain could command and use it

"bei tag und nacht,
auf Zuge und wacht,
zu und von dem Feinde,
zu wasser und Land,
in schantzen und Pässen,
Stürmen, Scharmutzeln, Schlachten
und sonst auf alle vorfallende gelegenheiten,
wie es rechtschaffenen Ehrlichen tapferen
Soldaten gebühret."[1]

("By day and night, on patrol and on guard, to and from the foe, on water and land, in entrenchments and passes, attacks, skirmishes, battles and on all other occasions, as befits a sturdy, honest and bold soldier.")

A soldier's career began with *Laufgeld* or travelling expenses which the new recruit received from the hand of the recruiting agent. Once his name had been entered in the register of the unit to be formed, the new recruit had to report without delay, by the shortest route and as one of a group of five or six others to the "mustering centre",

[1] State Archives Weimar, H. 44, Werbe-patent, dated 18. 2. 1625

84 The price regulations for supplies sold to soldiers in Leipzig, signed and sealed by Elector Johann Georg of Saxony in person (1631). Museum für Geschichte der Stadt Leipzig

the travelling expenses being used for this purpose. The commissioning orders expressly prohibited the new recruits from undertaking any "expeditions" on their way to the mustering centres. Since such activities were not unknown at the mustering centres either, the orders of the Duke of Bavaria of 1611 provided for the following schedule: The mustering centre of a regiment should be kept open for new arrivals for six days. This gives an idea of the "catchment" area of a recruitment campaign—journeys of three to five days or 100 to 150 kilometres. Weapons and equipment were to be issued on the seventh and eighth days. On the ninth day, the recruits were to be inspected, man by man, by the commander or his representative, the commissar. Finally, the procedure of forming a unit ended by the latter appearing before the troops, reading the "document of articles", presenting the "persons of high office" (the staff), handing over the standards to the ensigns and swearing in the soldiers on parade. This was usually done in the form of a solemn ceremony with musical accompaniment. However, the provost also had his say, warning the recruits in a stern voice of the ban on dice and card games, drinking, brawls and cursing.

The holder of a princely or Imperial recruitment patent set up his tents in those parts of the land which were densely populated and where there was a lot of traffic. Patents were nailed up at busy points and a drum was beaten to invite old soldiers and potential recruits to the recruiting table. In many cases, however, the authorities did not permit a drum to be sounded and the recruiting agent had to make do with a table in the local tavern.

The news that a recruiting campaign was in progress rapidly made the rounds, reaching out-of-the-way places, creating unrest and attracting the curious. The assembly of a crowd of people equivalent to the population of a small town immediately caused a supply problem. Certain occupations, such as the catering branches, the metal, cloth and leather trades, the goldsmiths and peasants, profited from the demand for food supplies and equipment resulting from the formation of a military unit. Since

93

85 Recruiting-drummers—a sure magnet for even the most obstinate. Copperplate engraving by Christian Richter. Staatliche Graphische Sammlung, Munich

[1] Du Praissac: Discours militaires (De l'Enseigne), Paris, 1618, copy in Deutsche Staatsbibliothek Berlin

[2] Bellus, Nicolaus: Kayserlicher Triumpff-Wagen und Victoria ... Teutscher Nation und Kriegs Helden Buch, Frankfort on the Main, 1632, copy in Municipal Archives Stralsund

94

the recruit, once he had received his travelling expenses or bounty and pay, was sometimes required to buy his own weapons and all his clothes and food, there rapidly developed a flourishing trade between the mercenaries on the one hand and the townsfolk and peasants on the other. Sutlers with their vans soon appeared on the scene and, as travelling dealers, plied their trade of buying and selling merchandise. Stolen property was also frequently disposed of through the same channels. Prices rose as the supply of goods became more critical and it became difficult to obtain the merchandise required. This boom, which was concentrated around mustering centres, ultimately proved to be at the expense of the local population since it happened only too quickly that the soldier took advantage of the superiority of his weapons and made use of the *jus belli*, plundering wherever the opportunity presented itself. This was a frequent occurrence since he was seldom paid regularly, the rate of pay was not very high and the value of money fluctuated. Thus the mustering centres, soon after they had been established, became the terror of whole areas. They were characterized not so much by military discipline as by gluttony and alcohol since here, too, there were usually people who were more interested in "living it up", as long as their pay lasted, than in the art of war.

A large measure of ability and experience was required from the well-paid recruiting agents and officers to make efficient fighting-units from the motley collection of recruits with their variety of social, national and religious backgrounds. It was no rare event for mercenaries to disappear again, taking their bounty with them. This also underlined the lack of uniformity since it was only in rare cases that it was possible or customary to dress the newly formed regiment or troop in the same clothes.

What kept the mass of troops outwardly together were the articles of war, the oath of loyalty towards the general and his flag, the authority and jurisdiction of the commander and a certain set of professional customs akin to those of a guild. The units carried a flag as a common symbol in the field; ribbons around their arm or hat distinguished foe from friend. The flag was a well-guarded symbol both on the march and in camp and especially in battle. The task of carrying the heavy cloth, swinging it in a dashing manner and holding it on high in the rough and tumble of battle as a sign of steadfastness was exclusively the duty of the ensign. This was why the customs of war usually exempted him from other duties. The ensign received the flag from the hands of the colonel in front of the assembled regiment on the mustering square and, if he lost his hands, he was expected to carry the flag in his mouth. If mortally wounded, he was to roll himself in the precious cloth to prevent it falling into the hands of the enemy as a trophy.[1]

Among the booty captured by the troops of the League under Tilly in the battle against the army of Ernst von Mansfeld at Stadtlohn (1623) was a large number of flags of double-thickness taffeta, the material mostly used at the time.[2] Three red flags were decorated with a blue flame-symbol, a design frequently found. A gold flag was embroidered with the Virgin in armour and the word "Revirescit" while on another Fortuna, the chief goddess of the free mercenary, was depicted, surrounded by crowned virgins. Another banner featured a mounted cuirassier and the famous slogan of the Roman legionaries "Pro patria mori—dulce & decorum est" (It is sweet and honourable to die for one's country). Others bore garlanded swords, olive branches and wreaths of laurel. Animal symbols, such as a pelican tearing open its breast—a symbol of heroism—with the words "Quod inte est, est pro me" underneath, were popular motifs. Croatian regiments carried flags showing—how symbolic!—a wolf in a threatening posture. Thus a regiment or troop, when finally complete, presented a colourful and lively picture in which the individual could still display his personal character in his clothing, language and habits.

This individuality declined in the course of military training with weapons of increasing complexity and in marching and combat exercises. These were for the mechanization of the movements and the elimination of the differences between the soldiers, the aim being to create a kind of fighting-machine. The regulations issued by the Prince of Orange in 1608 prescribed 33 drills for musketeers. According to Wallhausen's "Art of War on Foot", the musketeers had to practise 143 drills and the pikeman 21.[1] This marked the beginning of the transformation of the individual warrior into the "trained wage-soldier" of the decades which followed the war. The initial human material for the standing armies of the princes was supplied by the "great mass of mercenaries and vagabonds" (Franz Mehring) of the Thirty Years' War. Socio-economic and technical developments had resulted in the emergence of professional soldiers.

The highest degree of standardized exercise-techniques was attained initially by the élite troops of Spain and then by their adversaries, the forces of the United Netherlands. This was the pattern followed by King Gustavus Adolphus of Sweden in his reform of the army. The armies of the emperor or the princes, paid as they were at irregular intervals, were of a greatly inferior standard. They were unable to achieve the exemplary standardization and the expertise in the handling of weapons in battle of the forces mentioned above.

In the age of the manufactories, the major factors in combat were fighting ability, the commander's judgment and the resources in manpower and horsepower available. The use of weapons was based less on the application of science and technology than on the individual expertise of the mercenary. As a consequence of progress in military technology, a further "division of labour" took place in the various branches of the army; this was also reflected in its hierarchical organization. At the lowest level, there were the pikemen, equipped with a pike of five to six metres in length as a defence against cavalry attacks, and the musketeers who, in addition to their muskets and ancillary equipment, also carried a sword for close-combat fighting. The heavy cavalry were the cuirassiers, armed with a sword and two pistols while the arquebusiers, as "marksmen on horseback" who dismounted for man-to-man fighting, had only a short carbine and side-arms. The artillery, with its gunmasters, sergeant artificers and constables, was a guild-like force with a marked *esprit de corps* and was hired in complete units.

As a rule, contingents of foreign origin attracted a great deal of attention. There were the Greek horsemen from Morea, known as "stradiots". Dressed in the Turkish manner, they rode fiery horses and carried a lance of some four metres in length. Experts lauded the qualities of the Polish hussars and cossacks—one could find

86 Two boys take the "King's Shilling" from the hand of an officer. The verse predicts the moral ruination of the new recruits. Etching by Christian Richter. Art Collections Veste Coburg

[1] Cf. also new edition of "Wapenhandelunge" (1609) by Jakob de Gheyn with the title: Über den rechten Gebrauch der Muskete für den jungen und unerfahrenen Soldaten, Berlin, 1975

95

*Town, countryside,
man and beast,
is all destroyed: the Lord's duty
is done.*

From: Der verfochtene Krieg
by Friedrich von Logau

"dergleichen keine Reuterey in der Christenheit/wie auch in der Heydenschaft . . ./von schönen abgerichteten Rossen/mit köstlichem Zeug behenckt/schnell und auch wol armirten Pferden/mit Lantzen so achtzehn oder zwantzig Schuch lang sind.[1] ("no such cavalry in Christendom or among the heathens . . . with fine, well-trained steeds, beautiful harness, speedy and well-armoured horses, with lances eighteen or twenty foot long.") An even more astonishing sight for the contemporaries in the German theatre of war were the small warriors from Finland and Lappland who fought with bow and arrow. The Swedish soldiers were regarded as brave fighters who "preferred to die chivalrously rather than flee". The social background of such soldierly qualities was described by Gustavus Adolphus in a letter to Maurice of Orange, the outstanding Dutch commander. He wrote that he had not hired his soldiers for money nor recruited them in taverns with handsome promises. On the contrary, they were raised from the peasantry, accustomed to hard work and toil. They could withstand cold and heat, hunger and guard-duty, without difficulty. Unaccustomed to luxuries, the soldiers of his army were satisfied with less and quickly became used to obeying their commanders.[2] This was the situation throughout the country in the years immediately after 1630 when the invasion of the Empire began. The military campaigns and the great Swedish victories—Breitenfeld, Rain and Lützen—in which indigenous troops had a major part took a heavy toll of the nucleus of free peasantry. Sweden and Finland, sparsely populated as they were, supplied fewer and fewer men. A contemporary reported about 1640 that he had travelled through Sweden for days on end without seeing a single healthy and able-bodied man. There was also a decline in the serious steadfastness, the ardent zeal of fighting for God's own cause, for the liberation of the Evangelical faith. The open practice of conquest was too apparent for the soldiers to be impelled any longer by the noble aims of combat which had been proclaimed as the purpose of the struggle.

Troops on the march were a motley and changing body of men, not usually capable of marching more than five or six kilometres in a day. Wallenstein's campaign of 1626 from Zerbst to Upper Hungary in which the army covered 600 kilometres in 22 days—about 30 kilometres a day—was an exception. Heavy losses were the price which had to be paid for this speed. Of the 20,000 who started out from the Elbe, only 5,000 reached their destination and the combat efficiency of even these was very dubious.

[1] Wallhausen, J. J. von: Kriegskunst zu Fuss, p. 120

[2] Grimberg, C.: Svenska folkets underbara öden, vol. III (1611—1660), Stockholm, 1960, p. 125f. (first edition 1913)

BAGGAGE-TRAIN,
MARAUDERS
AND PUBLIC NUISANCES

A regiment in marching order was headed by the drummers, trumpeters, standard-bearers and the vanguard—the soldiers for this being provided by each company in turn. Then came the main body of troops, the column being protected at the rear by the rearguard (about 100 soldiers) following the main force at an interval in time of some 30 minutes or a complete hour. To maintain its combat efficiency, a regiment needed a large number of carts and horses and spare horses had to be taken for every cuirassier and for the staff. The baggage-train became an indispensable socio-economic body for a military formation on the march and prospered and increased in its own particular fashion. Even before the war, a regiment of 3,000 men was followed by a crowd of 4,000 non-combatants on foot and in carts. In the last year of the war, there were 40,000 men entitled to draw rations in the Imperial-Bavarian army while the more than 100,000 soldiers' wives, whores, man servants, maids and other camp-followers had to feed themselves.

It was obviously no longer a question of a militarily and administratively essential baggage-train of carts, horses and auxiliary personnel but of an appendix which had resulted from the relative overpopulation of late feudal society and from those people who had been uprooted by the war. In addition to the towns, the residence-cities of the rulers and the markets, the marching columns and camps of the mercenaries had become a part of those phenomena which offered an existence to those masses living or vegetating outside organized society. A regiment was followed on foot or in hundreds of carts by a baggage-train which included the families of the soldiers and officers, their servants, sutlers, soldiers no longer fit for military service, deserters from far away, tricksters, whores, gipsies, Jewish hucksters and so on—in short, a whole crowd of individuals who made a living from the daily needs, the gambling, the booty and the pleasure-seeking of the soldiers. Reports from the district of Ulm indicate that large numbers of children and young people were to be found in military camps. In the camp at Langenau in 1630, there were 368 horsemen, 600 horses, 66 women, 78 girls, 307 stableboys and 24 children.[1] This was an appendix which took no part in the actual fighting but appeared on the scene again soon after the battle was over in order to take from the dead whatever had been left behind by the victorious soldiers. Even in the occupation of quarters, the women of the baggage-train were quicker than the officers in taking possession of the best rooms so that the "whoremaster" in charge of the baggage-train had to intervene with his men, using their sticks and whips, and enforce the priority of the soldiers.

It was the custom for the rearguard and the baggage-train to make "raids" on the areas along their route. This marauding, so angrily condemned by Wallhausen, was done by soldiers, whores and youths, either individually or in small gangs. According to Wallhausen, this practice was very well regarded by the senior officers since

87 The provost and his assistant kept law and order in the armies and were feared for the draconic punishment they meted out. Etching by Christian Richter. Art Collections Veste Coburg

[1] Zillhardt, G.: Der Dreissigjährige Krieg in zeitgenössischer Darstellung. Hans Heberles "Zeytregister" (1618—1672). Aufzeichnungen aus dem Ulmer Territorium, Ulm/Stuttgart, 1975, p. 21

the cumbersome baggage-train and even some of the fighting units were able to solve the supply problem in their own particular manner. The boldest and most expert in requisitioning and stealing supplies from villages and farms—an activity which was not without its dangers—were known as *Mäusköpf* ("thief-heads"). Like "bees bringing honey to them", they often obtained plunder for the officers on their expeditions which was usually not available or in short supply in the vicinity of the troops on the march or in quarters—such as fresh food and delicacies, valuable personal articles and garments of high quality as favoured by rich peasants.

It was normally the case, however, that the marching-route or location of a large body of troops was not a secret for the peasants or townspeople. The roads were frequented by a considerable number of people "on the move", travelling scholars, journeymen and mounted messengers. They and persons who had escaped from an attack on a convoy of waggons spread the news of approaching troops before the latter actually appeared on the scene. In many cases, either on their own initiative or at the behest of the authorities, information systems were established by the peasants, using riders on swift horses, beacons or bell-signals. The only chance that the foraging *Fress- und Pressreuter* and "thief-heads" then had of making a big haul was by launching surprise raids on places far away from the marching column of troops. Wallhausen asserts that even "good soldiers" took part in these activities, underlining the seriousness of this constant disintegration of the units at the rear of a body of troops on the march. However, military requirements often conflicted with economic needs and the worse the supply position of the formation and the worse the fighting spirit of the troops, the more likely it was that the economic arguments would predominate. Thieving by soldiers of the kind described was pursued on an independent basis in the second half of the war in particular. Freebooters, highwaymen and footpads, operating singly or in groups and totally independent of military units, roamed the countryside and laid in wait for the unwary. They were the scourge of the population and the peasantry in particular waged a merciless minor war against them.[1]

The "marauders" were an illegal or semi-illegal but tolerated phenomenon. The *Gartbrüder* (marauding mercenaries), however, were able to refer, if necessary, to the verbal or written permission of the authorities to molest the peasants and townsfolk. These characters descended upon a particular area when it was selected by the military command for demobilization purposes. Units were demobilized either just before the beginning of winter if the eternal problem of winter-quarters could not be solved, at the end of a military campaign or when—quite simply—no more money was available for maintaining the unit in an active state. If funds were still available, the duly "demobilized" soldier received the usual pay of half a month. If the colonel was not able or not prepared to make this payment, he could expect mutiny and disobedience. Towards the end of the war, when the reduction of the number of troops in the field was imminent, the payment of the *satisfactio*, the pay still outstanding, became a thorny problem for the state. Oxenstierna, the Swedish chancellor, aptly remarked that the soldiers would not allow themselves to be demobilized without their pay: with "these fellows, no rhetoric, no logic, no Demosthenes nor even a Cicero is of any use".[2]

[1] Detailed information in Moscherosch: Philander, and in Grimmelshausen's Simplizissimus and Landstörtzerin Courasche and in Seltsamer Springinsfeld; Kraus, I.: Die Kriminalität des dreissigjährigen Krieges auf der Grundlage der Werke Grimmelshausens, Thesis. Heidelberg, 1950

[2] Lorentzen, Th.: Die schwedische Armee im dreissigjährigen Kriege und ihre Abdankung, Leipzig, 1894, p. 127

Demobilized soldiers were usually turned loose on the peasants. The colonel or commander tried to get rid of them in the manner employed by the States-General in 1629 after the successful siege of Hertogenbosch. About 6,000 mercenaries were allocated to the neighbouring and neutral Imperial territories of Mark, Cleves and Berg where they had to shift for themselves for the duration of the winter. Decrees issued by the authorities, as in the provinces on the borders of Turkish territory or in Brandenburg, obliged the civilian population to give food free of charge or a heller to any discharged soldier wandering through the countryside; he was also permitted to steal food. The *Gartbrüder* infesting the eastern provinces of Austria in the direction of Turkey were considered such a burden by Wallhausen that he was of the opinion that it was less costly and militarily more expedient not to demobilize the troops each year or at the end of a campaign. The mercenaries roaming around the country-side still retained their weapons and were mostly very impudent, alienating the population in much the same way as the marauders. Wandering around in groups, they were a dangerous nuisance for hamlets and isolated farms. The inhabitants had to give them what they demanded and, indeed, they themselves selected that they wanted

88 Cavalry engagement—a popular pictorial motif. Pistols and swords were preferred for fighting on horseback; the left hand to remain free for controlling the reins. Etching by Jan Martszen de Jonghe. Moravská Gallery, Brno

99

89 Soldier duelling with Death. The verse deals with the futility of the "bullet-proof" superstitions. Copperplate engraving by Conrad Meyer. Staatliche Graphische Sammlung, Munich

[1] Hohberg, M. von: Georgica curiosa aucta, Nuremberg, 1687, p. 74, copy in University Library Leipzig
[2] Rotwelsche Grammatica oder sehr leichte Anweisung . . . Frankfort on the Main, 1704; Wolf, S. A.: Wörterbuch des Rotwelschen. Deutsche Gaunersprache, Mannheim, 1954
[3] Schirmer, A.: Deutsche Wörterkunde. Eine Kulturgeschichte des deutschen Wortschatzes, 2nd edition, Berlin, 1946

to take.[1] Decrees issued by the prince ruling the area allowed his subjects to take action in self-defence against the *Gartbrüder* infesting his territory.

The wandering mass of the homeless and uprooted, without work and without anything to call their own, displayed a certain degree of segregation in their language as well. A new means of communication did not need to be invented since the vocabulary was supplied by the thieves' cant of the German branch which was understood even beyond the frontiers of the Empire. The war enriched its vocabulary to a not inconsiderable extent and helped to disseminate it. Even in the time before it, the secret flash language of the innumerable beggars and vagabonds had been adopted by the lansquenets. This jargon or *Rotwelsch* was incomprehensible for ordinary folk but many words from it found their way into the ordinary speech of the mercenaries and the working people. In the "Sixth Face" of his *Philander*, Moscherosch tells of a mercenary who, with a group of marauders, roams across the countryside stealing and murdering but, on quiet days, copies a "little language book". This was a kind of dictionary of soldiers' *Rotwelsch* and showed that most of the basic words were of German origin, although many of them had a changed meaning and there were many new forms. Most of the new ones of foreign origin, however, came from Aramaic and Hebrew (via Yiddish-German jargon), followed by Romany and the Romance languages.[2]

In the course of the war, the mercenaries not only became familiar with this "patter" but also developed a special soldiers' language as a result of their long association with the profession of arms. This had first evolved with the appearance of the lansquenets at the end of the 15th century and, in the course of the Thirty Years' War, had been enriched by an especially vigorous flow of technical expressions of non-German origin. The Romance languages (Spanish, Italian, French) supplied most of these and they are to be found in German and English alike: army, alarm (Ital. *all'arme* = to arms), artillery, bomb, brigade, baggage (which acquired its pejorative meaning during the war), deserter, dragoon, fort, front, forage, garrison, general, grenade, infantry, calibre, carbine, cavalry, command, company, cuirass, lieutenant, major and so on. From Hungarian and Turkish there came "hussar" (Hung. = the 20th) and "horde" (Turkish); "howitzer" came from Czech and originated during the Hussite wars while Polish contributed "sabre" and "ulan". The word "flint" is probably derived from the Swedish *flinta* as far as German is concerned but is of Anglo-Saxon origin in English. At this time, little English was yet spoken on the continent and Dutch was the dominating language on the seas. Foreign words accounted for most of the military technical expressions in German—underlining the universal nature of the war on Imperial territory and the supremacy achieved in various fields by its western neighbours.

In his everyday speech, the soldier also used a language which contained a profusion of non-German words, many of which have also survived in English ("to give no quarter"). These included a large number of curses, most of which were of blasphemous origin[3] and distortions of such words as *Gott* and *Dieu* (*Potz* and *Peu*).

This crude and undisciplined language, at which the devout Christian made the sign of the Cross when he heard it since it seemed that the Devil himself was speaking from the mouths of soldiers, was accompanied by a bizarre superstition, reflected by the trust in magic potions, amulets and mysterious utterances. The camps were visited by people who, in return for money, prophesied the future and claimed that they could make soldiers "bulletproof". The ancient belief in invulnerability was more popular than ever before in view of the invisible and deadly balls of lead flying around. To the profusion of superstitious ideas and aids listed by Gustav Freytag, there may be added the *spiritus familiaris*, an object which always had to be sold for a price lower than that paid for it; its last purchaser lost his soul to the Devil.

Fear of supernatural beings, of mysterious forces, of the barbarous punishments employed by the officers and of death at any moment and the prospects of booty and the easy acquisition of goods of any kind were obviously the most powerful factors which guranteed a certain degree of combat efficiency on the part of the mercenaries. Military drill, customs and traditions also helped to maintain discipline and resolution in battle despite the tendency to disintegrate which affected many mercenary formations.

Contemporary reports clearly indicate that significant differences existed in respect of their military qualities. George Gascoigne, the English Renaissance poet who himself served as a mercenary with the rank of captain, reports that mercenaries were classified in three categories: "Haughty Harte", "Greedy Minde" and "Miser".[1] This classification can certainly be applied to the Thirty Years' War and the mercenary scene in Germany. It would be to take a one-sided view of the situation, however, if the existence of a superior group of disciplined and hard-fighting mercenary units were to be denied. It is a striking fact that in the battles of the "Great War" which sometimes lasted an entire day, an astonishing degree of toughness and stubbornness was displayed by mercenary troops. On the other hand, there can be no doubt that the disastrous influence of the irregular actions of mercenary mobs or formations on the morale of the disciplined mercenaries became greater and greater and that they came to terms with the mass criminality of the second and third categories. By their very nature, even the serviceable units were nothing more than the trained instruments of a feudal predatory war and lacked the standards of a higher morality.

It is therefore not surprising that for the peasants, townsfolk, priests, scholars and poets their view of the soldier in this long war was dominated by the irregular and fearsome creatures which the war had attracted and generated. For the most part, it was the gangs wandering about the countryside who were responsible for the innumerable and indescribable barbarities and torturing of innocent people which, even today, are considered to have been the invention of this war. For the sake of completeness, however, it should be added that such practices had always been employed by the lords for the punishment of their peasants and by the courts of the municipal councils for the punishment of the townsfolk when they were found guilty of inciting opposition to the authorities. Sadistic torture had been a principal method, long before the war, of extracting confessions in trials and of inflicting punishment. Murder and manslaughter, legalized or sanctioned in various forms, were regarded as part of the life-style of the ruling class and as a means of maintaining authority.

The world could give the mercenary neither real freedom nor human feelings and he lived in a state of contradiction, aptly described by Grimmelshausen: "to kill

Soldiers' Choir

Off you go, lads and move forward,
Turn about,
prepare the slow-match:
fire a salvo, let the bullets fly,
And shout with
all your might.

From: "Pierie" by Daniel von Czepko

[1] Wijn, J. W.: Military Forces and Warfare 1610—1648, in: The New Cambridge Modern History IV

and to be killed in turn, ... to pursue and to be pursued, ... to rob and to be robbed ... their whole existence was centred around this."[1] And yet the idea of freedom continued to survive in the thinking of many of the mercenaries of the "Great War" for whom there was no longer a place in the standing armies of the absolutist regimes. To some extent, it was inherited from the lansquenet and it was stimulated by the great crisis of government of the feudal class. The Thirty Years' War, as a predatory war of the feudal powers, helped to fan the extreme contempt and hatred felt towards the military profession. In the eyes of the population, the mercenaries were *hostes Imperii* —the enemies of the Empire—and oppressors.[2] Ultimately, recruits for the princely armies could only be obtained by force, by the press-gang.

> "You will fade away like smoke
> and the warmth fades too
> And your deeds do not warm us."

> Brecht:
> Ballad of the Woman and the Soldier

[1] Simplizissimus, I/16

[2] Resolution über die Frag: Ob Diejenigen Reichs Stände ... für Rebellen zu halten? Flugschrift (leaflet), University Library Greifswald

PEASANT AND SOLDIER

PEASANT AND SOLDIER
AS DEADLY FOES

In such a conflict as the Thirty Years' War, which was mainly fought over the lowland areas and in which the fruits of agricultural labour were the direct source for the maintenance of the armies, the relations which existed between the soldiers and the peasants were of pre-eminent importance. In this connection, the rural population can be taken to include the inhabitants of the small country-towns, which were very numerous in Germany, since their low defence-capability offered little protection from a determined military attack. The larger towns were a different matter, however. It is true that they could be captured or obliged by a "voluntary" agreement to provide quarters for mercenaries but their fortifications, their age-old traditions in self-defence and the availability of money with which to purchase exemption from the obligation to provide quarters represented more or less effective ways of keeping even approaching armies at a reasonable distance while small raiding parties were even less of a problem.

In dangerous situations and when their lives were in danger, the inhabitants of the countryside sought refuge in the larger towns and sometimes in fortified monasteries and manor-houses. This was no easy step to take since the developed urban market and trade centres usually owned numerous villages in the neighbourhood as well and exercised sovereign rights over the peasants. Large sections of the urban population enjoyed advantages from urban production and trading privileges in comparison with the open countryside, especially within the distance of a mile around the town. The peasants saved their lives by seeking refuge in the towns but they were uprooted from their means of existence and at the mercy of the municipal authorities. From Frankfort on the Main, it is reported by a contemporary that "bei Wirthen, Krämern, Handwerkern und anderen war inzwischen das Schinden und Schaben (der Bauern) so gross, dass fast nicht auszusprechen".[1] ("It can scarcely be described how hard (the peasants) had to work for the tavern-keepers, merchants, tradesmen and others.")

The town-councils adopted a variety of attitudes towards those fleeing from the countryside, this depending on the actual situation at the time. In the spring of 1633, Swedish troops played havoc in Swabia and Bavaria, plundering hundreds of villages and castles and taking the booty to Augsburg where they sold it. Numerous peasants also fled there but they did not stay long since the bakers demanded a high price for their bread; the latter even preferred to sell in to the canteen-women who were better able to pay for it. Finally, the town council had the villagers expelled from the town since they had to be fed and were consequently a burden.[2]

Soldiers' song

Watch out, peasant, I am coming.
Get yourself out of the way, quick.
Captain, give us money,
while we are in the field.
Girl, come here,
Join me and the jug.

From: Heilmann I, p. 317

[1] Wetterfelder Chronik. Aufzeichnungen eines lutherischen Pfarrers der Wetterau ..., ed. by F. Graf zu Solms-Laubach and W. Mathaei, Giessen, 1882, p. 225

[2] Franz Sigl's, Franziskaners zu München Geschichte der Münchner Geisseln in schwedischer Gefangenschaft, ed. by M. J. Stöger, Munich, 1836, p. 47

A report from Leipzig of August 1633 describes how the peasants left the outskirts of the city to take shelter from the wild bands of the infamous Count Holck. Thousands, so it is related, fled northwards across the Elbe with waggons, carts or wheelbarrows, on foot or on horseback, many only with bundles on their backs or with their children in their arms. Large numbers of these unfortunate people fled through Leipzig, leaving the corn still standing in the fields or on the ground in sheaves or swaths. The townsfolk, fearful of higher prices and famine, were horrified that the peasants had even trampled down the corn so as to leave nothing behind for the plundering mercenaries.[1]

Very many refugees were attracted by the peaceful cantons of the Swiss Confederation. The inhabitants of Upper Swabia sought safety there on many occasions, as in the spring of 1642, "across the lake", even with cattle, horses and carts. However, those seeking refuge were not always welcome. In 1635, the authorities of the canton of Zurich had 7,000 "beggars" driven back over the bridge across the Rhine at Eglisau and into the devastated south-west corner of the Empire since there was already a shortage of food south of Lake Constance.[2]

The chronicler of the monastery of Salem, not far away from Lake Constance in the northerly direction, had this to say in 1636: "Weilen dan nun die kaysserischen soldaten also thürmisch und verüebig, dorften die underthonen nit wohnen, noch uff den derfern verbleiben, seien also auss den nägstgelögenen derfern, alss Mimmenhaussen, Neyffra, Weilldorf und Düffingen gnuog, wohl alle underthonen, in dass closter hierin gewichen mit weib und kind, hab, vieh, ross, Schwein und allem, wass sie hadten, dass also die sändhöff, spüthal, gerüchtstuben, frawenhauss, steinmezhauss, wangnerhauss, bschaidt, scheyren, schöpf, stadel und ställ, thorhäusslein, in summa alle örter krogetvoll gelegen, durch den ganzen grümb kalten winter (deren dan vil übel erfroren) und sommer bis uff den herbst . . ."[3]

The chronicler reports in 1646 of long columns of Bavarian peasants moving into the Alps where they believed they would be safe from the Imperial troops.

Terrible things must have happened in May 1648 in Munich. Crowds of people collected outside the gates of the city; waggons were everywhere in a crazy disorder and the poor carried all their worldly possessions on their bleeding backs. The elector and thousands of townspeople had fled to Salzburg.[4]

Most of these, when the news sounded good, would have returned to their villages with what remained of their possessions and, from the ruins of their houses and their devastated and spoilt fields, would have begun again to build a place where they could work and live. Looking down from an elevation, the hardboiled "scout" in Moscherosch's *Philander* caught sight of a dried-out fishpond—where it was easy to break up the ground—and of four peasants "harnessed to a plough like horses and tilling the ground . . ." And it happened only too often that the mercenaries descended on them yet again, destroying the work which had been begun again with so much effort. "For the goods of the peasants, so they said, belonged to the soldiers as much as to the peasants themselves."

Emergency organizations on a joint basis were also established in many places, such as the "Gemeinschaftliche Sache" ("Common Cause") of the peasants of Erling from 1627 until the end of the war. Some of them harnessed the few horses which had

[1] Kurtze/Jedoch eygentliche Warhafftige Beschreibung/Der dritten Bloquirung . . . der Churfürstlich Sächsischen Stadt Leipzig, 1633, copy in the Museum für Geschichte der Stadt Leipzig

[2] Die Tagebücher des Dr. Johann Heinrich von Pflummen 1633—1643, ed. by A. Sender, IInd part, Karlsruhe, 1951, p. 394

[3] Sebastian Bürster's Beschreibung des schwedischen Krieges 1630—1647, ed. by F. von Weech, Leipzig, 1875, p. 98f.

[4] Friesenegger, Maurus: Tagebuch aus dem 30jährigen Krieg, ed. by P. W. Mathäser, Munich, 1974, pp. 142ff. and 163

not yet been stolen and "ploughed almost all the fields" while the other peasants stood guard over the fields and those working in them.[1]

Of the numerous descriptions that have survived, the most notable is that of Grimmelshausen, a master of the art of realistic language, in the 4th chapter of the 1st Book of *Simplizissimus*. Even today, the drastic and ironical narrative style of the novelist vividly characterizes the horrifyingly businesslike and senselessly destructive actions of the marauders and his model could have been—or perhaps even were— the masterly engravings of Callot of Lorraine. The story in the reports is repeated a hundred times: the bands of mercenaries destroyed domestic utensils, tools and furniture, ruined stores and seeds, slaughtered or took away the cattle and the domestic animals, inflicted cruel tortures on the inhabitants or killed them and then set fire to the farm, which was usually built of wood, clay and straw. This was expressly forbidden by all the rules. In addition, it also frequently happened that young plants and ripe corn were deliberately trampled down by the armed plunderers or military detachments on the march and not without the senseless killing of the village inhabitants either. It is likewise occasionally reported that the healthy and able-bodied inhabitants were driven away and sold to the Turks "for eternal labour, far worse than death".[2] It is quite clear in this case that real happenings are mixed up with imaginary ones— not uncommon otherwise for contemporary authors—and the picture often offered by experience and narration, retelling and dissemination, becomes stereotype. However, the basis of the many contemporary reports is true; it is the contradiction, experienced and felt as irreconcilable, between the masses of the people and the soldiery.

Real and imaginary recollections are also reflected in the belief that the worst tormentors of the peasants were the Croatians, Cossacks, Stradiots and Hungarians while the Swedes were not any better. The foreign warriors attracted attention on account of their clothing, equipment, combat techniques and life-style so that their actions were also regarded as unusual. When a band of mounted troops suddenly appeared, daring, unruly and unscrupulous in word and deed, then they were "Croatians"—apparently devils in human form.

One of the most fearful and usually fatal tortures employed to extort confessions was the "Swedish drink" — the forcible filling of the gullet and stomach with waste products of human and animal origin.[3] However, there is no evidence that it was the invention of the "Swedes", i.e., of the mercenaries serving under Swedish command in Germany. The fact that the alarmed and tortured people of the country attributed the most repulsive deeds to foreigners may also have been the expression of the emergent national consciousness. Nevertheless, the profusion of fictitious descriptions was based on actual experience. The foreign mercenaries had no close links whatsoever with the land and the people in the German territories and easy booty was what they were after. Often bold and daring in battle, they changed into robbers when confronted with peasants and townsfolk. Some of them were even a pest in the countries they came from—such as the mercilessly foraging and plundering "Scots" in Denmark or the Lisowczyki in Poland. The mercenaries from the Balkans had developed their combat techniques and their freebooter style of acquiring provisions in the course of their permanent guerilla warfare with the Turks.

[1] Ibid, p. 40

[2] Theatrum Europaeum I, Frankfort on the Main (Merian), edition 1643, p. 1050

[3] Chemnitz, B. Ph. von: Königlich schwedischer in Teutschland geführter Krieg, IInd part, Stockholm, 1653, p. 521, copy in University Library Greifswald. For the Croates cf. Bauer, E.: Hrvati u tridesetoljetnam ratu, Zagreb, 1941

90 An attack on a peasant for his money.
Copperplate engraving by Christian Richter.
Staatliche Graphische Sammlung, Munich

Despite all the variety, the antagonism between the peasants and the soldiers was a feature common to all of them: *milites esse rusticorum diabolos*—the soldiers were the devil of the peasants. This mortal enmity is reflected in its brutal and unadorned form in the numerous dialogues between peasants and soldiers. "Zwerch", an inhuman marauder, says that "He is of the Devil who has mercy on a peasant" or "... who does not strike down everything and especially the peasant"[1]. The peasants had no choice but to resort to similar means to repel the inhuman oppressors and to give vent to the hatred that had built up inside them. In addition to the naturalistic description in Book 1, chapter 14, of *Simplizissimus* in which the peasants of the Spessart and Vogelsberg inflicted awful tortures on the soldiers wandering through the countryside, there is a great deal of other evidence available in which the peasants appear as merciless avengers.

The peasants were confronted with the war in a variety of ways: in the shape of regular military formations which—whether in friendly or enemy territory—demanded accommodation and food, as an exceptionally heavy taxation burden imposed by their own sovereign, or as openly impudent or treacherous raids and attacks carried out by armed bands on their own initiative. A specific feature of the Thirty Years' War was that these aspects of the war were mixed up with each other so that a composite picture emerged which did not correspond to later rules—by which the military and civil spheres were to be kept separate. Despite the chaotic situation, one thing is nevertheless clear: the war was not merely a confrontation between dynasties, states and princely alliances but also a protracted and far-flung war between peasants and soldiers. The theoretician Wallhausen considered that a mercenary unit on the march had to face two foes at the same time—the enemy in the field and the peasantry.

Ernst von Mansfeld, the prototype of a commander of such units and in the pay of the Bohemian Estates and King Frederick, promised "to leave the robbing entirely to them". And this is what they did, in the territory of their supreme commander, without any qualms of conscience or the slightest inhibitions. The anger of the peasants of Bohemia and the Upper Palatinate towards such "protectors" obviously increased rapidly. There is a report of 1620 from the area of Saaz with its many woods of 400 "Mansfeld" men being eliminated by armed peasants. The agent of the Elector of Saxony, Friedrich Lebzelter, wrote to his master on 24 May of the same year that several thousand peasants had assembled at Tábor, that they were "zimlich wohl armiret und hätten einen gar tapferen ansehnlichen Bauersmann zu ihrem Führer" ("fairly well armed and had a very brave and respectable peasant as their leader"). Sentries and red and white flags gave the camp a really military appearance. The first demand made by the peasants to the officials who had come from the Government in Prague to calm them was that Mansfeld and his plundering soldiery should be expelled from the country. The peasants themselves offered to take over its defence. The rebellious Estates in Bohemia flatly rejected this offer, a decision for which they had to pay dearly in the warlike events that followed.

An almost classic example of organized resistance to the parasitic soldiery was supplied by twelve villages in the Sinngrund district between Rhön and Spessart. When the Duke of Saxe-Lauenburg, serving on the Imperial side, set up his recruit-

[1] Moscherosch: Philander, p. 280

ment and mustering centres in Franconia in 1626, the infamous "foraging" of the new recruits on their own initiative immediately became a problem. The peasants of those twelve villages decided to organize their resistance to these pernicious activities— "to put together their bodies, possessions, honour, property and blood if any of these villages were to be raided by the soldiery . . ." They called on the inhabitants of the neighbouring villages to join their alliance. If this did not happen, these outsiders had to reckon with an attack "in strength and with energy" by the conspirators should the latter be driven from their farms and houses by the soldiery. Each village provided two officers and had to supply sufficient provisions, hand-firearms and ammunition. The oath taken by the peasants expressly forbade the plundering of enemy baggage-waggons nor were they to strike and strip captured soldiers and their women. The leaders of the peasants were obviously aware of the detrimental effect on the combat efficiency of their forces of such practices, inspired by blind hatred. In actual fact, the clashes with the peasants persuaded the mercenary forces not to indulge in further raids. The news of the courageous resistance of the peasants even reached the emperor and he ordered his regiments to avoid Franconia so as to prevent further "mischief".[1]

The guerilla warfare waged by the "Harz peasants" against convoys and raiding parties was a protracted and stubborn struggle. The towns of Quedlinburg and Stolberg and the Auerberg were used by them as bases and they could find safety in the woods covering the mountain slopes. In 1626, the peasants and miners of the central Harz area had built up courier lines and a network for reconnoitering embracing Halberstadt in the North and Nordhausen in the South. Even at the beginning of the 1630's. the chronicler writes of the "uprising of the Harz peasants" and of how dangerous it appeared.[2]

In 1632, the Bavarian peasants began to wage a general small-scale war against the victorious Swedish soldiers invading the country since the latter had proved to be intolerable oppressors. It was the intention of Gustavus Adolphus to weaken the Duke of Bavaria by ruining the country. The latter, in turn, regarded the self-defence of the peasants, which he expressly called upon them to undertake, as an important instrument for the prevention of even more damage. Religious motives also played a part in this. The peasants mercilessly killed the mercenaries appearing singly or in groups and there are also reports of cruel torture. Several hundred villages fell victim to the vengeance subsequently taken by the Swedish troops. The smoke of burning buildings and devastated villages marked the progress of their reprisals.[3] Hatred for the soldiery continued to smoulder, however.

In the winter of 1633/34, the Imperial forces also sought winter-quarters in the ravaged districts of Bavaria. But on this occasion both soldiers and peasants starved in the exhausted countryside. The mustering of a Spanish-Italian regiment on 30 December 1633 presented a strange sight: on one side, the officers, "respectable people in splendid clothes"; on the other, emaciated figures, wrapped in rags for the most part, some even wearing women's garments. It was said that 30 died every day. The peasants attempted to cast off this pitiful and cruel burden by a great rebellion. At the beginning of December, storm-bells summoned the suffering people between the Isar and the Inn to assemble in camps and to organize themselves in armed mobs.

Mein Manheit zeig ich hier, Du schandhir sage ahn
Wo ist der schelm Der dieb, der hirnd dein Loser Man.

91 A robbing soldier attacks a woman and her child. Copperplate engraving by Christian Richter. Staatliche Graphische Sammlung, Munich

[1] Müller, K.-A.: Das Söldnerwesen in den ersten Jahren des dreissigjährigen Krieges, Dresden, 1838; Heilmann, J.: Kriegsgeschichte von Bayern, Franken, Pfalz und Schwaben, IInd vol., 1st section, Munich, 1868
[2] Bellus: Kayserlicher Triumpff-Wagen, p. 136; Gottfried, J. L.: Historischer Chronicken Continuation . . . (1629—1633), Frankfort on the Main (Merian), 1633, p. 387, as Theatrum Europaeum II edition
[3] Riezler, S.: Geschichte Baierns, vol. 5, Gotha, 1903, p. 428f.; Chemnitz: Königlich Schwedischer . . . Krieg, vol. I, Alten Stettin, 1648, p. 18

Most of the peasants came with hay-forks and spiked clubs and some carried muskets. They demanded from the elector, whom they defiantly called "the peasants' greatest enemy", to withdraw all troops, including the Bavarian forces since none of them were worth anything, no matter who their commander was. Maximilian I was obliged to negotiate, mollify and make concessions, i.e., to withdraw the troops from the east bank of the Inn. Following this success, the militant peasants dispersed, like those of Sinngrund in Franconia, to return to their fields. Only one of the peasant formations remained intact in the forest of Ebersberg. It was overwhelmed, after stubborn resistance, by mercenaries at the end of February 1634, the same fate being shared by all the insurgents west of the Inn as well.[1]

At the beginning of the 1630's, the districts along the Upper Rhine and in the Black Forest were also marked by widespread unrest among the peasants. In 1633, it was the turn of the Breisgau area, the district around Schlettstadt and the Sundgau area.

After the Battle of Nördlingen, the unruly Imperial soldiery who had driven out the French troops in July 1635 plundered 150 villages and market centres in Alsace and Burgundy. Even a chronicler favouring the Imperial side wrote that such actions had become "a free trade" ("freyen handtwerckh erwachssen"). He notes, however, that the peasants killed "any of our people that they met" ("alles, was sie von unserem volckh antreffen") and that it "could no longer be called war but was more like robbery".[2]

In the first half of 1635, the peasants of the county of Cilli in Styria rebelled, demanding a reduction in the rate of interest and statute-labour. This area was far away from the fighting of the "Great War" but, being on the Turkish border, it was constantly threatened by surprise attacks. Castles and monasteries went up in flames and it was only by the intervention of troops originally recruited for the defence of the Slovenian frontier that the rebels were scattered and defeated. The use of the Viennese city guard was also considered. On the instructions of the authorities, the mercenaries meted out retribution in the usual barbarous manner, on this occasion adding death by drowning to their repertoire.[3]

What titanic resolution must have been possessed by the peasants when they did not give up in the face of such practices by the authorities and when persecuted by the tortures and cruelty of the busy soldiery but continued, time and again, to wage a bitter struggle with them, a struggle which sometimes took the form of a full-scale war. The moral stature of this achievement is not affected either by the fact that there was an obvious increase in the terrorism which characterized many of the peasant uprisings. This was a reaction to the barbarism of regular and irregular warfare. To preserve the lives of those carrying out work with a sensible purpose, it was necessary to eliminate the parasitic mercenaries with their senseless killing and destruction. In this defensive struggle, the class of the German peasants with its many strata had to pay a heavy toll in life and limb. As suspected by Frederick Engels, it was clearly higher than the price paid in the princely reprisals immediately after the German Peasants' Rebellion of 1524—1526.[4]

In the struggles already mentioned and others, the peasants supplied ample evidence that they had not lost the organizational and military abilities of their fore-

[1] Riezler, S.: Der Aufstand der bayerischen Bauern im Winter 1633 und 1634, Munich, 1901

[2] Pflummen: Tagebücher II, p. 212

[3] Mell, A.: Der windische Bauernaufstand des Jahres 1635 und dessen Nachwehen, in: Mitteilungen d. Historischen Vereins für Steiermark 44/1896

[4] Engels, F.: Der deutsche Bauernkrieg, in: Marx/Engels Werke, vol. 7, Berlin, 1960

fathers. This was most clearly apparent in the peasant uprising of 1626 in Upper Austria. Known rightly as the "Peasants' War", it is to be considered as part of the overall military activities of the time.[1]

The emperor, as the ruler of the area, had handed over the "Land ob der Enns" to his Bavarian cousin and ally as a pledge since this was the only way in which he could repay the elector (who only desired this, too) for his assistance in the crushing of the Austrian and Bohemian rebels in 1620. Bavarian soldiers and tax officials, zealous "papist" vicars and Jesuit priests came to the *Ländl* to accelerate the return of the population to the bosom of the Catholic Church. The new Bavarian regime certainly put pressure on and harassed the aristocratic opposition as well but the main burden of Bavarian rule was nevertheless borne by the peasants. Protests were crushed by the mercenaries of the Bavarian governor, Count Herberstorff in the spring of 1625 and a cruel precedent was set at Whitsuntide of the same year. On the 14th of May, the governor commanded the male inhabitants of five parishes and two market-centres to come to the castle of Frankenburg, to the "Haushamer Feld", 5,000 persons duly appearing on the following day. After they had been surrounded by heavily armed mercenaries, 38 village-judges, councillors, well-respected peasants and also a journey-man-dyer were seized by force and obliged to cast dice for their life on black cloths under a linden tree. Seventeen losers met their death at the hands of the executioner, only two persons being shown mercy. The "Frankenburg game of dice" was intended to be a warning to the angry people of the country. The triumphant oppressors dared to take further action and mandates from the ruler of the area prohibited the practising of the Protestant faith. All those who refused to embrace Roman Catholicism were obliged to leave the area and their immovable property and, in addition, had to pay charges, including a *Freigeld* (10 per cent of their wealth). Mercenaries were lodged in the houses of the peasants and townsfolk to accelerate the forced conversion to Catholicism or the expulsion of the inhabitants. They impudently provoked those who were unwilling who—if they were well off—could only purchase a delay for their conversion at most. Otherwise, all that they could do was to move to the free cities of the Reich in Upper Germany where the forcible conversion to the Catholic faith was neither usual nor required by law. The peasants, bound by close links to their home, farm and village community did not leave the area despite alienation of a severe degree. They dared to fight for their rights and liberty.

In the spring of 1626, open rebellion was about to break out. One of the principal demands of the peasants was that the soldiers should be withdrawn from the area, for the maintenance of whom the "garrison tax" was to be paid. The peasants were well aware that the troops, now present in larger numbers and making unrelenting demands every day, were being used by their ruler to extort even more from them and to force them into an even greater state of subjection. Since their ruler and the actual holder of the country, by way of pledge, went about this under the banner of Catholicism, the Lutheran faith was a moral support in their "permissible natural defence", as the peasants wrote to the emperor, against a hostile and alien state-power.

The peasants carefully made secret preparations for the rebellion but it broke out prematurely in May 1626. Tens of thousands of peasants, armed with weapons or

The "Song of the Swedes"

The Swedes have come,
Have taken everything,
Have smashed in the windows,
Have taken away the lead,
Have made bullets from it
And shot the peasants.

F. M. Böhme: Deutsches Kinderlied, No. 1625 a

[1] Schmiedt, R. F.: Der Bauernkrieg in Oberösterreich vom Jahre 1626 als Teilerscheinung des Dreissigjährigen Krieges, Thesis. Halle, 1963 (typed); Eichmeyer/Feigl/Litschel: Weiss gilt die Seel; Der oberösterreichische Bauernkrieg 1626. Exhibition of Upper Austria in Linz Castle and Scharnstein Castle (Catalogue), Linz, 1976; Sturmberger, H.: Adam Graf Herberstorff, Vienna, 1976

capturing them from the enemy, assembled in the various camps and fought several successful battles against the troops of the governor and of the Emperor. Most of the towns opened their gates to them—including the town of Wels. A formation of 600 men moved into the latter—in military order in ranks of five or six men, with varying sets of equipment. They laid siege to the capital, Linz, but were unable to take it. The leader of the rebels, a peasant by the name of Stefan Fadinger from a farm in St. Agatha and a former soldier, called himself the "chief of the honourable community and peasantry of the Christian Evangelical Field Camp at Linz". The peasants took measures for the effective waging of their war and for the defence of their dearly won positions; committees and field command centres were established and field orders issued. In this manner, the traditions of the Great Peasants' War were revived in this small district. The seal of the peasants' camp at Weiberau, a place with many traditions, bore the inscription "Sigillum einer verfolgten Bauernschaft" ("Seal of a persecuted peasantry") and, in addition to peasant symbols (plough and mill-wheel), also depicted the sign of the Hussites, the goblet. The "black peasants" of the biggest group wore the typical headgear of the peasants of Upper Austria—the dark yodeller's hat and above them there waved black flags bearing a white skull. This grim symbolism and the traditional battle-hymn "Free us, Dear God, from Bavaria's yoke and tyranny and its cruel oppression!" with its last line "It has to be" expressed the fierce and desperate determination of the rebellious peasants to cast off the hated civil and military rule of Bavaria at any price, even that of their own life.

The detailed report by the Bavarian mercenary leader, Count Gottfried Heinrich von Pappenheim, who subsequently became the commander of the famous regiment of cuirassiers under Wallenstein, describes a typical armed clash between a mercenary army and a peasant force.[1] Well entrenched in the wood known as the Emlinger Holz, they sang psalms before the battle of Eferding on 9 November 1626. With their morale enhanced by the solemn singing, they stormed out of the wood and challenged Pappenheim's mercenaries *in furia* to do battle with them—"Come out, Pappenheim!" was their battle-cry. The "incredible boldness" with which the peasants attacked their foes, including the heavily armed *Eisenreiter* and the gun-crews, struck fear into the hearts of the mercenaries. They could only believe that the peasants were "bullet-proof"—"unnt den harten Felsen gleich" ("like hard rock"). Pappenheim admits that it was only by pleading with his soldiers and threatening them with fearful retribution that he was able to persuade them to move against the peasants again. The latter, in groups of eight to ten men, dared to attack an entire company (approx. 80 to 100 men) and caused great injury, wounding many horses and men.

The princely adversaries of the emperor endeavoured to win over the rebels to their side. King Christian IV of Denmark, from 1625 onwards the instigator of a great anti-Hapsburg coalition, sent an unnamed representative with full authority to hold negotiations with Fadinger and the mobilized peasant forces. This "foreign person" carried credentials which had been signed on 6 June 1626 in Wolfenbüttel and which promised the peasants "Succurs" in the name of the King of Denmark. However, it did not prove possible to co-ordinate the military actions and the attempt to form an alliance remained an episode.

[1] Enss, Caspar: Fama Austriaca, Cologne, 1627, p. 895ff., copy in Biblioteka Gdańska; Historia Teutsches Krieges, no place, 1645, p. 26, copy in Bayerische Staatsbibliothek, Munich

In the end, the peasant formations were regularly defeated by the trained, better armed and numerically superior mercenary units—but the desperate bravery of the rebels made them the moral victors, a fact which was also conceded by Pappenheim, a man who demonstrated his ability as a military commander. It was only on few occasions, he wrote, that he had seen fighting with "such obstinacy".

This fighting capability, which was also noted with astonishment or admiration by many chroniclers, was not easily countered. In the 1630's, the victorious campaigns of the Swedish armies awakened new hope in the peasants as far as the Danube. The peasants of Hausruckviertel again took out their weapons from their place of concealment in 1632 and began another rebellion, led by Jakob Greimbl who had already been active as an agitator in 1626. They were joined by the peasants of Mühlviertel. Local unrest again broke out in the same district in 1635/36. Some years before this, a mystic and visionary lay-preacher by the name of Martin Laimbauer had travelled through the villages there and passionately proclaimed that he had been sent by God to "free the land from servitude". However, it was not more than 700 in all who flocked to the new Messiah as he travelled through the countryside. Pursued by detachments of mercenaries, the little band of his most faithful followers which had taken shelter in a church at St. Georgen on the Gusen was mercilessly struck down —nor were the children spared. The victors took Martin Laimbauer and eight other prisoners to Linz where they were executed on the 20th of June of the same year. The executioner tortured their leader with red-hot irons, nailed his right hand to the execution-block before severing it with the axe and finally decapitated him.—The spark of hope continued to smoulder among the peasants. In the final year of the war, a peasant-leader was sent by conspirators to the robbing and plundering Swedes, who were camped outside Prague, to ascertain whether they were prepared to lend support in the event of a rebellion. As was to be expected, the Swedes failed to give any help at all. Among the aristocratic members of the Estates of Upper Austria, there must always have been the paralyzing fear of another peasant rebellion. When, in 1641, they considered mobilizing the peasants to defend the land and their estates against the groups of Swedish mercenaries, they demanded that the peasants should not be allowed to wear the dark hats which had identified them in 1626. At that time, the authorities feared that the spark of insurrection could cross the frontier and a bridge be struck with Bohemia which was always a restless breeding-ground of rebellion. This was also the reason why the Imperial government took care to have the frontiers between Bohemia and Upper Austria heavily guarded and strongly fortified.[1]

Bohemia was, of course, the country in which there was an endless chain of attempts to organize rebellions among the peasants up to 1630. To begin with, these were always directed against two foes—the Church with its policy of forcible conversion and the mercenaries. It was especially the taxes which had to be paid to the army, the transport services which had to be rendered, the food which had to be supplied and the insolent plundering plus famine and plagues which, between 1625 and 1627, led to a long sequence of outbreaks of anger in Southern and Eastern Bohemia. These insurrections were always directed against feudal authority as well, however. Castles and monasteries were stormed and set on fire, miners and woodcutters took up arms and weavers

The Other Song

No soldier should be sad
and weep everywhere,
Has he not rich peasants
in his enemy's hall,
Plancker Crabat
In ragged finery,
Strike hard, soldier,
God helps you, early and late.

From: Zwey schöne neue Lieder (1632), Leaflet

[1] Janoušek, B.: Ohlas hornorakouského povstání r. 1626 v jížních Čechách, in: Jihočeský sborník XXXIII/1964

moved around the country, secretly recruiting volunteers and leading them to the Danish camp in Silesia. In August 1627, a preacher by the name of Matouš Ulický appeared on the scene in Čáslav. He was certainly the author of that appeal to "people of the lower class" to prepare themselves for battle—like Jan Žižka and his brothers in the past—to safeguard not only their liberty but also their life and possessions, their women and children. The strict discipline and behaviour of the Upper Austrian peasants, especially under Stefan Fadinger, also recalls the Hussite spirit.[1]

In the 1620's, the "Wallachian" herdsmen of the mountains in Southern Moravia began their struggle against the Imperial mercenaries, a struggle which continued until the mid-1640's. The men of the mountains, who were brave and elusive, co-ordinated their raids and skirmishes with the Danes and the Swedes who were at war with the emperor. They even fought shoulder to shoulder with the mercenaries—but did not achieve any lasting benefit from this. Their weapon was a long, razor-sharp axe, which they otherwise used to protect their herds from the wolves and which they swung with consummate skill.[2]

PEASANTS
"SAVE THE LAND"
AT PRINCELY COMMAND

The Thirty Years' War between the various princes, waged with professional soldiers who were difficult to control and for whom there was scarcely any money, raised the question, for the governments of the Empire, of which was worse: these destructive mercenaries or subjects with weapons. The authorities sought to exploit the fundamental enmity between the soldiery and peasantry in the converse manner to which they employed it in cases of insurrection. The peasant—willing and endeavouring to protect his family, farm, fields and crops from destruction—was to save the land and himself with the approval and arms of the Government. Campaigns—known as *Landesdefensionen*—were organized time and again to provide military training for the young generation of peasants capable of bearing arms. Every name was entered in lists and registers by the authorities and the young men were required to present themselves at certain places on Sundays for training in the use of weapons. Depending on the degree of danger and the actual orders issued, every fifth, eighth, tenth or thirtieth man had to hasten to the assembly point of the committee when the alarm was raised by the ringing of a bell.[3]

This practice had already been used in the 16th century, especially along the troubled and exposed Turkish frontier in the extreme Southeast of the Empire. From the end of the century, the use of the country's subjects for its defence also proved useful in the Northwest in the struggle against the Spanish Hapsburg armies which were

[1] Petráň, J.: Matouš Uhlický a poddanské povstání na Kouřimsku a Čáslavsku roku 1627, in: Acta Universitatis Carolinae, Philologica et Historica 7/1954

[2] Dostál, F.: Valašská povstání za třicetileté války (1621—1644), Prague, 1956

[3] Schnitter, H.: Volk und Landesverteidigung. Studien zur Geschichte des Landesdefensions-wesens in den deutschen Territorien vom 16. bis 18. Jahrhundert, Berlin, 1977; Jähns, M.: Geschichte der Kriegswissenschaften, 2nd section, Munich/Leipzig, 1890; Frauenholz, E. von: Entwicklungsgeschichte des deutschen Heerwesens, 3rd vol., IInd part (Die Landes-defensionen), Munich, 1939; Oestreich, G.: Graf Johanns VII. Verteidigungsbuch für Nassau-Dillenburg, in: Geist und Gestalt des frühmodernen Staates, Berlin (West), 1969

92 The peasant reacts with helpless gesture to
the imperious demands of an officer. The village
houses of wood and loam have been set on fire
by the soldiers and are rapidly burning down.
Copperplate engraving by Rudolf Meyer.
Staatliche Graphische Sammlung, Munich

93—95 Murdering and robbing soldiers fall
upon peasant villages. Hans Ulrich Franck
was responsible for vigorous etchings having
little in common with the idyllic style in fashion
at the time. Germanisches Nationalmuseum,
Nuremberg

96 By the events of war the peasantry was forced to take actions of self-defence; in the beginning these were individual actions, later on they were executed in an organized form. Etching by Hans Ulrich Franck. Staatliche Graphische Sammlung, Munich

97 This bird's-eye-view conveys an impression, with astonishing military and topographic accuracy, of one of the battlefields of the Peasants' War in Upper Austria of 1626—the areas along the Danube from Passau to Linz—and also supplies important information regarding the mastery of modern military technology and fortification techniques by the militant peasants. Copperplate engraving by Wolfgang Kilian (1626). Germanisches Nationalmuseum, Nuremberg

Nᵒ 1. Statt Passaw.

1. Oberhauß.
3. Inndorff.
4. Der Tonaw fluß.
5. Yn fluß.
6. Haffnerzel.
7. Englharts Zell / so die Pauren die erste Schanz vnd Wacht gehabt.
8. Schloß Maschbach / so die erste Loßschüß geschehen seind.
9. Ein altes Schloß auffm Berg.
10. Die 5. Schiff / so hauptman von Tannozol commandirt.
11. Der Paurenschanzen bey der Ketten / so mit 4000. Man vnd 8. stuck besetzt.
12. Die Ketten vnd 2. Sail / damit die Tonaw gesperrt gewesen / doch zersprengt worden.
13. Das Schloß Newhauß.
14. Der Marckt Ascha.
15. Vrfahr gegen Ascha.
16. Attenßham.
17. Closter Willering.
18. Statt Efferding.
19. Die 5. schiff / so die Ketten zersprengt / vnd auff Linz ankommen.
20. Das Kays: Schloß Linz.
21. Die newe Palisada / so gegen den Trug- bawren gemacht worden.
22. Das werck / darinn der Trugbaur stehet / in welchem 6. stuck / vn vff den Trug- bawr 3. gestanden / alda Hauptman von Tannazoil Posta gewest.
23. Wo die Rebelle den anfang mit 12000 zu stürmen gemacht.
24. Der Wasserthurn / darauff 5. stuck ge- standen.
25. Die Palisaden bey der Pruck / darin 2 Stuck gestanden / darbey die 5. Succurs- schiff angelendt / alda Capitän Leuten- empt von Veldhofen gewest.

26. Der Salzstadl / darauff 2. stuck gestan- den.
27. Das Schulerthürl / Hauptmans von Schernberg Posta / wo die Rebellen mit 8000 Man / von 10 vhr / biß vmb 4 vhr gegen tag continuirlich gestürmbt / vnnd letztlich mit grossem verlurst abziehen müssen.
28. Herrn Grundmans Hauß / welchs von den Rebellen starck besetzt gewest / auß welchem in einem Außfall Herr Haupt- man von Schernberg erschossen worde / letztlich mit stucken die Bawren darauß getrieben.
29. Der Schmidthurn / da man mit Toppl- hacken den Rebellen grossen schaden ge- than.
30. Die Schanz / so die Pawren bey dem Galgenberg an der Tonaw gemacht / darauß sie mit stucken die Tonaw vnnd die Rebellen bestreitten können.
31. Ein Lauffgraben in die grosse Schanz / so sie ober dem Capuziner Closter gebau- et / darinn sie 14 stuck Geschütz wider den Trugpaur vnd das Schloß plandirt.
32. Ein Lauffgraben / biß zum Schmidthor.
33. Ein Schänzlein / darinn 4 stuck gegen dem Schmidthor gericht gewest.
34. Ein Schänzlein inn der Ledergassen / darinn 2. stuck gestanden.
35. Die Schanz im Vrfar / darinnen die Rebellen 8. Stuck gehabt.
36. Der Rebellen Palisada gegen der Pru- cken / darinnen sie 2. Stuck gehabt.
37. Die Tonaw Prucken / so von den Sta- halterischen abgebrennt worden.
38. Der Capuciner Closter / darinnen des Rebellen Haupt Quartier gewesen.
39. Danzhauß / Capitein Apian Posta.
40. S. Marthin.

Eigentlicher Abriß/als im 1626. Jar
die Pawren in Osterreich ob der Enß/Rebellisch ge-
west/Herrn/Herrn Graven von Herberstorff/rc. Statt-
halter zu Lintz/mit 6000.starck/alda belägert/Herr Statt-
halter grossen Mangel an Proviant gehabt/vnd auß Be-
velch Jrer Churfl: Durchl: in Bayrn/rc. Herrn Hauptman
Bärtlme von Tannazol/Jhr Gn: den 18. Julii/obbemeld-
tes Jars mit 5. Schiffen/darauf 300. Man succurriert vn
proviantirt hat/Er Hauptman sich durch die Pauren ge-
schlagen/vnd jhrer der Pauren vber die Tonaw gehabten
gespanten Ketten vn Sailern zersprengt/vnd nacher Lintz
angelangt. In gleichem wie die Pawren/so die Statt Lintz
belägert/den 3.tag drauff/Sturm geloffen/vn nach weh-
er 5. Stund/sie mit verlurst etlicher hundert Mann/
erumb abzihen müssen.

Wolfgang Kilian fecit A° 1626.

98 Contemporary illustration of the unsuccessful
siege of Linz by rebelling peasants in June/July
1626. They also failed to capture the castle (on
the right of the picture). Germanisches Nationalmuseum, Nuremberg

99 Pamphlet of 1627: weapons, also of Hussite
pattern, flags with the surviving battle-cries and
songs of the rebellious peasants of Upper Austria
in 1626. The text refers to the Great Peasant War
of 1525/26. Some of the weapons and names are
fictitious and there is an anti-peasant tendency.
Germanisches Nationalmuseum, Nuremberg

Contrafactur der Stad Lintz, wie die von den Ensischen Bawren belagert bestürmbt und wieder abgetrien worden, 1626.

Glücks Hafen

Des vor ein hundert Jahrn vorgangenen Bauren kriegs, Sambt Eigendlicher Contrafactur und Abriß der vornembsten officirn und Befehlshabere, ob wol der gewehr und Waffen deren sich itzo die Rebellischen Bauren im Ländlein ob der Enß, in diesem Hir= lauffenden 1626. Jahr, bey jhrer vermeynten Kriegs Expedition gebrauchen.

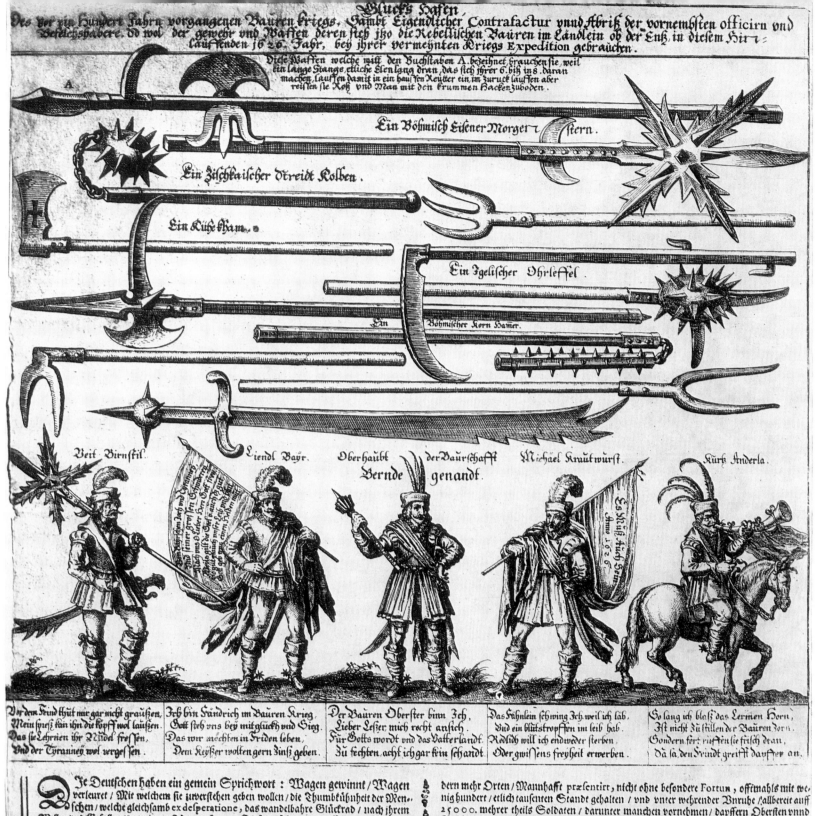

Diese Waffen welche mitt den Buchstaben A. bezeichnet, grauchen sie weil ein lange Stange, etliche Elenlang dran, das sich jhrer 6. biß in 8. daran machen, lauffen damit in ein hauffen Reutter ein, im zuruck lauffen aber reissen sie Roß und Man mit den krummen Hacken zuboden.

A

Ein Böhmisch Eisener Morgen Stern.

Ein Zischkaischer Streidt Kolben.

Ein Kühe Cham.

Ein Igelischer Ohrleffel.

Ein Böhmischer Korn Hamer.

Veit Birnstil.   Liendl Bayr.   Ober haubt der Baurschafft **Bernde genandt.**   Michael Krautwurst.   Kürtz Anderla.

Vor den Feind thut mir gar nicht grausen, / Mein Spieß kan ihn die Köpff wol lausen. / Das sie schreien jhr Blud fressen, / und der Tyranney wol vergessen.	Ich bin Fändrich im Bauren Krieg, / Gott steh uns bey mit glück und Sieg. / Das wir möchten in Friden leben, / Dem Keyser wolten gern Zinß geben.	Der Bauren Oberster binn Ich, / Lieber Leser, mich recht ansich. / Für Gotts wordt und das Vatterland, / Zu fechten, acht ich gar kein schandt.	Das Fähnlein schwing Ich weil ich lab, / Und ein blutstropffen im leib hab. / Redlich will ich endweder sterben, / Oder gwissens freyheit erwerben.	So lang ich blaß das Lermen Horn, / Ist nicht zu stillen der Bauren Zorn. / Sondern fort rüstten sie frisch dran, / da sa, den Feindt greifft dapffer an.

Die Deutschen haben ein gemein Sprichwort: Wagen gewinnt / Wagen verleuret / Mit welchem sie zuverstehen geben wollen / die Thumbkühnheit der Menschen / welche gleichsamb ex desperatione, das wandelbahre Glückrad / nach jhrem Willen und Gefallen / zu zwingen sich unterfangen. Dieses möchte nun / auff jetzigen Bawern Auffruhr im Ländlein Ob der Enß / nicht unfüglich gezogen und accommodirt werden / Dann daß derselbe einig und allein auff das Glück fundiret / wird niemandt leugnen / Und darff keiner weitleufftigen Wiederholung / was nunmehr vor hundert Jahren vorgangen / Sondern ist der damahlige Verlauff / allenthalben Weltkündig / unnd zu ewigem Gedächtniß / von dem vortrefflichen Historico Sleidano / mit allen Umbständen / außführlich beschrieben hinderlassen / Dißmahls nur mit wenigen jetzigen Zustandt zuberühren / So ist sich nicht unbillich zuverwundern / daß dieses nunmehr ablauffende 1626. Jahr! Seyt dem Monat Majo: und so kurtze Zeit hero / obgedachte Ober Enserische Bawern / fast unversehens im Städtlein Ascha / sich zusammen rottirt / die Waffen ergriffen / von 500. uff Ein: Zehen: und mehr Tausend dermassen gesterckt / daß sie mit der gantzen Macht nicht allein unterschiedliche Städt / Flecken und Dörffer angefallen / mit Fewer und Schwerde verfolgt / unnd zu Grund gerichtet / Sondern sich auch zum öffentlichen Schlagen / im freyen Feld bey Bawerbach / Lintz / Spieß / Effertingen / Gemünden / auffm Zuckerbergt / der Welserheyd / und an dern mehr Orten / Mannhafft präsentirt / nicht ohne besondere Fortun, offtmahls mit wenig hundert / etlich tausenten Standt gehalten / und unter wehrender Unruhe / allbereit auff 25000. mehr theils Soldaten / darunter manchen vornehmen / dapffern Obersten unnd Befehlichhaber / jämmerlich erschlagen haben / Inmassen davon hin: und wider in Schreiben und offenem Druck gnugsame Nachrichtung vorhanden.

Gleich wie nun bey einem Glückshafen gemeiniglich jederman / auß grosser Begierde / etwas stattliches zu erheben / sich keine Kosten tauren lesset: Also haben ihnen auch die Bawern / ohne Zweiffel / Gottes Ehr / Religions: und Gewissens Freyheit / zum Zweck vorgesetzet / und dahero eine rechtmessige / eyferige Defension, gänzlich eingebildet. Dieweil aber der Gestalt / das Date Caesari quae sunt Caesaris, & quae Dei, Deo &c. Item, die Vermahnung Pauli / Jederman sey unterthan der Obrigkeit etc. unbesonnen übergangen / alles auff Glück und Gerathwol gestellet / So stehet der Außgang in Gottes Händen / der helffe / daß mit diesem zu endlauffenden alten Jahr / das landverderbliche Kriegswesen / unnd was dem anhängig / gänzlich abweiche / Hingegen das annehme Newe / den längst gewündschten / edlen / werthen Frieden / sampt gutem Vernehmen und auffrichtigem Vertrawen / zwischen Obrigkeit und Unterthanen / zu des heiligen Römischen Reichß und dessen Gliedern / gewündschtem Ruhe und Wohlstandt / einsten wiederbringen möge / AMEN.

Gedruckt im Jahr / 1627.

100/101 Peasants' revenge —
merciless retribution for raiders
and marauders. Etching (detail)
by Hans Ulrich Franck. Staatliche
Graphische Sammlung, Munich

sent to re-impose the rule of the Spanish king in the seven liberated provinces of the Netherlands. In the territories which were influenced by or directly concerned in the national revolutionary war of liberation of the Netherlands, rulers such as that of Nassau-Siegen (Count John VI and Count John VII), Hesse-Kassel and the Counts of the Palatinate at Rhein were able to raise peasant units who showed that they could fight bravely in battle. With reference to the peasants of Westerwald, Prince Maurice of Orange, an outstanding exponent of the art of war, said that they were more skilled in the use of guns than the Dutchmen.

It was obvious that it was easier to finance and maintain "land-saving organizations" of this kind than mercenaries who were hired for fairly long periods. This also explains that the ruling princes made use of them on repeated occasions. However, these defence obligations were a considerable burden for the peasants. In addition to the regular practices on Sundays, they also had to provide transportation and carry out entrenchment works. This is why the peasants endeavoured to avoid being selected.

The history of the defence obligations in Bavaria appears to have been a particularly tense affair since the ruler of the country increasingly interfered in the life led by his subjects, regimenting, commanding and threatening them without respite. In 1604/05, much energy was expended in registering the peasants for the armed defence of the country. It was decided by Duke Maximilian that the traditional costume of the peasants—narrow breeches tied at the knee and closely fitting doublet—was unsuitable for warlike purposes and that it was to be replaced by generously cut clothing of the "Gallic style". The cost of this change was to be borne by the peasants. They, however, declared that they were unable to bear such an "intolerable burden" and would agree to buying new clothing only when their old clothes were unserviceable. The ducal authorities answered this with strict executive decrees: tailors were only permitted to make clothes of the approved style; young peasants who did not wear laced breeches and doublets of generous cut were not allowed to take part in public dances. Despite this, the peasants remained stubborn and obstinate and even in 1611 a decree had to be issued, instructing them to accompany their captain to church on Sundays. For the church service, they had to carry side-arms and wear a hat (instead of a cap) and "laced" clothing. The "breeches question" had developed into a state affair without the duke being able to achieve what he wanted, however.

In the open countryside, it was not so easy to persuade the peasants to go into action against the enemy. At most and for their own reasons and in their own fashion, they carried out skirmishes, laid ambushes and waged guerilla warfare against invading armies, as happened in 1632 in the case of the Swedes. In the autumn of that year, the elector admitted that he had been unable to use his subjects "to any effect at all" in a military sense and the expense incurred had been in vain. The officials and officers were instructed to collect the weapons from the "selected" peasants and have them taken to the armouries.[1]

The elector of the Palatinate took no less trouble in preparing the peasants of the remote Upper Palatinate for the defence of their area. They were recruited in troops and carefully fitted out with uniform clothing. After Frederick of the Palatinate had been defeated at the White Hill in 1620, it was planned to march the peasant detach-

[1] Heilmann: Kriegsgeschichte II/2, p. 808ff.

ments to Bohemia to oppose the victors of the Imperial League. However, the government at Amberg had unwelcome news for the elector of the Palatinate. The troop from Grafenwöhr totally refused to obey any commands. In the opinion of the peasants, their oath only obliged them to defend the Upper Palatinate. In general—according to the report—they were not well disposed towards the authorities and could easily be incited to *inclinationibus* or insurrection. The attempt to integrate young peasants in mercenary units was a total failure. Once again, it proved impossible to bridge the antagonism between these two social groups. The peasants simply disappeared or openly deserted and complete troops or detachments refused to obey the commands of their officers or even beat them up.

These and many other happenings demonstrate that there was never a clear division between the military mobilization of the peasants and their open revolt against the authorities. It was by no means the case that all the peasants handed in the weapons in the use of which they had been drilled—despite the importance attached to this by the authorities. Well aware that the subject who knew how to use the pike and the musket was the biggest source of danger for the existing order (and not the free mercenary who had no roots), the watchdogs and the crowned heads of this order were very cautious indeed in their use of the mechanism of defence—as if they were holding a piece of hot metal in their hand which could be used for only a short time at most.

PEASANT
SELF-DEFENCE AND
ADAPTABILITY

When the peasants took defensive measures on their own initiative and paid little attention to the decrees of the state, they acted quite differently to when they fought within the defence framework organized by the authorities. From their original needs for protection and peace, the peasants evolved a variety of independent and well-considered forms of defence. It was only in retrospect that the princely and municipal administrations were obliged to legalize these forms—usually because they themselves had been unable to make an effective contribution to the defence of the country.

In times of imminent danger, while the men laid in wait for the enemy in ambushes, the women and children hurried to carefully selected hiding-places in caves or in the moors and woods, taking their animals with them. In some places, the peasants built "thorn defences" through which the mercenaries could only pass one by one. Certain death awaited them.[1] So that enough time was available to reach the hiding-places and refuge-centres, warning-systems had to be established, linking one village with another. Lookouts in high trees, on hills and church-towers communicated with each other by fire or smoke signals. Village judges, inn-keepers, priests, officials and peasants

[1] Khevenhiller, F. C.: Annales Ferdinandei, vol. XII, Leipzig, 1726, p. 144

questioned everybody that was "on the road"—pedlars, beggars, monks, itinerant merchants and butchers, herdsmen, couriers, foraging soldiers, gipsies and postilions[1].

The weapons needed for survival in the small-scale warfare carried on almost everywhere against the mercenaries were mostly of the traditional type: halberds, pigstickers, hayforks and small-calibre muskets and pistols. Hand-firearms and guns were used by the peasants mainly when they were drawn up in organized formations, as demonstrated by the Peasants' War in Upper Austria. Peasants who hastened to the defence of fortified positions brought sledge-hammers, axes, long nails, bundles of straw and pitch with them.

Stubborn, intelligent and inventive, the peasants saved their own lives and those of others in a situation where the wars waged by their rulers were on the increase and at a time when life was cheap. This was an expression of moral greatness and historical achievement of which only the popular masses in town and countryside were capable. The historiographer Eberhard Wassenberg, who is otherwise very temperate in his assessments, confirms that many enlightened minds, who believed in human progress, regarded the peasant as the alternative to the mercenary. After describing the destruction wreaked by the Swedish soldiery under General Banér (whom he compares with the rapacious kings of the Goths Totila and Alaric and Attila, king of the Huns) in Northern Germany, he unexpectedly adds a sentence which does not reflect the historical reality but is rather a visionary assumption or wishful thinking: "Der-halben so stund auch das gemeine Volk und die Bauern auf/damit si des mänschlichen Geschlächts algemeinen untergang mit algemeinen Waffen hinwäg nähmen möchten."[2] ("This is why the ordinary people and the peasants rebelled to prevent the general ruin of mankind by force of arms.")

The uncertainties of war, the frequently recurring misery which became more and more serious and an outlook which was distorted by religious contradictions brought peasants and mercenaries into contact with each other which was other than the mortal enmity between them. Of this there is more than ample evidence. In actual life, when certain circumstances prevailed at certain places, they avoided each other or had to live side by side, they feared each other or had to collaborate. The Wetterfeld chronicle is evidence of just how accustomed village inhabitants became to the turmoil of war: Military formations crossed or encroached on the territory of the county of Laubach on more than eighty occasions and the villagers had to abandon their homes eighteen times in the years after 1634 alone.

In the towns, it was rather the rule than the exception that the armed townsfolk fought side by side with hired mercenaries. However, their relations were not really marked by a comradely spirit since the townsman had to provide accommodation and money for the mercenary. The former regarded the latter as being lazy while the trained soldier accused the civilian of cowardice and clumsiness. In the defence of many towns, it also happened that peasants seeking refuge or summoned for the "Defension" also lined the ramparts, towers and walls. The town of Weilheim was besieged in November 1646 by French and Swedish troops but was courageously defended by mercenaries, townsfolk and peasants. When the town did at last fall, the besiegers killed all the persons bearing arms that they found within its walls.[3]

[1] Bog, I.: Die bäuerliche Wirtschaft im Zeitalter des Dreissigjährigen Krieges, Coburg, 1952

[2] Wassenberg, E.: Teutscher Florus, Danzig (Hünefeld), 1645, p. 307, copy in University Library, Greifswald

[3] Friesenegger: Tagebuch, p. 147

Siege of Freiberg

Freiberg has a strong town-wall,
Many townsfolk and peasants
came to defend it.
It was hard-pressed;
The enemy had to withdraw in
shame and mockery.
So rejoice, you miners,
Always keep God in your hearts!

From: Tränen des Vaterlandes
(Verse 3)

[1] Historischer Chroniken Continuation, p. 444

[2] Friesenegger: Tagebuch, p. 33f.

[3] Gaedertz, K. Th.: Johann Rist als niederdeutscher Dramatiker, in: Jahrbuch des Vereins für niederdeutsche Sprache VII/1881, p. 138

[4] Wassenberg: Teutscher Florus, p. 504

At times, peasants were also to be found in the train of mercenary troops moving through the countryside and plundering on their way. In 1626, Duke Christian of Brunswick "lodged" with his troops in Minden after rich booty had been acquired in Hesse. They had set fire to castles along the Weser and sacked five "noble houses". A report states that "many Hessian peasants" took part in this, obviously exploiting the desperate situation of their masters to avenge themselves for the hardship and suppression they had suffered.

The social aspect of their motivation was even more apparent in the case of the Bohemian peasants in 1631. When Saxon troops, as allies of Sweden, occupied the country, numerous exiles returned with them. Now freed from years of oppression by the Imperial regime, the peasants took their revenge, storming and plundering the estates and castles of their "overlords and priests" and even killing some of their owners who had not fled quickly enough. Many Imperial soldiers suffered the same fate.[1]

When victorious Swedish troops marched into Bavaria, the divided opinion of the peasants was revealed by the following incident: the peasants of the village of Machtlfingen wanted to take the booty plundered from the village by drunken Swedish freebooters. However, they met the soldiers in company with peasants from Herrsching who called the Swedes their "brothers" and were consuming the food that the latter had stolen. They even fetched beer from the villagers to drink with the soldiers.[2]

Schiller, in "Wallenstein's Camp", also portrayed how the peasants adapted in this manner to the pre-eminence of the soldier in the countryside. It is the peasant, accusing and damning the soldiery, who nonetheless relies on his wiles and experience of the uncouth mercenaries to dare to walk among the colourful and dangerously restless "mob of soldiers" (to quote the peasant's son) with the following in mind: "When they take what is ours in bushels, we have to get it back again in spoonfuls." And, together with his little son, he strikes up conversation with a group of Tyrolean musketeers—"merry fellows who like to chatter"—with the intention of dicing with them—since he is the possessor of "lucky" dice. Caught cheating, the peasant only escapes the gallows because the cuirassiers are too contemptuous of him to hand him over to the camp executioner. This was the motif used by a contemporary dramatist (Johann Rist) when he has one of his peasants say: "Ey laht se nehmen, ick nehme wedder".[3] ("So let them take it away, I will get it back again.")

Since the field commanders and the generals could rely on scarcely any cartographic documents, they had to make use, in many cases, of the local knowledge of the local people. Peasants were forced or persuaded to guide them through pathless woods and marshes to prepare an ambush, to find a short cut or to lead a reconnaissance detachment to enemy positions. Peasants were also used as spies since their presence attracted little attention, peasants being found everywhere. At the siege of Freusburg castle in the Electorate of Trier in the Westerwald (1643), a peasant showed the besiegers the place where they could force their way in. Subsequently caught, he met his death on the gallows.[4] From many other examples, it may be concluded that peasants performed such services for any side and sometimes these services could be purchased.

In its centuries' long struggle with the peasants, the feudal class had also learnt that peasants could be harmed by peasants when the affair was managed in the right way. Individual peasants, who saved their own skin in this manner, even allowed themselves to be used as the executioners of members of their own class—as shown by the vengeance inflicted by the mercenaries on the rebellious Sundgau peasants in 1633. The steward of Altenstein castle near Ebern in Franconia wrote the following report on 16 September 1632: When 20 Imperial horsemen ride out, "all the (Catholic) peasants, labourers, women and maid-servants run with them" in the hope of obtaining plunder in the Protestant villages.[1]

The peasants gradually learnt to live with the war and its excesses and there is evidence that they profited from it by selling their produce. Dismayed and resentful, the loyal chronicler of the monastery of Salem observed at the end of the 1630's how the peasants living on the estates of the monastery who had not left their farms (he calls them "thieves" and "good finders") removed everything from abandoned farms which was not nailed down. When the soldiers abandoned their camps, these peasants collected everything which could be used or sold and hawked it in Constance—iron utensils, crockery of any kind, tools, ropes, cow-harness, saddles, wheels, carts and even religious pictures.

The chronicler also relates that many took the road to Constance so that they could feed their families. There they purchased victuals, living animals, tallow and candles with the intention of selling these goods again in the military camps. There is a report from Bavaria of 1645 that horse-dealers travelled from village to village, buying up horses which had become rare and expensive and selling them "in large numbers on the Swiss market". Although the dealers profited from this, the peasants escaped the obligation of putting their animals, free of charge, at the disposal of their ruler or of the robbing mercenaries. It could also happen that the peasants bought back from the soldiers the animals which had been stolen from them and others.[2]

When the peasant—by force or of his own volition—became the partner of the soldier, he was a suspicious, inconvenient and sometimes malicious partner who could scarcely conceal his hatred of the other. With an inventiveness which never failed, he outwitted the boisterous soldiery on many an important or minor occasion and the contemporary allegory simplified the peasant/soldier relationship by depicting the peasant as the hare, lamb, mouse or dove which was at the mercy of the more powerful soldier in the shape of a dog, wolf, cat or hawk.[3]

In the dialogue already mentioned between the peasant and the lansquenet, the latter asserts that destruction can be continued "until all peasants are lansquenets"; the peasant reveals the absurdity of this gloomy prognosis with the words: "And when no child is born, then it will be a good time."[4] Neither the one nor the other could happen. It was the peasant who triumphed—although at great cost—since it was he who created and protected life.

In his poem "Wohlklingende Pauke", Nikolaus Peucker uses the allegory of the garden to extol the work of the peasant and to depict its triumph over the pernicious purpose of the mercenary. In times of war, the once cultivated land is covered in weeds, bushes and trees but when the war is ended, the garden re-emerges in new splendour when tended by the peasant and safe from the thieving attentions of the mercenary. The latter has to disappear or submit to the commandment of peaceful labour. The

The defences of the Electorate of Saxony

May God now give you understanding and strength,
That you may serve these defences as a true servant,
Come, come!
Serve God and your prince as you should,
that you do not break your oath,
But reinforce it at all times,
as honest, honourable people,
Come, come!
Attend willingly for practice,
And also when there is danger,
Let none be absent or spare himself.

From: Tränen des Vaterlandes
(tune: The Sun shines on a hard frost,
Verses 19 and 20)

[1] Berbig, K.: Bilder aus dem 30jährigen Kriege in Thüringen und Franken, Ztschr. f. Gustav-Adolf-Vereine, No. 38

[2] Heilmann, I.: Die Feldzüge der Bayern in den Jahren 1643, 1644 und 1645, Leipzig/ Meissen, 1851, p. 232f.

[3] Hohberg: Georgica, p. 12

[4] A merry song and dispute between a peasant and a lansquenet, in: Tränen des Vaterlandes, p. 323ff.

mercenary, "the poor fool", is obliged to rake and thresh in the service of the peasant, to chop and cart wood; and his distress is without end.[1]

Transitory though the soldier's life was, it nevertheless left behind deep scars in the life of the working masses. Its alien traits came to the fore: violence, unscrupulous greed, cold-blooded mercenariness, brutalization of feelings, loss of class ties. To quote the words of a soldier's song:

> "Haus und Acker
> Verlass ich wacker
> Und kei (kehr) mich nichts drum.
> Greint mein Gredel,
> Ich schlag's zum Schädel
> Dass's taumelt herum."

("House and field, I boldly leave, Caring nothing for it, If my girl weeps, I hit her on the head, That makes her stagger.")

It seems here that the farmer's boy has already become a brutal thug of the type commonly found in the armies of the "Great War". Nevertheless, the undertone of violence born of despair with which he takes leave of his former life is unmistakable. Very few indeed were able to reverse this step. Most of the peasants who had become mercenaries would have resisted the attempts at the end of the war to resettle them in Bavaria, Hesse and the Palatinate and probably ended up with the mass of the other mercenaries in wars outside Germany, assuming that they did not become members of the numerous gangs which survived after 1648.

It is to be noted that the return to working life, in the social conditions of the time, meant nothing less than a return to serfdom. In Johann Rist's popular drama "Irenaromachia" (1630), which was used by another poet, Erasmus Pfeiffer, as the basis for his "Pseudostratiotae" (1631), there are moving scenes in which peasants and soldiers steal the booty from each other. In the Second Act, a dialogue develops between Irene (Peace) and Rusticus (a peasant). The former reminds the peasant of the blessings of peace but the latter retorts that in times of peace the authorities did not know how to treat the poor "Husslüde" (civilians) and that this was why a good war was better than "solck böss Frede" ("such a wicked peace"). He asserts that in a raid it was possible to get more in a week than in six months of hard work in peace.[2]

Influences such as this, alien as they were to the peasant mentality, distorted the consciousness of the peasants precisely in those areas where the "war of the rulers" was at its worst. The soldier moved between the peasant and his sovereign lord. The struggle for dear life with the invading mercenaries prevented the peasants from recognizing the fundamental and insurmountable antagonism between them and their "own" rulers and the suppressed classes wasted their energy in numberless individual actions. The result of this was that no great peasants' wars occurred in Germany in the centuries which followed. This ebbing away of peasant aggressiveness in the class-struggle may well be considered the most detrimental socio-political consequence of the Thirty Years' War.

[1] Peucker, N.: Wohlklingende lustige Pauke (1650—1675) . . ., ed. by G. Ellinger, Berlin, 1888, p. 27ff.

[2] Gaedertz: Johann Rist

PROFITEERS AND TECHNICIANS
OF THE WAR

IMMOVABLE
AND MOVABLE
PLUNDER

The war, lasting an entire generation, accelerated as a whole and in its individual parts the possibility for the mighty of becoming even mightier and the risk, for the oppressed, of becoming even weaker. Above all, it resulted in significant shifts in the distribution of landed property, the principal form of ownership of means of production. These great shifts in ownership relations, which proceeded at a faster rate during the war, resulted in turn in mass-migration by the population and in noticeable changes in the social and intellectual life of large numbers of the people. The political and religious offensive of the Catholic Church and temporal feudal powers in the course of the counter-reformation was essentially aimed at the recovery of the property of the papal Church which had been "alienated" after the Reformation and the secularization of the authorities. Consequently, as already indicated by the numerous skirmishes which preceded it, the Thirty Years' War had to be, by and large, a "struggle for the property of the Church" (Marx).[1]

However, it was by no means the case that this struggle only concerned the feudal class, which had split into rival groups professing different creeds. It was also the affair of the broad masses of the people since, on the basis of the specific ownership relations and the religion prescribed by the authorities, there existed—for three generations already—well-established socio-political, official and charitable institutions and enduring every-day customs and habits according to which people organized their work and their hours of recreation and edification and celebrated joyful and grievous events. The politico-religious contradictions led, for a period of decades, to two different methods of chronology being used at the same time. The "eternal Gregorian calendar", introduced by Pope Gregory XIII in 1582, was rejected by the non-Catholic rulers, theologians and scholars, despite its express recommendation by such authorities as Tycho Brahe and Kepler. These non-Catholics regarded it as the work of Satan and based their official celebrations and annual events on the Julian calendar which had long since been out of date. Between these two calendars, a difference of eleven days had developed in the course of time. It is not difficult to imagine the additional confusion and discord, even at work and in the family, caused by the "calendar quarrel" and not even the Reichstag of 1613, which was commissioned to deal with the affair, was able to settle it. It was only in 1699 that the Parliament of the Imperial princes declared that the Gregorian calendar was binding within the territory of the Reich.

He who wages war fishes with a golden net.

Saying, 16th/17th century

[1] Marx, Karl: Chronologische Auszüge zur deutschen Geschichte vom Ende des 15. Jahrhunderts bis zum Westfälischen Frieden aus der "Weltgeschichte für das deutsche Volk", ed. by Friedrich Christoph Schlosser. 1st edition (vols. 11—14), in: Marx/Engels: Über Deutschland und die deutsche Arbeiterbewegung, vol. I, Berlin, 1973, pp. 428 and 436

Serious attempts to gain possession of the disputed ecclesiastical territories took place already during the first half of the war. The pioneer of the wide-ranging "Hague Alliance" of the anti-Hapsburg powers of Europe, King Christian IV of Denmark, concentrated on the wealthy bishoprics of Northern Germany. Beginning in 1625, the "Lower Saxon-Danish War" ended four years later with the defeated king waiving all claims in the Peace Document of Lübeck to all territories of the Reich. The victorious emperor, urged on by the most militant Catholic-Hapsburg circles in Vienna, now prepared to take the initiative. In 1629, he issued the Edict of Restitution which called for the return of all the territories taken from the Catholic Church since 1552. For some of his sons and other members of the various branches of his family, Ferdinand had already selected well-endowed sinecures. The "Restitutioners"—commissioners, scribes, zealous Jesuits and priests—went to work wherever Imperial troops were in control—in the whole of Northern Germany and also south of the River Main. The extent of the "alienated" possessions—churches, monasteries, properties, movable property, libraries, schools, literature, archives and funds—were reconstructed according to old documents. It was a great deal which found a new owner and which had to be given back.

In 1629, non-Catholic church services and ceremonies were banned by the Imperial commissioner in Augsburg who also took possession of the church keys. The Evangelical preachers had to leave the city and three of them immediately appealed to Ulm. Several hundred soldiers of the bishop and the governor occupied the gates and the monastery buildings and patrolled the streets. One morning, the townsfolk around the Fish Market awoke to find that a new gallows had been erected there. The list of prohibitions was first directed against the "fanatics" and sects and then against secret Evangelical baptism of children, trading in "heretical books", the discussion of religious questions and the singing in public of German hymns while Latin texts had to be approved by a censor. Only the teaching of the Catholic religion was permitted in the schools and the colleges. However, the measures taken at Augsburg were also an admission of a lack of initial success against underground and secret "heresy". Apart from this, there was a shortage of Catholic priests for the daily duties. There were occasional instances of open resistance and scuffles. The restitution, which had been planned on such a large scale, was not systematically enforced since the Swedish army had begun its march on the territories in question in 1630/31. It was rather the source of additional conflict than the instrument of profound change.

The edict had touched the nerve of princely and feudal power and it was not surprising that the united opposition of the Protestant rulers again swelled up, as at the Electors' Assembly at Regensburg and at the Leipzig Convention of Protestant princes at the beginning of 1631. Finally, although this was more on account of the pressure exercised than of their own volition, the mighty Protestant potentates of the Reich from Brandenburg and the Electorate of Saxony became the allies of the King of Sweden in the same year.

Following the mighty blow struck against the forces of the emperor and the League by the Swedish army at Breitenfeld (near Leipzig) on 17 September 1631, the way was open to Thuringia, the Swedes passing through the "Pfaffengasse" ("priests' lane") or the Main-Rhine district where the territories of the Catholic bishoprics of Bamberg, Würzburg and Mainz were located, each richer than the next. The King of Sweden regarded the territories obtained *jure belli* as military booty and treated them as he liked, disregarding all the laws of the Reich.

In the train of the victorious Swedish forces, there were such proud princes of the Holy Roman Empire as the counts of Hanau, Nassau, Hohenlohe, Solms and Wertheim, the princes of Hesse, Brunswick, Lüneburg, Baden and Anhalt and above all the dukes of Saxe-Weimar who desired temporal wealth and immortal fame and, at the same time, were well aware of their precarious position. Duke William's father had produced twelve sons and it was not long before the view was taken, in the castle of Weimar, that they could not all remain "in their own duchy". Duke William, appointed governor of Thuringia and Erfurt in October 1631 by the King of Sweden on his way westwards, rapidly established here a court of some pretensions, which had not been possible hitherto, and a Department of War. Already in November, he was again urging Gustavus Adolphus to let him have all the possessions of the Catholic bishopric in Thuringia and the frontier zone of Franconia. He received nothing since Gustavus Adolphus—quite correctly—did not consider him important enough. Duke William remained at his shaky command-post, out of favour and of limited use.

More fortunate, to begin with, was the career of his younger brother Bernhard, who likewise fought on the Swedish-Protestant side. Already a colonel at 28 years of age and from April 1632 a general under Gustavus Adolphus, he was the latter's diligent pupil and, after Gustavus Adolphus's death in battle, he led the Swedish army to victory at Lützen. Bernhard's services were rewarded and in 1633 he was given the "Duchy of Franconia", formed from the bishoprics of Würzburg and Bamberg, as a fief from the Swedish crown but without the mighty fortresses of Würzburg and Königshofen. These remained in Swedish hands as bases and watchful look-out posts. However, the state established in the entire southern part of the Reich (the Holy Roman Empire) following the triumphal progress of the Swedes collapsed after the defeat at Nördlingen and Bernhard was once again a prince without a land. In 1635, a new chance appeared in the shape of France which was now directly involved in the war. At the end of that year, Louis XIII provided him with the means to raise an army of 18,000 men, with the Landgraviate of Alsace and with the administration of Hagenau, plus all the powers of the previous occupant. In return, Bernhard fought on behalf of France along the Upper Rhine and captured the fortress of Breisach, known as "the cushion of the Holy Roman Empire". The necessary liquidity was advanced by the Lyons banker Bartholomäus Herwarth—a descendant of the once-famous merchant family of Augsburg. He had spent 1632 in Frankfort on the Main to observe the course of events and business and perhaps to profitably invest capital. As it was, Herwarth came to the conclusion that the Empire resembled a gigantic cow which ate nothing but grass and spent the whole of its time chewing the cud. The Lyons banker moved to Paris and rose to be General Controller of the Royal finances. Duke Bernhard of Saxe-Weimar died of a pestilence in 1639. His second dominion in Alsace did not survive him, the commanders of his disintegrating army fighting over what was left.

102 The Stock Exchange—the heart of the trade metropolis of Amsterdam which was active throughout the world and where there was a flourishing arms business. Copperplate engraving (17th century). Güstrow Museum

103 Commemorative column designed by the architect Matthias Staud in memory of the crossing of the Rhine by the Swedish army (1631). Güstrow Museum

In contrast to this, the Count Palatine John Casimir of Zweibrücken had a great career at the side of the Swedes. As the husband of the half-sister of Gustavus Adolphus, he was the holder of important offices in Sweden itself and he headed both the financial administration and the minting establishments for copper coins. His place in the succession to the Swedish throne was documented by the fact that Queen Christina, who abdicated in 1649, appointed the son of the Palatine, Karl Gustav, as her successor.

The electors of Brandenburg, alternating between the emperor, Sweden and Poland, achieved a significant increase in territory—the bishoprics of Magdeburg, Halberstadt and Minden. However, the Swedes only allowed them to have the eastern part of the Duchy of Pomerania which had been ceded to them by an irrevocable settlement.

The greatest advantage was obtained by those mighty princes of the Holy Roman Empire to whom the emperor had to pledge himself, especially in the eventful period of the first twenty years when he asked for the help of two powerful princes in the struggle with the rebels of Bohemia and the Palatinate. The elector of Saxony presented the emperor with a bill of almost four million florins and thus made sure of the two Lusatias, which belonged to the Bohemian crown. With rare pedantry, the Duke of Bavaria presented Emperor Ferdinand II with a claim for 15,080,778 florins, 40 kreuzers and one heller. Ferdinand acknowledged a debt of only twelve millions, plus interest of five per cent on this sum. His Bavarian cousin was given Upper Austria and the Palatinate on the right bank of the Rhine for a few years and the Upper Palatinate and the status of Elector for ever in place of Frederick, the despised Count Palatine and King of Bohemia. The princely families and leaders were no less interested, however, in also acquiring possession of movable property.

When the army of the League, headed by the Duke of Bavaria captured and plundered the beautiful city of Heidelberg with all its traditions in the fields of the arts and sciences, General Tilly took what was probably the finest jewel of the Palatine capital —the illustrious "Biblioteca Palatina", also known as the "mother-library". The devout Duke Maximilian resisted the temptation to keep it as booty and presented it to Pope Gregory XV. The most precious part of the "Palatina", including more than 3,500 manuscripts, crossed the Alps on the backs of mules and arrived in Rome, where it was given a special place in the "Vaticana". A later conqueror, Napoleon Bonaparte, took part of it, as plunder of war, to Paris in 1797. This was returned to the "Palatina" following his overthrow while some 850 German-language manuscripts were returned by the Vatican in 1816.

The duke of Bavaria benefited from this gift since the pope was now more willing to help finance the military activities of the League. Between February 1621 and August 1623, the League received 620,000 florins from Rome while the emperor was given somewhat less—615,000 florins.[1]

In the appropriation of art treasures, libraries and archives, the Swedish conquerors proved to be past masters. They had gone about this in a systematic manner as early as the 1620's in the course of their campaigns in the Baltic area. The king ordered the treasures, books and objets d'art of the Jesuit colleges, cathedral chapters and canons and monasteries of Riga, Courland, Prussia and Ermland to be confiscated, packed in

[1] Duch, A.: Die Politik Maximilians I. von Bayern und seiner Verbündeten 1618—1651, 1st part, 2nd vol., Munich/Vienna, 1970

crates and dispatched to Sweden. The Swedes took "rich booty in books, precious paintings and other things" in Oliwa and Pelplin in particular.

This plundering was continued on a greater scale as the army moved across the Empire. That the castles and universities in the Catholic bishoprics along the Main and Rhine held rich treasures was known to Gustavus Adolphus in 1620 at the latest when he journeyed right across the Empire.[1] Marienberg and Würzburg fell into the hands of the conquerors on 18 October 1631 and already on the 16 November the Swedish king issued a letter of donation for the University of Uppsala, transferring to it the ownership of the most valuable collections of books from the colleges and from the university and episcopal libraries and manuscript collections. On 13 December, the Swedish army marched into Mainz. Numerous guards were immediately assigned to the library of the Jesuit college there and the doors of the building sealed. A royal letter of authority is still in existence which bears the date of that very day, instructing the court chaplain and the court physician to confiscate "all the libraries and private books found in the (electoral) castle and in the deserted colleges, schools, monasteries or otherwise in the deserted houses of Mainz". The precious booty was subsequently dispatched northwards in long waggon-trains accompanied by strong escorts. It was a similar story with cultural treasures from Silesia and Bohemia.

The Saxon and Swedish conquerors anticipated plunder of inestimable value in Prague in particular since it was in the capital of Bohemia that Emperor Rudolf II had assembled what was probably the most valuable collection of art treasures, instruments and curiosities of Europe. It was estimated that the art collection alone contained three thousand paintings, including pictures by Leonardo da Vinci, Michelangelo, Titian and Lucas Cranach the Elder. The emperor took most delight in the works of Dürer and these formed the heart of the vast "art cabinets", which were never fully catalogued, in the halls and rooms of Prague Castle. A rough estimate of the total value after Rudolf's death (1612) suggested a figure of 17 million florins. It was in this year, too, that the disintegration of the Renaissance collection began. The Hapsburg family were the first to help themselves to a large share and their example was followed in 1619 by the Government of the Bohemian Estates, then by the administration of Emperor Ferdinand II and subsequently by the Saxon occupation authority of 1632. However, the collection was still impressive and, in its essentials, was still intact. It received its death-blow at the end of the Thirty Years' War when the Swedes captured the "small side" of Prague, the castle and the rich monasteries on the neighbouring hills in mid-July 1648.

According to their own estimates, the Swedish troops under General Königsmarck took booty worth seven million Imperial thalers. One of the rarest items was the *Codex Argenteus*, the handwritten Visigothic manuscript of the Bible produced by Bishop Ulfilas in the 6th century, featuring letters of silver and gold on purple parchment. In 1669, it found a permanent home in the University Library at Uppsala. The most valuable of the plundered books were brought here, others going to Strängnäs, to the Royal Library at Stockholm, to the School Library at Linköping and to Åbo. Private individuals who appropriated such treasures included Königsmarck himself, who built palaces from the profits of war in which to keep his shares, high-ranking politi-

[1] Johan Hands Dagbok under K. Gustav II Adolfs resa till Tyskland, Historiska handlingar 8/3, Stockholm, 1879

Farewell

Innsbruck, I must leave thee,
I drive down my streets and into a
strange land.
My joy is gone,
when things are so bad for me.

Folk song, 16th/17th century (Verse 1)

cians, diplomats and generals such as Nils Brahe, Carl Gustav Wrangel and Magnus de la Gardie. The inventory of Queen Christina, who embraced the Catholic faith and took some of the art treasures with her to Rome in 1652, listed innumerable jewels, medals, books, 71 bronze statuettes and 427 large paintings. It was not at all the case that the treasures passed into the hands of people who would cherish them. Long journeys by sea and overland and the indifference or greed of the personnel accompanying and guarding them caused untold damage.[1]

It has happened that Sweden's territory has been spared foreign invasion and the plundered works of art have been safer there than they were in the places where they were originally kept. For many works of art, it was a stroke of good fortune that they did not pass into the hands of such rough adventurers as Count Ernst von Mansfeld or Duke Christian of Brunswick. The latter, known as the "dashing Halberstädter", made a rich haul in the Catholic chapter-house of Paderborn on 31 January 1632. His horsemen wreaked havoc with chasubles and sacred vessels and he himself had precious statues of the apostles and saints melted down to provide metal for coins with the inscription "Gottes Freundt und der Pfaffen Feindt" ("God's friend and the priests' foe"). In this manner, so this freebooter boasted, he was helping the apostles to go all over the world at last and to convert the heathens.

CHANGES
OF OWNERSHIP AND STREAMS
OF REFUGEES

The most profound changes in ownership as a consequence of war and a succession of rulers took place in the prosperous heart of Central Europe—in Bohemia.[2] The noble lords there lent their rebellions against the increasing threat of Hapsburg and Catholic control of the country and the Church in 1618—1620 a genuinely feudal touch by confiscating the landed estates and riches of the Catholic Church, its religious Orders and its temporal supporters.

The victory of the army of the emperor and League at the White Hill over the forces of the Bohemian Estates and their elected king Frederick (called the "Winter King" since he only reigned for one year) was followed by an exceptionally drastic redistribution of feudal possessions in the opposite sense. Not only did the Catholic Church receive a generous part of the estates confiscated by the emperor, a rich reward was also given to a small number of noblemen who had remained loyal to the emperor and to colonels and generals who were owed pay and favours by the emperor. The Confiscation Commission, armed with full powers, took possession of some 500 estates in Bohemia worth an estimated 43 million florins. This was no less than three-quarters of all the land in the kingdom. Similar happenings took place in Upper and Lower

[1] Walde, O.: Storhetstidens litterära krigs-byten. En kulturhistorisk-bibliografisk studie, part. I, Uppsala/Stockholm, 1916

[2] Bílek, T.: Dějiny konfiskací v Čechách r. 1618, Prague, 1882/1883; Polišenský, J.: Třicetiletá válka a český národ, Prague, 1960

132

104 Satirical pamphlet in the popular form of a pictorial riddle attacking the Bohemian exiles who had been driven from their homeland (1620). From: H. von Zwiedenick-Südenhorst, *Gegenreformation in Deutschland*, Ullstein Weltgeschichte

Austria and in Moravia where estates worth five million florins were expropriated. In Bohemia, it was the numerous knightly families in particular who were decimated. Some 680 noble families and innumerable townsmen lost their property. It was these strata, however, who had deep roots in the national solidarity and traditions of the Czech people.

Many of the expropriated knightly families responded to the confiscation of their property and forced conversion by fleeing the country, many of them finding refuge and the prospects of a new career in the Swedish army. Of the 49 officers from Bohemia serving in Swedish armies, five were counts, four were lords, 24 were knights and 16 were of middle-class origin. Derfflinger, who later became a famous field-marshal of Brandenburg, came from Upper Austria and was believed to have been of peasant origin. He served in the Swedish cavalry from 1632 onwards. The redistribution of property in the Austrian territories is documented by the expulsion or flight of 36,000 families and the appearance of new landowning noble families, such as the Althans, Dietrichsteins, Collaltos and Enzmüllers, and also of new-rich war-profiteers such as the Muschingers and Megiers. The escape route to the North and West over the mountains from Bohemia, Moravia and Austria was also taken by tens of thousands of parish priests, teachers, peasants, merchants and artisans. They sought asylum in the Free Imperial Cities of Franconia and Swabia, in the Protestant principalities and especially in Saxony, which was close to their homeland. Towards the end of the war, 20,000 houses were abandoned in Lower Austria alone.[1]

In the 1620's, the streams of refugees from Bohemia mainly consisted of noblemen or middle-class people, parish priests, lawyers, physicians and officials. Bringing their most valuable possessions with them, they arrived in groups and waggon-trains in Zittau, Pirna, Freiberg and Annaberg—knowledgeable people, many of whom were wealthy. The emperor, however, was not prepared to tolerate the removal of valuable "goods and movables" from his kingdom and instructed the Elector of Saxony to list and hand over the "possessions and movables of the rebels". With the exception of Leipzig, many of the town councils complied with the electoral command which then followed. However, the ruler kept the valuables for himself, outwitting the emperor in this manner. The princely and municipal officials also took their share. A significant

[1] Hantsch: Die Geschichte Österreichs, vol. 1, Vienna, 1959, p. 350

remainder, mostly gold and silver plate, was regularly offered at the Leipzig fairs up until 1629.

The most important place of refuge for the first great wave of emigrants from Bohemia was Pirna, which was not far away and where 2,000 exiles were counted by the town council at the beginning of 1629. In Dresden, the Czech religious community rose to 642 in 1632 and in Zittau in 1628 to 360 members. They included important scholars, well-respected Protestant preachers and printers, some of whom brought Czech type with them so they could continue their trade in Pirna. Jan Ctibor of Prague was one of these. It was not easy for the immigrants of Czech origin to settle down permanently in German cities nor did they desire this. They continued to hope of return to their native land and accompanied the victorious Saxons or Swedes to Bohemia but were forced into exile once again when the latter were defeated. Even when the army of the Swedes, their "religious kith and kin", robbed them, too, in 1639, they did not abandon their hopes.[1]

The inhabitants of the Saxon cities at first viewed the new arrivals, who included proud nobles and well-dressed merchants, with curiosity and sympathy but soon became less well-disposed towards the strangers. They were blamed for many a misfortune and vicissitude. Songs went the rounds, mocking the "lost band", the "ragamuffins" and the "rebellious wretches". The Lutheran clergy in particular suspected them of the "infiltration of Calvinism". For fear of pestilence, an increase in prices and competition, the exiles were not permitted to settle within the town-walls and they had to accept the lesser safety of the suburban areas. Groups of knowledgeable artisans moved to the Erzgebirge district, founded new industries, fabricated musical instruments, produced lace and manufactured toys. Others travelled as far as Poland, the territories of Prussia and to the Dutch provinces which had been freed from Spanish rule.

Following the Imperial decree of 31 July 1627—the day of St. Ignatius, the founder of the Jesuit Order—against the non-Catholics, such famous scholars as Pavel Stránský left their native country. He initially found a position as a parish priest at Pirna but his illustrious book, the *Respublica Bojema* was published at Leiden in 1634. It was probably in this year that Jan Stránský left Pirna and moved on to Poland, like the great Jan Amos Komenský before him. It was in 1627, with the first wave of emigrants, that Wenzel Hollar, who later became a renowned engraver, turned his back on Prague with its glorious traditions in the field of art. He spent the following decade in some of the great cities of the Reich (Frankfort on the Main, Cologne, Strasbourg) and was later able to obtain commissions and find a new stimulus in England and Holland. The great army of exiles of non-aristocratic origin were those who suffered particular distress and they were the real losers of the insurrection of the Bohemian Estates and of the war in general.

[1] Winter, E.: Die tschechische und slowakische Emigration in Deutschland im 17. und 18. Jahrhundert, Berlin, 1955

GLORIOSA IN VITA —
INFAMATO IN MORTE:
WALLENSTEIN

In Bohemia, where a succession of such changes made it increasingly more difficult for the exiles to return, new names with new coats-of-arms appeared alongside some old ones in the lists of the aristocracy: Karl von Liechtenstein, Jaroslav Martinic, Pavel Michna. Even complete foreigners moved into the feudal residences vacated by expelled noblemen—soldiers such as Don Balthasar Marradas and Christoph Thurn, the lords von Eggenberg, Trautmannsdorf, Metternich and many other lesser figures. Czechs who had hitherto possessed little wealth rapidly bought up great estates at a cheap price from the riches which they suddenly acquired: the Trčkas, Herman Černín and especially the Waldsteins.

One member of this Bohemian family, Albrecht Wenzel Eusebius, was not given a square yard by the Emperor but was nevertheless the greatest beneficiary from the victory at the White Hill.[1] Loyal to the house of Hapsburg since the start of his career, he put regiments, which he himself recruited and financed, at the disposal of the emperor and fought bravely for the latter's cause in the war against Venice and the Turks. Even during the rebellion by the noble Estates, he took the side of the emperor—in return for which his adversaries confiscated the Moravian estates of Albrecht von Waldstein—later known as Wallenstein. Now, after the collapse of the rebellion and the flight of the "Winter King", he was given a rich reward and this increased according to the number of soldiers which the colonel and "Gubernator of Bohemia" raised and equipped for the emperor. The latter became the debtor of his Bohemian military commander. However, it was during this period (1621—1623) that a vast number of profitable and, in some cases, excellently run estates were confiscated and were sold by the tax authorities at a price below their real value in order to raise money without delay. With a sure instinct, Wallenstein seized the opportunity and acquired from the emperor, as pledges and irrevocable property, one estate after another and more and more domains and villages. Like many others, the colonel carried on speculative buying and selling operations and by 1623 owned a quarter of the kingdom of Bohemia, forming a coherent complex around the towns of Friedland, Reichenberg and Jičín. For this, he received from the emperor the *fidei Commissum masculinum perpetuum*. On 12 March 1623, an Imperial decree conferred the status of a principality of the Holy Roman Empire on the complex which had been put together within two years and in 1627 the territory was raised to the level of a duchy, whose holder and his eldest son were entitled to call themselves the "Reigning Duke of Friedland". In the war against Denmark, the most active power in the "Hague Alliance" of 1625 which was directed against Spain and the Hapsburgs, the now Imperial general rendered even more services to the emperor. On 16 June 1628, he was given as a fief the duchies of Mecklenburg from which the hereditary but outlawed dukes had had to flee. He was made a

To his waggon he harnessed the monstrous wild creatures of the Dukes of Lauenburg. The Counts of the Empire, up to their ears in debt and lamed, reared up and shook themselves, they allowed the long, strong leads of Wallenstein to be thrown over them. Mansfeld, adventurous, with magical roaring, pierced their heart, greed glued their tongues to their mouths.

From: Alfred Döblin: Wallenstein, Third Book

[1] Of the latest literature on Wallenstein, the account by Golo Mann, which also includes cultural aspects, is outstanding: Wallenstein. Sein Leben erzählt von Golo Mann, 3rd edition. Frankfort on the Main, 1971; new list of sources concerning the varied career of Wallenstein in: Documenta Bohemica IV, Prague, 1974, and V, Prague, 1977

member of the Estates of the Empire and was permitted to keep his hat on in the presence of the emperor.[1]

His was a comet-like career unparallelled before and the reasons for it have never really been clarified. In addition to the taxes and the sale of exemptions from the billeting of mercenaries which were imposed on cities, villages and districts everywhere, apart from booty taken in war and an advantageous marriage with the daughter of Count Harrach (1623) who possessed great influence at the Imperial court, it was the minting of sub-standard coinage on a gigantic scale and with Imperial permission which contributed to the great wealth accumulated by Wallenstein.

The preparation for war and the recruitment and maintenance of soldiers had long since exhausted the Imperial coffers. On account of the low land-prices, little profit had been made from the sale of the confiscated Bohemian estates and the cash obtained for them was soon used up. But the war demanded new and even larger sums—a practically ideal opportunity for dynamic speculators not afraid of taking a risk. It was in these circles that the plan took shape to suggest to the emperor that he hire out the privilege of minting coins. Without devoting much thought to the matter, Ferdinand II agreed and on 18 January 1622 a contract was signed between the Imperial court chancery on the one hand and Hans de Witte, a merchant, court supplier and money-lender of Prague, and his 14 partners on the other. In return for a fee of six million florins, the right to mint coins for one year in Bohemia, Moravia and Lower Austria was granted to a "Coinage Consortium". It was given the monopoly for the purchase of newly-mined silver at fixed prices and of silver fragments in the territories of Bohemia and Austria and was permitted to mint 70 florins from a mark of fine silver (in actual fact 123 florins were produced from this). This meant that the florin fell to a quarter and even a tenth of its nominal value. It is true that Wallenstein belonged to the consortium but he was not one of the main beneficiaries from the deterioration in the coinage. The lion's share of the two million profit was claimed by Prince Liechtenstein, the Imperial governor of Bohemia. The Government again took the minting of coins under its own control in the summer of 1623 but not without carrying out a comprehensive reform. The financing of the war had been made possible for a further year and the burden had been passed on to the ordinary people.

In the second half of the 1620's, Albrecht von Wallenstein, the "uncrowned king of Bohemia", was the commander-in-chief of all the troops in the Holy Roman Empire. In this "first generalship", he accumulated additional profits as a "war-businessman" but it was not easy, month in and month out, to procure wages, provisions, clothing, weapons and ammunition for dozens of regiments so that they could be used for the plundering of the country and against the enemy. For an Imperial army on a permanent basis, there was developed an organization which was far-flung and with wide ramifications. It was a question of extracting money from hundreds of sources. The "great commander" Wallenstein was joined by a "great financier". In Prague, at the centre of this organization which spanned the whole of Central and Western Europe, there sat Hans (or Jan) de Witte, to whom reference has already been made. A member of the Reformed Church and of Dutch origin, he was its inspiration.[2]

[1] Documents in Státní ústřední archiv Prague, Pobočka Mnichovo Hradiště, RA Valdštejnové

[2] Ernstberger, A.: Hans de Witte. Finanzmann Wallensteins, Wiesbaden, 1954

105 Cardinal Richelieu. Triple portrait, painted in preparation for a monument which was planned. Oil painting by Philippe de Champaigne. National Gallery, London

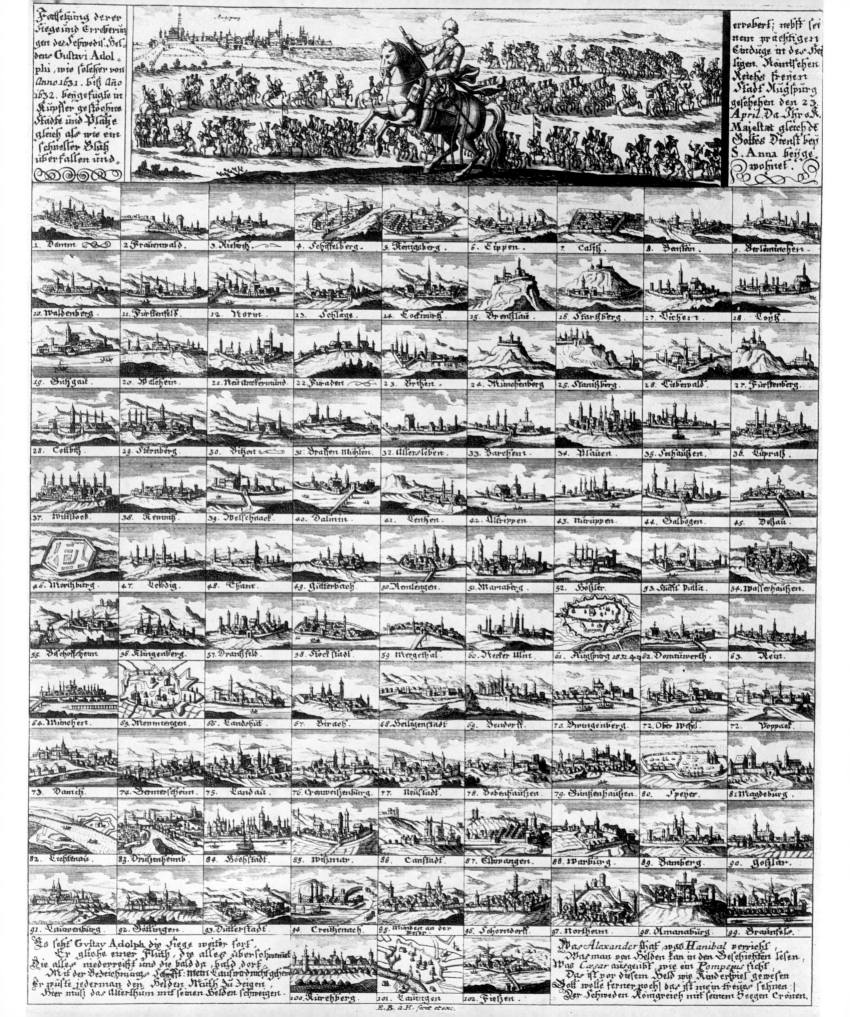

106 Pamphlet with miniature illustrations of the cities—even the smallest—captured by Gustavus Adolphus at the head of the Swedish army on German territory. Copperplate engraving by the monographist E. B. à H. Germanisches Nationalmuseum, Nuremberg

107 Battle-order at Lützen (16 November 1632): The Imperial army under Wallenstein was drawn up in compact squares in the Spanish manner with the infantry in the centre and the cavalry on the wings; the Swedish army under Gustavus Adolphus and Duke Bernhard of Weimar was in two long lines, with the artillery in action in front of the first of these. Copperplate engraving. Güstrow Museum

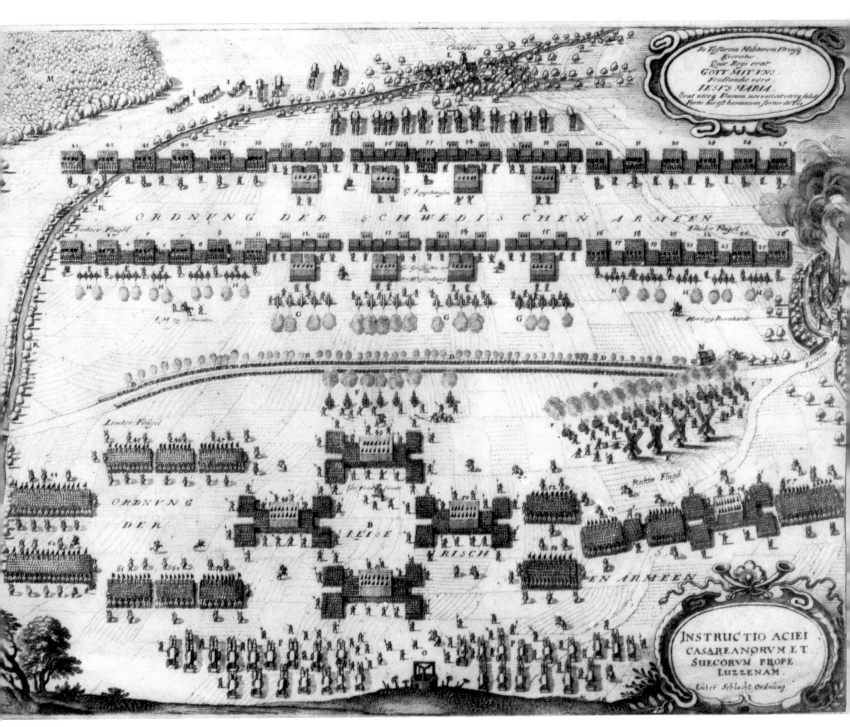

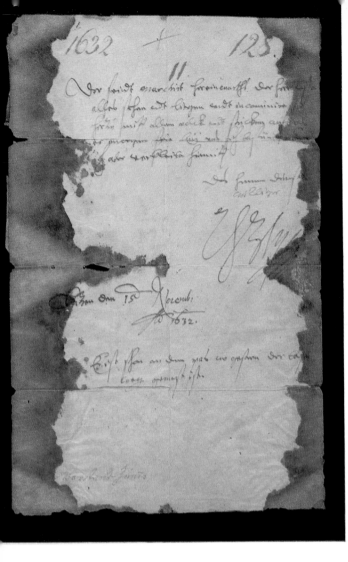

108 With a marching-order (stained with blood at the edges) hurriedly issued on 15 November 1632, Wallenstein (AHzF—Albrecht Herzog zu Friedland) ordered Fieldmarshal Count Pappenheim to Lützen where the battle was fought. The Swedes won but Gustavus Adolphus was killed—as was Pappenheim. Heeresgeschichtliches Museum, Vienna

109 The painting depicts a dramatic scene from the battle of Lützen. The Swedish king who suffered from short-sightedness, gets behind the Imperial lines. A musketeer (in the foreground to the left) fires the first aimed shot, then a group of horsemen surround the richly dressed combatant and inflict upon him the deadly blows. The naked corpse of the king is discovered only after the end of the battle in the darkness. Painting by Jan Asselyn. Herzog-Anton-Ullrich-Museum, Brunswick

110 Black breastplate of Gustavus Adolphus with silver decoration. The figures and inscription proclaim the bearer as the champion of God. Staatliche Museen, Heidecksburg

111 "Streiff", the magnificently saddled charger ridden by King Gustavus Adolphus in the battle of Lützen. Kungl. Livrustkammaren, Stockholm

112 The most realistic portrait of Gustavus Adolphus. Etching by the monographist L. S., incorrectly attributed to Lorenz Strauch. Original in the Schoolhouse of Madenhausen/Upper Franconia, Germany. Copy in the Germanisches Nationalmuseum, Nuremberg

113 The successful defence of the mountain-
town of Freiberg/Saxony in 1642/43 was
brought about by the skill and bravery of the
miners in the construction of earthworks and
tunnels. The surrounded town, called the
"rats' nest" by Torstensson, always maintained
contact with the outside world via underground
passages. Oil painting by Peeter Snayers.
Heeresgeschichtliches Museum, Vienna

114 Numerous sieges took place during the
war. Ulm was impregnable. After 1605, the
mediaeval town-wall was enclosed by a second
ring of defences with eleven sloping, earth-
covered bastions and three ravelins to protect
the gates in the trench of the earthen wall. The
costly project was based on Dutch and Italian
models and was supervised by the engineers
Jan van Valkenburgh, Johann Faulhaber and
Joseph Furttenbach. From: Mathäus Merian,
Topographia Germaniae

Die pfaffen Gass.

Huy juch habt gütten mütt der Lew mit seiner macht,
Der hatt nühn in die flücht vnd in den Lauͤfft gebracht,
Das seiste Closter volck wol in der pfaffen gassen,
So laufft vnd trölt euch nühn auͤs Eüwern festen passen,
Von Eirem Feigenbaum von Eürem Reben stock,
Geht vnd heület nühn auͤch in Eürem pfaffen Rock
Gebt euch in gütten schütz weil mans noch thüt erlauͤben,
Ehe man Euch in dem Nest ereilt vnd thüt berauͤben,
An Euͤver täglich schnarchen vnd pochen macht ein endt,
Macht euch nicht mehr so breit das blat hat sich gewendt.

Der andere pflegt zü jagen der thütt ietz lauͤffen vor,
Wie der Hünd der da schnapt nach eim stück vnd ver lohr,
Was er Züvor im maul So gehets Euch Geitz pfaffen,
Die ihr der Geistlichen güter wollet hinraffen,
Die Thür steht ietzünt auͤff wolt ihr so kombt herein,
Ihr solt vns dieser Zeit wilkomme gäste sein,
Doch schawet fleissig zü das ihr Euch nicht verirret,
Vnd im geschwinden lauͤff gefährlichen verwirret,
Es ist ein Lew dort auͤs der mochte euch ertappen,
Ehe ihr in Euͤvere höln geschlichen mit euͤverer Kappen.

Nach dem die Capuciner sich vor 8 Jahren zu Francfort am Main wider der Oberigkeit willen ein gedrungen
So hat man sie itzo wider ihren willen zur Statt hinaus gefürt, vnd in ein Schifflein den Main hinunder nacher
maintz gesendt geschehen den 13. Iuny A° 1633.

119 This portrait of Wallenstein as a general in the field, engraved after a painting by van Dyck is probably the best-known but bears least resemblance to the subject since the artist based his work on totally inaccurate sketches. Contemporaries describe the general as being quite different: gaunt and tall in figure, demanding respect and spreading fear and with a penetrating and often fiery look. He preferred eye-catching clothes—with a red sash and a feather in his hat and with a long, scarlet cloak over dark clothing. From: Mathäus Merian, *Theatrum Europaeum* III

116 The work of the illustrious master-craftsman Antonio Piccinino: a sword said to have belonged to Wallenstein. Museum für Deutsche Geschichte, Berlin

117 The great coat-of-arms of Wallenstein on the fountain in the garden of his palace at Prague (1630), crowned by a prince's hat (symbol of rank) and bearing the inscription "Albertus D(eo) G(ratia)"—by the Grace of God. The ox-heads are a reference to his possession of the Mecklenburg duchies.

118 Frydlant castle in Northeast Bohemia (present-day state)—centre of the estate of the same name acquired by Wallenstein in 1622. This made him a Bohemian potentate and it was from the name of this estate that he took his first ducal title.

ALBERT. DVX FRITLAND. COM. WALLEST. ETC

Pet. de Iode sculp.   Ant. van Dijck pinxit   Mart. vanden Enden excudit Cum priuilegio

120—122 Night of the murder in February
1634 at Eger.

First Act: Raid by officers disloyal to Wallenstein on colonels still faithful to the general
while they are unsuspectingly at table. All are
murdered.
Second Act: Captain Deveroux stabs Wallenstein in his bedroom in the Pachelbel House
with a halberd, shouting the words "Die, you
perjured knave!" His man-servant was also
killed.
Third Act: The corpses of the slain men are
dragged out of the house. Etchings by Mathäus
Merian the Elder in: *Theatrum Europaeum* III

123 Troops embarking in sailing-ships with Imperial flags. Copperplate engraving by Johann Wilhelm Baur. Staatliche Graphische Sammlung, Munich

124 Tripod-hoists and pulleys were part of the equipment used by the artillery. After: J. Furttenbach, Architectura martialis (1630). Municipal Archives, Stralsund

125 The movement of guns from one position to another was an exceptionally onerous task and frequently had to be performed with winches and the power of human muscles. After: J. Furttenbach, Architectura martialis. Municipal Archives, Stralsund

126 Mortars for high-angle fire were aimed with the aid of a device which used plumb lines and angle scales. After: J. Furttenbach, Halinitro Pyrobolia (1627). Municipal Archives, Stralsund

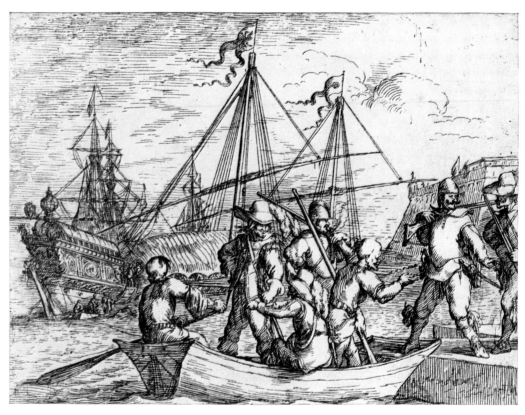

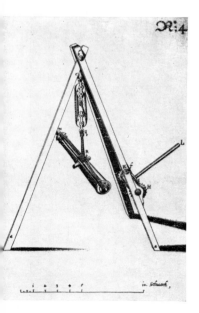

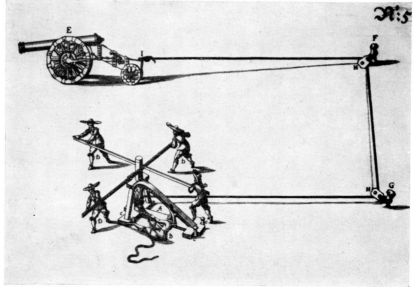

127 Artillery position in the battle, surrounded by troops. A sergeant artificer is loading a cannon. Copperplate engraving. Staatliche Graphische Sammlung, Munich

128 Artillery fire at long range—as here on the town of Wasserburg on the Inn, occupied by Bavarian troops and Polish Cossacks (1648) —accuracy and effect were not remarkable. The artist has omitted the large number of horses and waggons necessary. Copperplate engraving. Historisches Museum, Frankfort on the Main

following page:
129 Gun-accessory with engraved scale, showing charge and directional data. Gilded brass. The work of Ulrich Kliefer, master-craftsman of Augsburg. Städtische Kunstsammlungen, Augsburg

Gelegenheit der Statt Wasserburg, vnd wie die Königl: Schwed: vnd Frantzösche Armen ein Versuch darauff gethan den 5. Junij vnd de 8. dito wider abmarschiret Año 1648.

A. Drey Schwere Schwed: Stück damit in die Statt gespilt worden
B. Frantzösche Stück damit das Reitter v. Polacken lager vnter der Statt getheilt worden.
C. Zwo Frantzösche Brigaden.
D. Zwo Schwedische Brigaden.
E. Batterie aufm galgenberg.
F. Grüb worin die Schwedischen posten gefaßt.
G. Ziegelhütten, vnd Blendung.
H. Bayerische Schantz aufm berg.
I. Die Statt Waßerburg.
K. Das Schloß.
L. Capuciner Closter.
M. Polacken lager.
N. Der Ihn fluß.
O. Tirolisch gebürg.
Q. Abgehawene Dannen baume.
R. Teich.
P. Schloß Bastion, worauf mit halben Carthaunen auff die drey Schwedische Stück gespilet worden.

The taxes to be raised by the army by virtue of an Imperial decree were the chief financial source of the steadily increasing forces—authority and the army grew. Taxes—now levied as a regular payment—seemed to be preferable since they only "dipped in the barrel" and did not empty it entirely—as was the case with plundering and billeting, for instance. It was desirable to maintain a minimum of productive force so that fresh demands could subsequently be made. The Imperial regiments were stationed or on the march in Bohemia and Silesia, in the Free Cities of the Empire and in the enemy territories. Hans de Witte, with his far-reaching credit relations which extended as far as Augsburg, Vienna, Nuremberg, Hamburg, Frankfort on the Main, Breslau, Antwerp and Amsterdam, obtained cash, equipment and provisions. Through the collection of taxes, *per semper*, he was to be reimbursed for the money advanced.

At the beginning of Wallenstein's first generalship, this system of circulation functioned satisfactorily for the most part. De Witte's agents, of whom the most important were Walter de Hertoge in Hamburg and Abraham Blommaert in Nuremberg, were given bills of exchange for the money made available. The payments were made during the fairs in Frankfort, Leipzig and Naumburg and at the great markets in Linz and Vienna. The particular faith of the landowners was no hindrance to the flow of money. If there was a hold-up in the flow of cash, this was not for reasons of religion. The more taxes that were levied, the greater the resistance that developed. The Estates, princes, cities and peasants found ways, means and pretexts of obtaining reductions in the sums demanded, in delaying payment and in even refusing payment altogether. Some cities, such as Stralsund (1628) and Magdeburg (1631) paid a part and prepared for armed resistance. The Imperial commanders, who usually kept back a part of the taxes for themselves, threatened exemplary retribution and used even more dreadful curses. However, it was of little use to the commander-in-chief and his skilful financier when cities or districts were ravaged or punished by having large numbers of troops billeted there. Under no circumstances did they contribute more money and the system of war contributions began to break down.

Hans de Witte's limitless credit declined and then collapsed. Following de Witte's suicide in Prague on 11 September 1630, there was little left for his creditors to claim. Without delay, the emperor had the "starken Concursus Creditorum" de Witte's announced in the Free Cities of the Empire. One of the greatest fortunes of Central Europe, founded on long-distance trade and money-lending in particular, had been destroyed by the war.

While the Berlin trading company of Weiler and Essenbrücher, suppliers to Field-Marshal Hans von Arnim who fought in the service of several rulers, met with a similar fate, a glance at the business records of de Brier, a Frankfort firm of merchants and jewellers, reveals a different picture. They manufactured, obtained or supplied jewels and luxury articles and at times even saltpeter, horses, butter and oxen, to de Witte, Blommaert, numerous high-ranking officers and princes. For the fairs of 1627 to 1632 alone, the following turnover is noted: Frankfort Lent and autumn fairs each 15,000 to almost 38,000 Imperial thalers, at Leipzig fairs about half of these figures, up to 3,000 Imperial thalers at the Peter-Paul market in Naumburg. Interruptions which followed did indeed reduce the profit but were not a real danger to this family

A farewell song for Wallenstein

*That's what happens when
one is too ambitious,
The Devil silently comes
and trips him up.
No tree grows up to Heaven,
The axe is already there,
to fell it to the ground.*

*O Wallenstein,
you were a stone for everyone,
Death takes from you misery
and pain,
the burden of the magnificence
of this world.
May God have mercy on your
poor soul,
Forgive you, for Christ's blood,
all your guilt and errors!*

From: Tränen des Vaterlandes, Soldiers' song.
(tune: They are sent for storm and strife,
Verses 8 and 9)

[1] Geschäftsbuch des Hauses Daniel de Brier,
State Archives Vienna (Haus-, Hof- und
Staatsarchiv), HS, W 1058

undertaking. De Brier, together with other merchants, had founded a trading company in 1620 with a capital of 36,000 Imperial thalers. This capital grew to 517,000 Imperial thalers by 1636.[1]

Wallenstein, in particular, was surrounded by luxury on an incredible scale although the electors, who had gathered in Regensburg on 13 August 1630 in supra-confessional unanimity of the never-ending burden of the Imperial army, had forced the emperor to dismiss his commander-in-chief who had established a splendid camp-state at Memmingen. The bitter fate of de Witte and his lamenting heirs moved nobody; Wallenstein, on the other hand, continued to obtain so much profit from the fertile fields, meadows and commercial fisheries in the "paradise of Bohemia" with its gentle hills, from his possessions in Mecklenburg and from the capital invested at Venice and Amsterdam that he could afford to live on a royal scale which was apparent to everybody.

An imposing memorial to the architectural initiative of Wallenstein, who continued to retain the favour of the emperor, still stands today on the "small side" of Prague. This is "Wallenstein's Palace", a spacious building of gloomy magnificence bounded by a profusion of streets and crowded by innumerable small houses. Four gardens, 26 houses and a lime-burning establishment were demolished to provide space for the monumental palace which—designed by the Italian architects Spezza and Pieroni—was built in less than three years (1622—1624). Soldiers were brought in when builders and owners were reluctant to act and demolition was started even when burgher-houses were still inhabited. The completed palace had innumerable rooms, a chapel, a splendid astrological cabinet, stables for 300 horses, a riding school, loggias looking out on to magnificent gardens, a park with pleasant walks, exotic plants, fountains and statues by the Dutchman Adriaen de Vries. The dominating colour of the interior decoration was blue—the fine leather, the gobelins and other tapestries, the silks, and the carpets from Italy, the Netherlands and the Ottoman Empire were all in this colour.

On the ceiling of the baronial hall, the painter Bartolomeo Bianco had depicted Wallenstein as triumphator, standing in a chariot drawn at a furious pace by the horses of the Sun. Contemporaries counted a court of a thousand people, including counts, gentlemen-in-waiting and pages of noble family. It is reported that a hundred dishes were brought at every meal and old soldiers were always welcomed. But this unparalleled luxury was to no avail: the owner of the palace was averse to music, dancing, celebrations and banquets. His worn-out nerves could not stand noise so that the streets and squares around the palace were cordoned off by chains and had to be covered with straw to deaden the sound of walking feet. Wallenstein suffered from serious infirmities when only forty years of age, these certainly including gout and perhaps syphilis as well.

In Güstrow, his residence in Mecklenburg, he had a wing added to the Renaissance castle he owned there but the walls only reached the first storey while in Wismar the "Palacium" did not get beyond the planning stage.

The new palace at Jičín, the capital of his Duchy of Friedland, reached the stage at which it could be inhabited. The whole of the town was transformed, along the lines of other administrative centres in Bohemia and within a short time, into a modern settlement before the very eyes of the inhabitants and visitors. Hundreds of architects, artisans and day-labourers were constantly at work converting wooden buildings into stone structures with tiled roofs, erecting new ones, levelling roads, clearing spaces for squares and laying out avenues and parks.

While Wallenstein's regiments impoverished the surrounding countryside and its inhabitants by extorting taxes from them, work was continued on the project of establishing an intact model state in Northeast Bohemia in accordance with the will of a severe and demanding ruler. Contemporaries called it the *terra felix*—a fortunate part of the Earth—whose prosperity was founded on the ruin of other regions. However, it was a difficult matter to shield the duchy from the ravages of war and after the death of its ruler the tide of the misery of war swept across this oasis which had hitherto been spared. The new owners of Wallenstein's possessions had neither sufficient power nor the economic intention to continue the project which had been implemented with such an iron will.

Already within a few days of the murder of Wallenstein, who had been outlawed by the emperor, on 25 February 1634 in Eger, commissioners of the Imperial army appeared on the Friedland estates to confiscate the property of the "traitor". A new and massive change in ownership was imminent in Bohemia. Within two weeks of the death of the greatest Bohemian landowner and even before the thanksgiving service ordered by the emperor could be held, a profusion of gifts were distributed by the grace and favour of the emperor—also to the evident murderers. It was subsequently estimated that the estates confiscated from the dead "traitors" Wallenstein, Trčka, Kinský and Illo were worth nearly 15 million florins. The fall and awful death of Wallenstein is more than the "tragic story of a man who could have died as the king of Bohemia". He had become a great danger for the conservative forces of the Catholic-Hapsburg phalanx as an areligious figure, as an independent and disquieting manager and organizer type of great personality who regarded himself as neither Austrian nor German but was rather inseparably associated with the destiny of a national class. With him and his companions in death, there disappeared the last powerful group of the traditional Bohemian aristocracy. The landowners that succeeded them were almost exclusively foreigners—soldiers, senior Imperial officials, Germans, Italians and Walloons.

SUCCESSFUL
"CHILDREN
OF FORTUNE"

The most important part of Wallenstein's possessions—24 domains and 50 estates—passed into the hands of the Trautmannsdorf, Schlick, Gallas (later Clam-Gallas), Adlersheim, Butler and Černín families, the Trčka estates—estimated at four million florins—were acquired by the Piccolominis and Colloredo-Waldsees and the landed property of the dead Count Kinský (Vchynský) went to Johann Aldringen.

The latter began his career as a clerk in the chancery of Luxembourg but in 1618 he was to be found fighting as a soldier in Northern Italy and the Tyrol. His destiny ultimately led him to Wallenstein and he became a field-marshal. He demonstrated his greed on a number of occasions but especially during the three-day *sacco di Mantova*, the pillage of Mantua with its untold riches, in June 1630. He shared the booty with Mathias Gallas. It was calculated that he had a million florins in Italian banks.

This Gallas was a member of the lesser nobility and his family held a fief from the prince-bishop of Trient. The fortune of war was kinder to him than would have been expected from his abilities. In the service of the League and of the emperor (or Wallenstein), he reached the rank of a count of the Empire and commander-in-chief in place of the outlawed Wallenstein. Hesitating between fear of the former and greed for his property, he helped the emperor, from his high position, to destroy Wallenstein. Four of his sons married into leading families of the Bohemian nobility and his eldest son became the Duke of Lucera. He himself, called "the ruin of the army" by his contemporaries and soldiers, indulged increasingly in drinking-bouts, gambling and notorious amorous adventures.

Unlike Aldringen and Gallas, Octavio Piccolomini was of aristocratic origin. This ancient family of Siena had supplied popes, such as the learned Aenea Sylvio (Pius II) and Octavio's brother was archbishop of Siena. In the service of Spain and the emperor and also as a long-term informant of the papal Curia, he rose to the rank of field-marshal—precisely at the time when he actively pursued the conspiracy against Wallenstein. Apart from the estates in Bohemia, Octavio also received many other gifts from Spain and from the emperor. He did not enjoy his great riches in Italy and Bohemia or his marriage with the still youthful daughter of the Duke of Saxe-Lauenburg (1651) for very long, since he died in 1656.

The Imperial field-marshal Peter Melander (Grecized from the original Eppelmann) came from a peasant family in the district of Nassau. A Calvinist, he entered the Imperial service in 1640 and rose to become the commander-in-chief of the entire army. He himself estimated that he had acquired 700,000 florins in cash during the campaigns of the last years of the war. The emperor raised the territories acquired by Melander—Esterau and the bailiwick of Isselbach—to the status of a county of the Holy Roman Empire.

Many others could also be named who were promoted and liberally rewarded by the emperor for their victories or because of perplexity or a lack of anybody more competent. This generosity is to be explained by his desire to prolong the war.[1]

The Swedish crown was not lacking in generosity either when it took captured estates and with them rewarded the loyalty of its meritorious, unscrupulous and able soldiers and diplomats. These included Carl Gustav Wrangel, who followed the advice of his father who said "If you take something, you've got something", Johan Banér and Colonel Ramsay, who was given estates in Mecklenburg. After the death of the king in 1633, the Chancellor Oxenstierna could scarcely save himself from the flattering and demanding gentlemen who pestered him: "Da war fast kein Stand, oder nahmhaffter Officirer und Bedienter, der nicht einige Aembter, Abteyen, Clöster, Herrschafften und dergleichen begehrte; da dan, je höher die person, je grösser auch die praetensionen waren".[2] ("There was scarcely any one of rank, any well-known officer or official who did not aspire to a few offices, abbeys, monasteries, domains and so on; and the more exalted the person, the greater his aspirations.")

Hans Christoph, Count von Königsmarck, may serve as an example of all of these. This son of a noble family of the Altmark initially tried his luck under the Imperial colours but it was in the service of Sweden that the cornucopia of Fortune really poured over him. In the course of several successful campaigns, he occupied the domain of Querfurt in 1640 and retained it until the end of the war. In the mid-1640's, he captured the bishoprics of Verden and Bremen for the Swedish crown. As a reward, he was appointed governor of these territories which he exploited by means of heavy imposts. He also acquired possession of more than half the estates belonging to the bishopric of Verden and also the administrative district of Neuhaus on the Oste in the bishopric of Bremen. For other services, the emperor rewarded the general with estates in the Empire, in Sweden and in Estonia. Mention has already been made of Königmarck's vast wealth on the "small side" of Prague. At his death, his fortune was estimated at 1.6 million thalers in cash, estates and bank capital, not including his possessions in Estonia.[3]

The endless wars waged by Sweden during its period as a "great power" were accompanied by a rapid increase in the wealth of the traditional aristocracy and upstarts who had rendered meritorious services. The Crown and the cities, not to mention the peasants, suffered a decline in wealth, income and political power. The aristocracy, with the spoils of war, patronized the arts but their splendour was based to no small degree on foreign sources of income.

Exalted rank and a commission with the authority to command did not suffice to make efficient armies out of the great mass of have-nots who flocked to the colours. A large number of experienced and seasoned experts in the art of war—a stratum of professional soldiers—were also needed. They were of exceptional diversity in education, origin and character. This isolated group of soldiers with similar interests left its mark more than once in the course of the war. The death of Gustavus Adolphus in 1633 left the Swedish army in an insecure position and it came to the conclusion that its interests had not been observed by the haggling diplomats of the Alliance of Heilbronn ("who sat in the parlours behind the stove"). The officers then formed a con-

[1] Hallwich, H.: Gestalten aus Wallensteins Lager, Leipzig, 1885; Elster, O.: Piccolomini-Studien, Leipzig, 1911; Schmidt, R.: Ein Kalvinist als kaiserlicher Feldmarschall im 30jährigen Krieg, no place stated, 1895

[2] Lorentzen: Die schwedische Armee, p. 35

[3] The most conclusive synthesis so far is in Redlich, F.: The German Military Enterpriser and his Forces, Wiesbaden, 1964

Ondt föra krijg ur Böker,
och hämpta barn ur Apotheket

*The waging of war is not learnt
from books*

Saying

spiracy under the leadership of their commanders. At this, the Great Treasurer Brandenstein travelled to the regiments stationed along the Danube to make a general account with them. The award of extensive territories worth almost five million Imperial thalers appeased the discontent only temporarily. Another serious crisis occurred in the summer and autumn of 1635 when most of Sweden's German allies deserted her and concluded peace with the emperor. The same happened again on the death of the energetic General Banér (1641).

The military specialists revealed themselves as self-willed and highly disagreeable partners towards the end of the war in particular, as in the July deliberations in 1647 at Eger (Cheb) when the commanders of the Swedish army put their claims for reimbursement—a number of North German bishoprics and Silesian duchies plus ten to twelve million Imperial thalers—before the diplomats at the Peace Congress of Westphalia. They also won the right for the army, as *tertia pars tractantium*, to have its own representative there as a third party in addition to the negotiating parties.[1]

THE ART OF WAR,
LOGISTICS
AND WAR ECONOMY

In that stratum of the professional soldiers who lived on and for war, there were many who were of common origin. Schiller, in the person of Colonel Butler, has one of these "children of Fortune" proudly say of himself: "From lowly service in the stable, I rose through skill in war to this dignity and rank, the plaything of capricious Fortune." General Banér called his army "this extended state" and, according to C. V. Wedgwood, it possessed "the characteristics of a self-confident class". According to the law of a large number and a long time, individual members of this corps of indispensable specialists in war, who were mostly not of princely birth, developed into great generals: in the Empire Tilly, Wallenstein and Montecuccoli, in France Turenne and Condé, in Spain/Italy Spinola and in Sweden—although greatly outclassed by the achievements of Gustavus Adolphus—Wrangel, Horn, Banér and Torstensson.

The problem of logistics also explains the strategic rule of employing the army rather as an instrument to apply political pressure by exhausting countries rather than as a purely military fighting-machine. The principle of war of avoiding battles as far as possible was based on the economic fundamentals of the motto of warfare at that time. Leading military theorists and outstanding generals such as John of Nassau and Maurice of Orange believed that it was better to defeat an enemy by famine than with weapons. Battles, as a "great game", were only to be risked as a last resort, they did not rank any higher than a skilful marching manoeuvre. The relation between

[1] In addition to Redlich and Lorentzen also: Šindelář, B.: Vestfálký mír a česká otázka, Prague, 1968

economics and strategy had assumed such a form in the last years of the war that —as Schiller put it—"the war was only continued to provide work and bread for the troops, that by and large one argued only about the advantages of the winter-quarters and that the finding of good accommodation for the army was more highly esteemed than the winning of a major battle".

All the important leaders, re-organizers and theorists of the mercenary armies largely based their concepts on an older model—that of the Roman forces. The scholarly treatises on the art of war in the 16th and 17th century display an astonishing knowledge of military history and many of their authors also translated and published the works of Antiquity. Ancient principles and the high combat efficiency of the Roman legions evidently lived on in the organization of armies, in camp orders and in the rules of training and tactics. Models, with lead soldiers, were used to reconstruct individual operations executed by the Byzantine Emperor Leo the Wise and Maurice of Orange organized his troops in The Hague on the pattern of the spearmen of Philip of Macedonia and of the Roman swordsmen. It was in the nature of the subject that the numerous writings on artillery and fortifications were based to a much lesser extent on ancient models and took Italian, Spanish, Dutch and French achievements as their main inspiration.

As it was, the majority of the army commanders of the Holy Roman Empire had little knowledge of this theoretical literature and relied on their own experience and the practice of German warfare with its many shortcomings.[1]

Success in war was largely determined by organizational talent and business acumen. A hierarchy of profiteers emerged with the supreme commander selling commissions which conferred the authority of a colonel on the holder. During the time of Wallenstein, who issued about two hundred such patents or commissions, there was a mad atmosphere of speculation which to Karl Marx seemed not unlike the trading in railway shares of the 19th century. Many a noble hastily sold his estates to get the cash for the purchase of a commission.[2] The colonels, for their part, pursued the recruitment of their regiments with markedly economic objectives in mind, usually in an undisguised and unscrupulous manner. Since the rulers engaged in the wars only paid the money they owed for the soldiers on rare occasions, the stratum of the colonels became, as it were, state creditors.

The appropriation of money by the medium-rank commanders was standard practice. A shortage of supplies and consequent plundering on the one hand and waste in prosperous billeting areas on the other were characteristic of the chaos in military logistics. This was one of the principal reasons why the average costs per soldier in the Thirty Years' War were far higher than on subsequent occasions under more advanced production conditions. According to Gustav Freytag, these costs were twice as high in the 17th century as in the 19th.

It was in the military staffs in particular that expenses were incurred on an ostentatious scale which was disproportionately high. The commanders usually maintained a "camp state" which did not at all perform just a directly military function. It was a small-scale feudal court, adapted to field requirements and including many layabouts, "spivs" and whores. The maintenance of a brilliant and numerous staff en-

English pickled herring (1621)

To Styria and England
have I sent many messengers for steel,
For theirs is of others the best
And can be splendidly hardened…

From: Scheible: Die Fliegenden Blätter, No. 22,1622

[1] For detailed information on warfare, cf.: Razin: Istorija voennogo isskusstva, vol. 3

[2] Marx: Chronologische Auszüge, p. 440

hanced the military prestige of a commander since it won for him the respect of his adversaries and rivals and made his employ a more attractive proposition for mercenaries seeking service.

The Imperial decree of 9 November 1630, which was intended to restrain the unreasonable demands for money made by the commanders, laid down the following rates for the staff of a cavalry or infantry regiment:

	florins	horses	florins	horses
colonel	600	17	500	12
lieut.-colonel	150	10	120	9
sergeant-major	50	8	—	—
quartermaster	50	6	40	2
military judge	30	4	40	3
chaplain	30	2	24	2
provost (military police)	30	6	60	8 (plus 4 assistants)
waggon-master	30	4	24	2
executioner	12	1	12	1
jailer	8	—	—	—
Steckenknecht	8	—	—	—

The captain of a troop of foot-soldiers could claim 160 florins, the lieutenant 60, the ensign 50, a sergeant 21, a corporal 12, lance-corporals and bandsmen 7 florins 30 kreuzers and ordinary foot-soldiers 6 florins 40 kreuzers. There was a great difference between the pay of the ordinary soldiers and that of the officers.[1]

On the basis of the above decree, the staff of a cavalry regiment with 60 mounts at its disposal drew more than a thousand florins pay per month. More than six times this sum was needed to pay the general staff of a field-army of six regiments (about 15,000 men) and almost 180 horses could be taken along. This conveys an impression of the large number of draught animals and mounts needed. The above figures do not include the sums acquired by members of the staff and their parasitic families on their own initiative. Only rough figures can be quoted for the total number of mercenary formations which developed into standing armies. Wallenstein alone had some 40 regiments under his command in 1630 and accordingly 20 million florins were needed annually for their pay. At the time of Wallenstein's second generalship, Sweden and its allies had similar numbers of troops on active service.

According to the calculations on which the Swedish Chancellor Axel Oxenstierna based his negotiations with the Evangelical Estates of Upper Germany in March 1633, the allied army was to consist of 56 infantry regiments and a half and 216 cavalry companies. The monthly upkeep of the infantry units was estimated at almost 400,000 Imperial thalers and that for the cavalry at about 423,000 Imperial thalers, totalling some 814,000 Imperial thalers (or about 1.22 million florins) in all for their pay per month. According to these calculations, the Allies had to find almost 15 million florins per year for the upkeep of the Swedish troops and the units from Heilbronn. What was

[1] Bellus: Kaiserlicher Triumpff-Wagen, p. 305 f.

demanded from the enemy Estates of the Empire in respect of taxes, billets, transportation and other services is not listed and is also difficult to estimate. Both allies and adversaries had to make their contribution to the feeding of a body of troops totalling at least 150,000 men.[1]

From this and other sources, it can be concluded that there were a quarter of a million soldiers in the Empire during the 1630's, plus just as many people, if not more, in the baggage-trains. With an estimated total population in the Holy Roman Empire of some 20 million, this means that 2.5 to 3 per cent were serving with the colours of the various war-lords. In comparison with modern conditions, this proportion does not seem particularly high. However, it represented a disproportionately heavier burden since the productivity of labour at that time was far less and production surplus to one's own requirements and the feudal contributions was not at all a general phenomenon. Apart from the Republic of the United Netherlands, whose well-drilled and disciplined soldiers received regular pay, the warring powers of Europe usually applied the principle of military economics which stated that *bellum se ipse alet*—war must nourish itself.

Masses of soldiers as an isolated and non-productive part of the population, war, camps and military campaigns as the rapid consumers and destroyers of products—all this raises the question not only of who financed and paid them but also of who produced the weapons, equipment, clothing, waggons and ships. Research has only provided a fragmentary answer to this so far.

The economy of war necessitated the "development of productive forces as forces of destruction" and the centralized organization of the collaboration of large numbers of people (Marx). In no other field of feudal society, whose basis was the small-quantity production of goods, were such mighty driving-forces active as the economy of war in respect of the quickest possible development of new techniques, structures and resources on a large scale.

The Empire had formerly been the world-leader in mining, metallurgy and metal-working and the miners, foundrymen, gunsmiths, armourers, the smiths of the various branches and the carpenters were still able to meet the requirements of the warring rulers and cities to a large extent. In addition to the traditional centres such as Nuremberg, Suhl, Aachen, Cologne, Augsburg, Ulm, St. Joachimsthal, Eger, Essen, Solingen, Venice, Tuscany, Brescia and Liège, new ones emerged such as Dresden, Munich, Graz and Vienna. The bell-founders of numerous cities paid more attention to the casting of cannon and mortars, e.g., the Löfflers and Herolds in Nuremberg and the Schelshorns in Regensburg.[2]

New demands were made on ore-mining, which had been gradually declining since the middle of the 16th century, and the smelting-masters in Styria, the Harz Mountains, the Erzgebirge, the Upper Palatinate and Hesse-Nassau received bigger orders. It happened more frequently than hitherto that agents contacted the middlemen and master-craftsmen to agree on deliveries and conclude contracts. Merchants and their agents zealously searched the whole of Europe for sources of supply, partners and markets. Copper, iron and lead in particular but also sulphur, slow-match material and saltpeter were urgently needed and prices rose. The commerce in these products

[1] Landberg, H./Ekholm, L./Nordlund, R./Nilson, S. A.: Det kontinentala krigets ekonomi. Studier i krigsfinansiering under svensk stormaktstid, Kristianstad, 1971, especially the contributions by Ekholm and Nordlund

[2] Franz, G.: Der Dreissigjährige Krieg und das deutsche Volk; Beck, L.: Geschichte des Eisens in technischer und kultureller Beziehung, 2nd section, Brunswick, 1895; Schwerpunkte der Eisengewinnung und Eisenverarbeitung in Europa 1500—1650, edited by H. Kellenbenz, Cologne/Vienna, 1974; Thomas, B.: Die deutsche Plattnerkunst, Munich, 1944; Hayward, J. F.: European Armour, London, 1951, German: Die Kunst der alten Büchsenmacher, 1st vol., Hamburg/Berlin (West), 1968; Müller, H.: Deutsche Bronzegeschützrohre 1400—1750, Berlin, 1968; Hoff, A.: Ein waffenhistorisches Handbuch, Feuerwaffen II, Brunswick, 1969; Schedelmann, H.: Die grossen Büchsenmacher, Brunswick, 1972; Waffen und Uniformen in der Geschichte. Exhibition of the Museum für Deutsche Geschichte. Berlin, 1957

was a continuing source of prosperity for such cities as Danzig, Hamburg, Bremen, Amsterdam and Frankfort on the Main. The "Golden Age" of the Netherlands was founded not only on worldwide peaceful commerce but also on the boom in trade associated with the war.[1]

A great deal of footwear, leather equipment and harness, felt, cloth and linen (for tents) was continually needed. Cereals, straw, hemp and especially draught animals and livestock for slaughter had to be procured in large quantities on occasions. Many waggon-teams, flat barges and proud ships and even beasts of burden for carrying material across the Alps were needed at short notice. The preparation and the waging of war consequently hit the population not only in the form of war-taxes, billeting, plundering and alienation—many people also had to contribute their productive labour for the purposes of destruction without having any certain and lasting advantage from this. The war not only had a destructive influence on the "peaceful" spheres of labour—it also struck at those with a "war priority" wherever it came.

The "ideal" equipment of an infantry regiment of some three thousand men, including 1,500 musketeers, 300 riflemen, 1,200 pikemen and a further 200 halberdiers conveys an impression of the great variety of equipment needed by such a unit:[2]

10 flags	1,500 muskets
10 partisans and	1,500 musket-rests
50 halberds for the commanders	1,500 bandoliers
31 drums	1,500 powder flasks and slow-match material
20 pipes	1,500 leather bottles
1,200 sets of ordinary harness	300 short muskets
1,000 long pikes	600 powder or priming flasks and
200 ordinary halberds	slow-match material
200 pairs of metal gauntlets	1,851 tunics

Such a regiment might have taken up to 1,600 horses with it and these would have been looked after by hundreds of grooms and stable-boys.

In 1625 at Würzburg, the following prices were charged: 61 Imperial thalers for a flag, two Imperial thalers for a partisan (a kind of halberd), one Imperial thaler for a halberd, four Imperial thalers for a drum, five Imperial thalers for a pike and three Imperial thalers for a musket. One cwt. of powder cost 40 Imperial thalers and the same quantity of musket-shot and slow-match material six Imperial thalers each.

From a bill sent by the Nuremberg cannon-founder Leonhard Loewe to the Duke of Weimar in the 1640's and from other sources, an impression can be obtained of the variety and expense of artillery equipment. For two half-cannon-royal, Löwe's bill listed the following items: 638 florins for raw material (copper, zinc, lead), 732 florins for foundrymen's wages and 1,273 florins for the services of carters, locksmiths, smiths, carpenters, ropemakers and other tradesmen. The charges for labour were accordingly much higher than the cost of the material. For each half-cannon-royal, there was also reckoned: one hundred iron cannonballs (each weighing 24 pounds), 40 cwt. of powder, 25 cwt. of slow-match material, one gun-carriage, one hoisting-crane, one pair

[1] Kellenbenz, H.: Unternehmerkräfte im Hamburger Portugal- und Spanienhandel. 1590—1625, Hamburg, 1954; Barbour, V.: Capitalism in Amsterdam in the Seventeenth Century, Baltimore, 1950; Klompmaker, H.: Handel in de Gouden Eeuw, Bussum, 1966; Bogucka, M.: Gdánsk jako osrodek produkcyjny w XVI—XVII wieku, Warsaw, 1962; Idem: Handel zagraniczny Gdańska w pierwszej połowie XVII wieku, Wroclaw/Warsaw/Cracow, 1970

[2] Wallhausen, J. J. von: Kriegskunst zu Fuss, p. 97; Heilmann: Kriegsgeschichte II/2, pp. 909 and 926f.

Vngleicher Zeug bleibt nicht beysamen.

GLATZ. in Böhmen.

19

Frigora bombardam rumpunt permixta calori; Sic fugit algentem calda puella senem.

Was macht daß ein groß stück zerspringt?
Hitz und Kalt von einander tringt.

Also ein Weiblin Jung und heiß
Verläst ein Alten Kalten Greiß.

130 The bursting of gun-barrels from the use of too much powder was a common occurrence. Despite a considerable amount of specialist literature on the subject, gunners usually relied on empirical experience. From: Daniel Meissner, *Thesaurus philopoliticus*. Biblioteka Gdańska

of wheels, several hundred entrenchment tools (choppers, picks, spades, shovels), waggons, 15 to 20 men for manning it, for moving it and for constructing a field fortification for it and several dozen draught-horses. According to the estimate of Georg Schreiber, the material needed per round fired cost five Imperial thalers and an average of 50 rounds could be fired daily. The cost was therefore far higher than in later centuries.[1]

The "patent" for the master-gunner, first issued by Emperor Charles V, gave this military technician a social prestige higher than that of a guild. Master-gunners always had three or four assistants at their disposal and their wives and children were permitted to ride on the military waggons and ammunition carts, apart from the rest of the baggage-train. They did not have to stand in the long queues for provisions, either, and were served first. In every region occupied by a conquering army, it was the custom for the bells to be regarded as the property of the chief gunner. When a town was captured, he was entitled to dispose of the war material in the arsenals and powder-magazines as he thought fit. The *ars artilleriae* was accordingly more closely bound to the dense concentration of labour and production-installation of the manufactory type than other branches of the war economy.

It would appear that Nuremberg was the biggest business-centre for weapons, ammunition and military equipment in the Empire. As early as the 16th century, it is known to have had two depot-centres, six arsenals and numerous other depots (zwingers, towers and fortifications, church-towers, the town-hall and castles outside the town). War-production and trade in every kind of war material was one of the most respected activities of the town administration. As in the past, it boasted a highly efficient metal trade and the armourers in particular supplied an increasing market in every direction of the compass and worked for customers of every creed and social

[1] State Archives Weimar, H 172 and H 587; Schreiber, G.: Anleitung und kurtzer Bericht/ Vom Geschütze und desselben Proportionen . . ., Brieg, 1666, 3rd chapter, copy in Museum für Deutsche Geschichte, Berlin (library)

rank. Their customers included: 1618—1620 the Bohemian Estates and their Reformed King Frederick; at a later date Lutheran rulers such as the Elector of Saxony, the Duke of Württemberg, the "court gun-stock maker" of the Catholic Emperor; the Bishop of Bamberg was sent 150 suits of breastplates from the arsenal in 1631. The town council decided what and at what price material from the municipal stocks was to be sold. At the same time, a number of private dealers were active in Nuremberg and the two sides often worked together, as in May 1631, for example. The war was in full progress and Duke Julius Frederick of Württemberg requested the delivery of 400 to 500 arquebuses. There were sufficient weapons available in the arsenal but their locks were defective. Since the council did not wish to cheat such a highranking customer, the deal was put in private hands so that the origin of the weapons could be concealed. However, the keeper of the Württemberg arsenal did not fall for the trick and refused to buy. The council also acted as an official commercial intermediary between master plate-makers on the one hand and potential buyers on the other. Private individuals obviously acted as agents, too. The names listed in the records include Ulrich Löser, who supplied hundreds of sets of breasplates, pikes and muskets in 1631, Hans Heber, Sebald Hentzen and Jörg Endthner.[1] These were the same men who continually received waggon-loads of muskets from the gunsmiths of Suhl, Schmalkalden, Zella-St. Blasien, Schleusingen and Ilmenau but, once again, this was through the agency of buyers and sellers resident there. The names from Suhl most frequently mentioned were the Kletts, the Stöhrs, Valentin Cronberger and Hans Heychmann.[2]

As early as the end of the 16th century, merchants by the name of Klett—obviously members of one family—appeared on the scene in Zurich to negotiate the purchase of weapons from the city-council. Deliveries of weapons from Suhl were in fact a regular occurrence from 1590 onwards. Between 1603 and 1631, the city of Zurich obtained weapons from Suhl almost every year but the Kletts (Valentin the Elder, Valentin the Younger, Steffen, Wolfgang and Georg) also brought "Nuremberg merchandise" (individual pieces of armour, powder flasks) with them. This trade was disrupted from the 1630's onwards and the council had to turn to Venice, Milan and Brescia with commissions for the work of such illustrious families as the Cominazzo and the Contoni.[3]

Strongly guarded waggon-trains with the weapons for which there was a ready market in half of Europe rolled over roads which were becoming increasingly more dangerous to the princely residence-cities of Weimar, Dresden, and Berlin, to many of the Free cities of the Empire and—almost as a matter of course—to the camps of Gustavus Adolphus. In November 1632, the town-council of Suhl wrote to the Duke of Weimar that they were unable to provide draught-horses since a large consignment of guns (1,500 muskets) had been sent to Erfurt. A "Specification" which has survived from the same year, drawn up by the burgomaster and council of Suhl, mentions the sum of 34,583 Imperial thalers "for the gun-barrels supplied". When three to four Imperial thalers is taken as the price each, this amounts to some 10,000 gun-barrels just for the customers indicated above.[4]

The biggest orders received by the arms-centre of the Thuringian Forest, which produced such large quantities of weapons, included those from Wallenstein and Hans

[1] Soden: Kriegs- und Sittengeschichte der Reichsstadt Nürnberg, vol. 3, p. 274ff., p. 403ff.

[2] Lugs, J.: Handfeuerwaffen, vol. I, Berlin, 1968, p. 490

[3] Schneider, H.: Suhler Schusswaffenfabrikation in schweizerischer Sicht, 1st part, in: Waffen- und Kostümkunde 1/1968

[4] State Archives Weimar, H 172 and H 587

de Witte. In his own duchy and in Western Bohemia, the general and war-businessman brought about a mighty increase in the production and storage of weapons, ammunition, entrenchment tools, horseshoe-nails, clothing and footwear. The modern forges, mines, smelting-works and forges in Raspenau (Raspenava) and Hohenelbe, most of the town and village smiths in Friedland, tailors and cobblers worked for the constantly growing army operating in the northern part of Germany. Two of the lessees of the big production-plants, Talduci de la Casa and Zanetti, extracted the maximum output from the installations by imposing a strict regime on their workers. The waggon-trains took the merchandise to the Elbe, to Lobositz, Leitmeritz, Tetschen, and Pirna. Cereals, zwieback biscuits, clothing and war material were passed on to the boatmen of the Elbe who took the costly and often dangerous cargo to Dessau and Boizenburg.

Although work was carried out at a feverish pace in Northeast Bohemia and although foreign craftsmen were brought from Italy in response to the urging and threats by the ruler of the country, the army needed far more than could be manufactured here—and even that was often not of the best quality. Hans de Witte concluded large contracts with the Nurembergers, in particular via his agent Abraham Blommaert. The latter was one of the major depositors of the "Banco Publico" founded in 1621 and through which all payments of more than 200 florins had to be made. It was not least the big orders from Wallenstein which ensured that the bank had an annual turnover of 100,000 to 350,000 florins. When de Witte and Wallenstein disappeared from the scene, these sums fell to about 67,000 florins and later, in 1631, to 15,000.

In the spring of 1625, de Witte established contact with Nuremberg and from there followed what was probably the biggest order for the Thuringian gunsmiths—the complete equipment for seven regiments. Within five weeks and against the immediate payment of an installment of 10,000 florins, the breastplates, muskets, pikes and short-barrelled guns were assembled and sent to Eger. The Suhl contractors had even delivered the goods ahead of schedule. In these deals, the Suhl craftsmen asserted their demand for punctual payment which had led to disagreements with the middlemen and this was also why they sought direct contact with Blommaert.[1]

In general, the officers were disinclined to lead their troops and regiments into wooded mountainous areas but the commanders, whether they wanted to or not, had to have the important production plants in their possession or—if there was a danger that these would fall into the hands of the enemy—destroy them. To ensure the delivery of horseshoes and horseshoe-nails, Imperial troops moved into the Suhl-Schmalkalden district and Wallenstein issued safe-conduct passes for the ironworks in the Harz. In 1626, the troops of Christian of Brunswick destroyed the smelting installations at the Andreasberg, plundered the stores and destroyed the bellows. Kamenschlaken and Altenau continued to supply Tilly with gun-components, grape-shot, spades and petards (cases of explosive for breaking down gates). Plundering and raids also interrupted the activities of the Fischbach ironworks in Hesse which had changed over to the production of ammunition. Time and again, the detachments which attacked it demanded the supply of iron and cannonballs otherwise they threatened to destroy the plant. Scarcely had ironmasters and workers restarted production again in 1639 when, in 1641, everything was destroyed once more—the weir of the millpond pierced, the

[1] Ernstberger, A.: Hans de Witte. Finanzmann Wallensteins, Wiesbaden, 1954

Schmalkalden.

131 Schmalkalden (with its castle) was one of the most important centres of the metal trade in the Empire. Copperplate engraving (17th century). Güstrow Museum

bellows of the hammers slit and the stock of coal used for the camp-fires. In the reconstruction of the ironworks (1643), the lessons of experience were learned and the bellows were constructed in such a manner that they could be rapidly dismantled and taken to safety in the woods. There is historical evidence for the decline of the ironworks in the hard-hit Upper Palatinate and in Baden, too. Of the 36 forges in operation before the war in the latter area, only 13 were still in production in 1647.

In the 1630's, it was the turn of Suhl, the most important war-production centre of Germany, to experience the ravages of war. Plundering by Isolani's Croatians and fire destroyed the town on 16 October 1634. Only a forge belonging to one of the Kletts and a barrel-smithy, a grinding and boring-mill and a house belonging to it survived the flames. Five master-gunsmiths by the name of Klett—Johann Paul the Elder, his three sons and his son-in-law Johann Krech—left Suhl and settled in Salzburg. Those who stayed behind rebuilt their houses and the forges but it was a long time before the manufacture of weapons in Suhl regained its former pre-eminence.

Other highly productive centres for the fabrication of small arms on the edge of the theatre of war in the Netherlands and along the Lower Rhine achieved rapid growth in the course of the national war of liberation of the Dutch against Spain. These were Essen and Solingen. The gunsmiths of Essen, who increased in number from 24 in 1608 to 54 in 1620, worked mainly for the northern provinces and as far as possible on the basis of contracts with the governors of the Netherlands. Weapons had been supplied to Emden, one of the major arsenals of the Netherlands, since 1568. However, others who used guns from Essen included the Spanish regiment "Parma", the troops of the Evangelist Ernst von Mansfeld in Luxemburg and the mercenaries of the archbishop of Cologne. It was about 1620 that the arms production of Essen reached its peak with an annual output of almost 15,000 guns. After this it declined, slowly at first and then more rapidly. In the 1640's, production and export evidently became more stable again and towards the end of the war 1,000 to 1,800 barrels, complete muskets, arquebuses and pistols were exported annually.[1]

[1] Mews, K.: Die Geschichte der Essener Gewehrindustrie, Thesis. Münster, 1909

166

Merchants and businessmen from Cologne also made a profit from the conflagration of war in Germany. Around 1610, there is mention in the records of a large-scale supplier by the name of Vichet. At the end of the 1620's, Anton Frey-Aldenhoven, on the basis of his relations with Hans de Witte, approached Wallenstein with an impressive offer for which a contract, already initialled, had been prepared and bearing the date 29 October 1628. For 110,000 Imperial thalers, he offered supplies which he undertook to deliver by the Frankfort Easter Fair of 1629, for which he required two-thirds of the payment in advance. It was a question of 10,000 breastplates and sets of armour, 6,000 sets of lansquenet equipment (iron helmets, mail collars, backplates, breastplates and pikes with sharp iron fittings), 2,000 muskets with butts of cherry-wood and walnut plus ammunition (12 balls per pound), musket-rests and bandoliers of sealskin, 1,000 bandolier firearms (short muskets) with locks, polished barrels plus ammunition (14 balls per pound), wheel-lock spanners, barrel-scrapers, bandolier belts and hooks and, to end with, 1,000 pairs of pistols. The offer was a serious one since the agent Frey evidently maintained well-established relations with plate-makers and gunsmiths in the Spanish Netherlands, in Trier, Mainz, Cologne and Hesse-Darmstadt, he supplied the troops of the emperor and the League and also those of their foes, including the Elector of Saxony. Frey's project of 1628 was implemented by others and then only incompletely. Nevertheless, it demonstrates to what extent it was possible to exploit the productive force of man for the purposes of war.[1]

The Italian and Central European enterprises with their transactions, profit-rates, concepts and projects were surpassed by Sweden, a country with a population of about 1.5 million people and only a few large towns. It was copper in particular to which this country owed its growing importance. At a time when even a statesman of the format of Cardinal Richelieu had only a vague idea of this state, the Swedish crown was already making vast profits from the export of copper to the whole of Europe, including Spain. It was here that the metal was turned into coins or cannons cast from it with which to proceed against the Protestant powers. A trading company,

132 All the parties engaged in the war obtained weapons from Solingen. Copperplate engraving (17th century). Güstrow Museum

[1] Státní ústřední archiv Praha, F. 67/23 III

167

whose shareholders included members of the aristocracy, senior state officials, merchants and Church institutions, achieved high profits up to the mid-1620's since Sweden possessed almost a monopoly in copper production in Europe.

Between 1626 and 1631, Spain and other countries stopped importing bars of copper from Sweden and the price in Amsterdam fell by 37.5 per cent and in Hamburg by more than 40 per cent. The trading company was hurriedly dissolved in 1627 and the shareholders compensated by the Crown. The latter now began to mint copper coins itself. Already in 1629, more than half of the year's production and in 1632 the entire output of the mine of Falun was taken by the mints. The Crown used the reddish-coloured coins to pay the restless and mutiny-prone regiments in Livonia, Prussia and Poland and the miners. However, entire waggon-loads of bags filled with coins went with the Swedish army into occupied and "allied" areas of Germany so that the low-value money could be put into circulation. However, only the North German territories were flooded with it since the towns and rulers of Central and Upper Germany firmly refused to accept the suspect coinage—memories of the "coin-clipper" inflation of 1621 to 1623 still being fresh.

Even a century later, the most productive copper-mine at Falun was called "Sweden's greatest wonder" by Carl von Linné, the famous scientist. During one of his twelve visits to the mine, Gustavus Adolphus exclaimed: "What king possesses such a palace as this!" With a total adit-length of 3.5 miles and 1,200 workers, the mine of Falun was the largest in Europe.[1]

Contemporaries were also fascinated by the sight of the copper and iron smelting-works. Charles Ogier, the secretary of the French diplomat d'Avaux, expressed his admiration for the great installation at Finspång. Raging currents of water poured into the throbbing, thundering buildings there to drive hammers, boring and grinding mills. Mighty hammers and rollers shaped plates and massive blocks of iron; with deafening noise, men with great hand-held mallets and steel axes worked the rolled material into the shape of musket barrels. The great installations, impressive as they were and operated by the harnessed power of Nature, in Södermanland, Östergotland, in the Mälar-Hjelmare region and in the Uppland ore-region did indeed serve a single purpose—the production of weapons for the "theatre of war" which was extending over a greater and greater area.

For the "Royal Swedish war waged in Germany", Gustavus Adolphus had little need of arms and military equipment of German origin since the natural wealth of Sweden was combined with Dutch business capital and the co-ordinated labour and skill of thousands of master-craftsmen, journeymen and labourers. At the end of the 16th and the beginning of the 17th century, especially after the beginning of Gustavus Adolphus' period of rule, an increasing role was played by specialists in the field of metallurgy coming to Sweden from the Netherlands and Germany such as Anton Monier from Brabant, Siegroth senior and junior from Hesse and Arnhold Toppengiesser of Aachen, once the leading European centre for brass and bronze casting.[2]

The arrival of three hundred Walloon families marked a turning-point in Swedish iron production. This wiry, thickset and blackhaired "smithy folk" with flashing brown eyes supplied not only Tilly with those brave men on the battlefield who con-

[1] Heckscher, E. F.: Sveriges ekonomiska historia från Gustav Vasa, vol. I, Stockholm, 1935; Boëthius, B.: Gruvornas, hyttornas och hamrarnas folk, Stockholm, 1951

[2] Roberts, M.: Gustavus Adolphus. A History of Sweden. 1611—1632, vol. II, London/New York/Toronto, 1958; Peltzer, R. A.: Geschichte der Messingindustrie in Aachen und den Ländern zwischen Maas und Rhein, in: Zeitschrift des Aachener Geschichtsvereins 30/1908

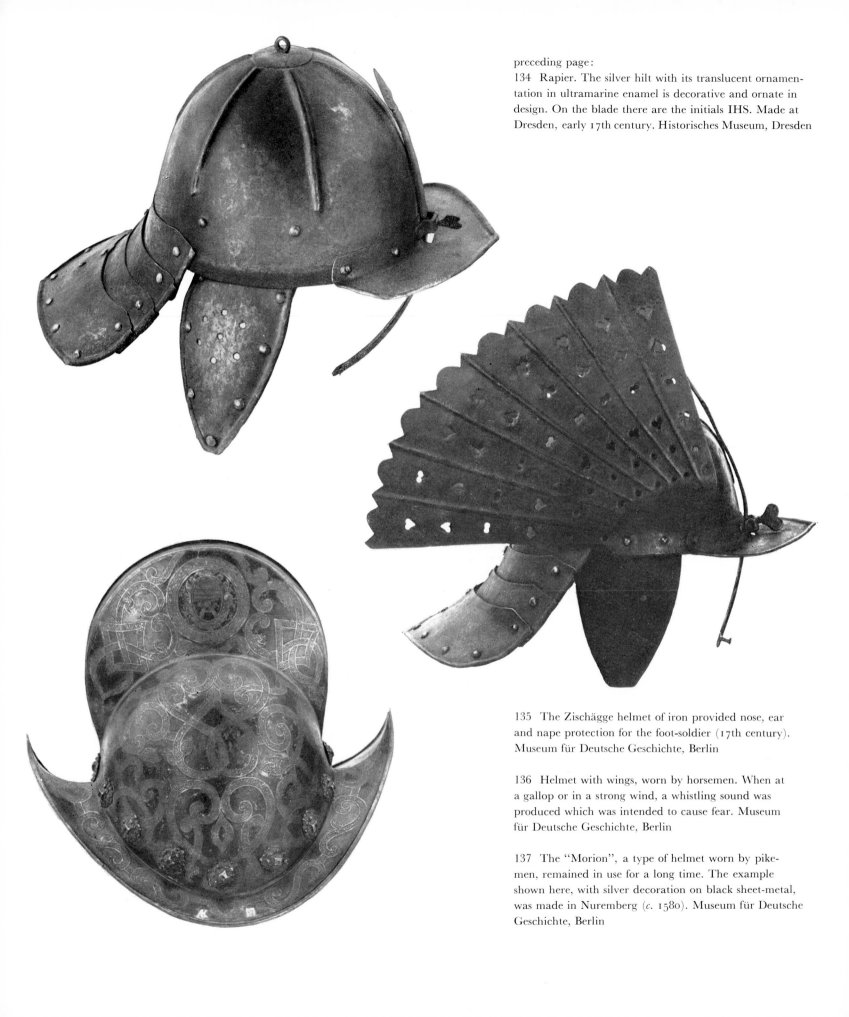

preceding page:
134 Rapier. The silver hilt with its translucent ornamentation in ultramarine enamel is decorative and ornate in design. On the blade there are the initials IHS. Made at Dresden, early 17th century. Historisches Museum, Dresden

135 The Zischägge helmet of iron provided nose, ear and nape protection for the foot-soldier (17th century). Museum für Deutsche Geschichte, Berlin

136 Helmet with wings, worn by horsemen. When at a gallop or in a strong wind, a whistling sound was produced which was intended to cause fear. Museum für Deutsche Geschichte, Berlin

137 The "Morion", a type of helmet worn by pikemen, remained in use for a long time. The example shown here, with silver decoration on black sheet-metal, was made in Nuremberg (c. 1580). Museum für Deutsche Geschichte, Berlin

138 Cuirassier's armour, as worn by the heavy cavalry of Count Pappenheim, a force consequently known as the "Pappenheimers". Museum für Geschichte der Stadt Leipzig

139 Rapier. The iron hilt displays ornamental figures on a black ground: Fortuna, Triton, Nereida and Leda with the Swan. Hilt by Daniel Sadeler, Munich, 1610. Historisches Museum, Dresden

140 Wheel-lock gun with blued iron parts and gilded, oval fittings. Made by the gun-maker Georg Gessler who also worked for Wallenstein. Dresden, 1611. Historisches Museum, Dresden

141 Barrel of one of the light Swedish field-guns with leather jacket, the use of which in battle was one of the innovations in warfare made by Gustavus Adolphus. Kungl. Livrust-kammaren, Stockholm

142 Lifeguard's parade halberd with the coat-of-arms of the Electorate of Saxony (1617), as used by bodyguards and escort personnel. Museum für Deutsche Geschichte, Berlin

143 Service partisan, usually carried by officers as a sign of authority. Museum für Deutsche Geschichte, Berlin

144 Pikeman's armour with breastplate, back-piece and protection for the upper arm. Light in weight and flexible, it gave the foot-soldier a fair measure of protection against thrusting and edged weapons. Staatliche Museen, Heidecks-burg

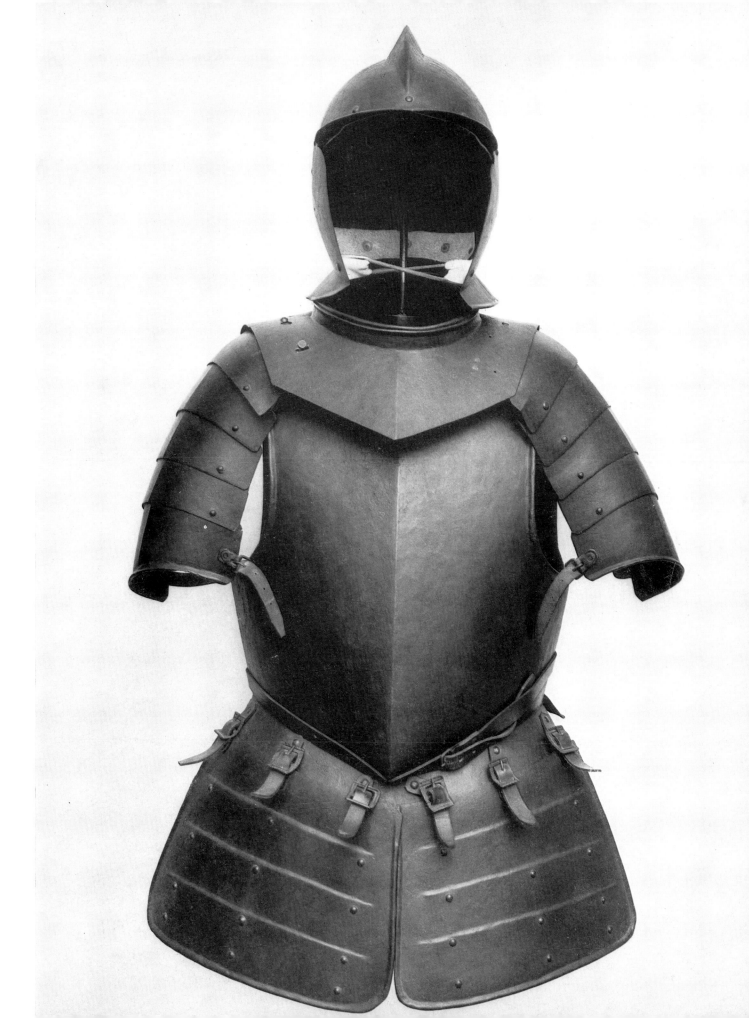

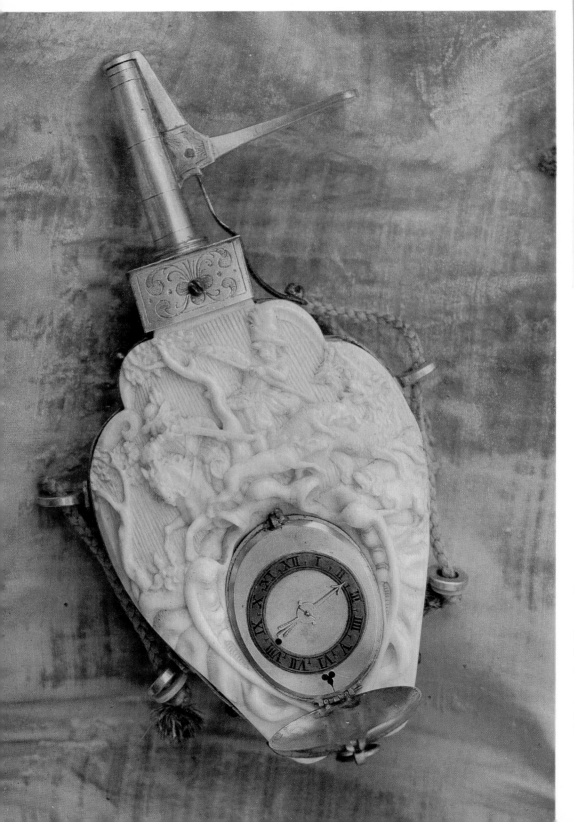

145 Powder-flask of ivory with built-in watch. Made at Augsburg. Early 17th century. Historisches Museum, Dresden

146 Military figures even on table ornaments—here as an artistic detail on a sauce-boat in the form of a ship. Städtische Kunstsammlungen, Augsburg

147 Powder-flask of horn with cords of German origin. 17th century. Historisches Museum, Dresden

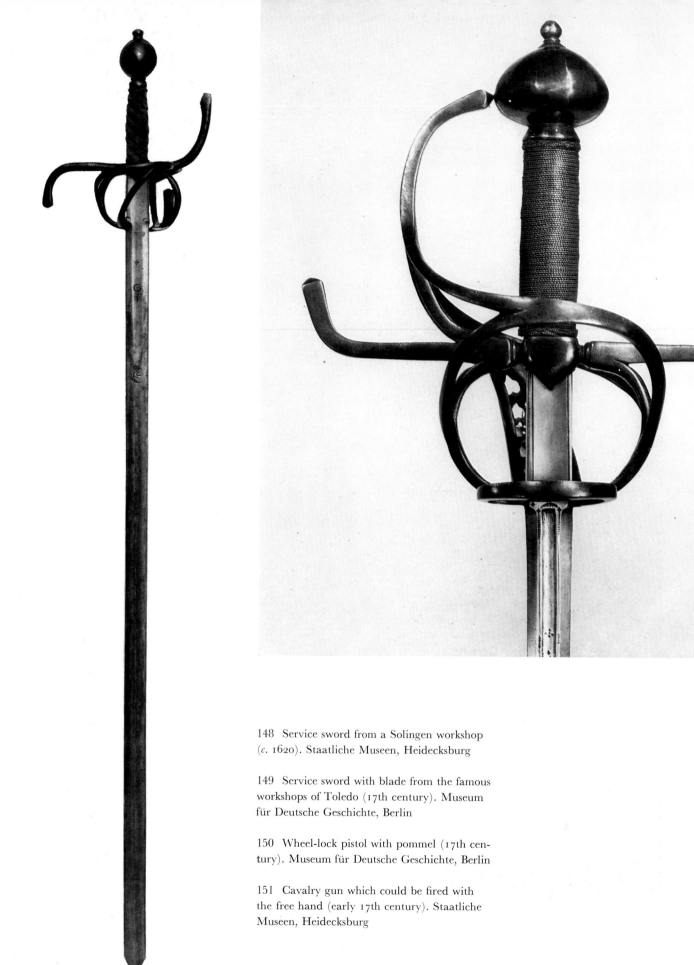

148 Service sword from a Solingen workshop
(*c.* 1620). Staatliche Museen, Heidecksburg

149 Service sword with blade from the famous
workshops of Toledo (17th century). Museum
für Deutsche Geschichte, Berlin

150 Wheel-lock pistol with pommel (17th century). Museum für Deutsche Geschichte, Berlin

151 Cavalry gun which could be fired with
the free hand (early 17th century). Staatliche
Museen, Heidecksburg

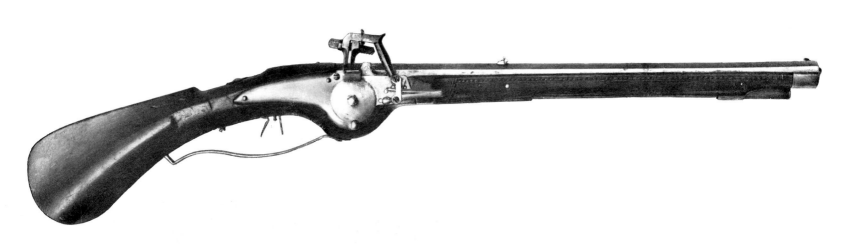

152 The cannon foundry of the Trip family in Södermanland. One of the first "industrial" paintings by Allart (Aldert) van Everdingen. Rijksmuseum, Amsterdam

Johann Carl Zeuchmeister und INGE-
nieur in Nürnberg. Ward Gebern A: 1587. 13 Januarÿ.

S. TRINITATIS
A: MDCXXX.
IN INCL. RATISB.

Wann vor Heerd und vor Altar soll der Erden-Donner spielen
auf die Feind': erfindet Stücke dieser Teutsche Archimed.
Wann der Andacht Feuerpfeil will zu Gott gen Himmel zielen:
Durch des Teutschen Hirams Hände dort ein Bete-Tempel steht.
Schau und ehre dessen Bild: seinen Geist das Werck dir weiset
Jene Witz Eraus dem Kriege und aus Holland hat geholt:
Diese Er vom Vatter erbte, der in ihm noch leben wolt.
Fama, weil Kunst Kunst wird seyn, diesen Sohn und Vatter preiset.

Seinem Geehrten Herrn Schwehr vattern zu   J. Sandrart sculp.   Zu freundschuldigem Ehrendienst hinzu
Ehren überreichet durch Michael Endter.   Anno 1662.   gethan durch Sigmund von Bircken. C.P.

153 This portrait of the Master of the Ordinance and engineer Johann Carl of Nuremberg bears a panegyric poem by the well-known poet Sigmund von Bircken. Carl deserves mention for his modernization of the military equipment and fortifications of the Free City. He laid down a very rare model collection of high artistic quality of weapons and military equipment ("Little Arsenal") which supplies ample evidence of the skill of the metalworkers of Nuremberg. Germanisches Nationalmuseum, Nuremberg

154 Mortar for high-elevation gunnery or for firework projectiles.

155 Gun with oval barrel on gun-carriage.

156 Organ-type gun with 14 barrels arranged in rows, all of which could be fired at the same time. All illustrations are part of the Carl Model Collection, Germanisches Nationalmuseum, Nuremberg

157 Gun-deck of the "Vasa". She was built in 1625 on the orders of Gustavus II Adolphus, set out on her maiden voyage on 10 August 1628 but sank before she had even left the harbour. It was not until April 1961 that the ship could be raised again. The photo shows the starboard side of the lower gun-deck with the gun-carriages. Sjöhistoriska museet, Stockholm

tinued to shoot when they had only stumps of legs to stand on but was also the source of experts in advanced forging and smelting techniques. The necessary working-capital for establishing new plants in the vicinity of the richest ore-veins was provided by great merchants and bankers such as Louis de Geer and Willem de Besche—both Dutchmen—who were pious men, demanding patrons and ice-cold reckoners in a single person. The king gave them the monopoly for the entire arms production of Sweden in 1627.[1]

The contract stipulated that de Geer (de Besche died in 1629) should provide the complete equipment for 15 infantry regiments and 3,000 horsemen but more than this was in fact supplied. Between November 1629 and the end of 1630 alone, the well-trained army intended for the "German war" received 20,000 muskets, 13,670 pikes and 4,700 sets of cavalry equipment. Sweden was even in a position to export hundreds of heavy iron cannon from Finspång and Nyköping. The great armaments enterprise of de Geer, who had his headquarters at Norrköping, included many other factories in addition to the two mentioned.

The development of heavy military equipment, which followed the progress in the art of fortification, was closely interrelated with advances in mathematics and the natural sciences. This is evident from a number of works on military technology, an outstanding example of which—on account of its high theoretical standard—is the *ars magnae artilleriae* of the Polish engineer Kazimierz Siemienowicz who had passed through the *haute école* of the Dutch. The book, which examined the achievements of intensive warfare, was first published by Janssonius at Amsterdam in Latin (1650) and French (1651), then by David Zunner at Frankfort on the Main in 1676 in German and later appeared in English as well. Siemienowicz started by listing those sciences which he had zealously investigated: arithmetic, geometry, mechanics, statics, hydraulics, pneumatics, graphics (technical draughtsmanship), metrics, civil and military architecture and fortifications, optics, natural philosophy and chemistry—and of course also the *nobiliora opificia*, i.e., the graphic arts since many guns, accessory equipment and gunnery measuring and aiming instruments (compass, quadrant, triangle, protractor, square and spirit-level) were masterpieces of the art of metalworking. Siemienowicz concerned himself with a total of 260 books of which 55 per cent dated from Antiquity, only six per cent from the Middle Ages and 39 per cent from the Renaissance (Italian authors in particular). In addition to his direct predecessors such as Adriaen van Roomen, Daniel Speckle, Andrea dell' Aqua, Diego Ufano, Mathias Dögen, Furttenbach, Wallhausen and many others, the author based his work on the mathematical and physical findings of Kepler, Galileo, Geronimo Cardano and Simon Stevin. These and others had introduced decimal fractions, improved trigonometrical tables, derived integral calculus from physical phenomena and had successfully described the movement of solid bodies in mathematical terms. The discovery of the laws of ballistics was primarily derived from firearms which were observed with the greatest interest by scientists on thousands of occasions. To begin with, it only proved possible to clarify the problems of the "external ballistics" — the movement of the missile and the influences acting on its trajectory outside the weapon. Chemistry, which was still in the early stages, was not yet in a position to examine the problem of "gas", to correctly

133 Louis de Geer. Idealized portrait of the great Dutch-Swedish arms-magnate in the simple dress of a Calvinist. Copperplate engraving by Jeremias Falck. Staatliche Graphische Sammlung, Munich

[1] Dahlgren, E. W.: Louis de Geer. 1587—1652. Hans liv och verk, 2 vols., Uppsala, 1923; Murray, J. J.: Amsterdam. In the Age of Rembrandt, London, 1972; Kilbom, K.: Vallonerna. Valloninvandringen stormaktsväldet och den svenska järnhanteringen, Stockholm, 1958

interpret the process of combustion and to clarify the properties of air. And although the secrets of air in particular were unveiled by pioneering discoveries during the period of the war (Guericke, Torricelli, Boyle), it was still a long way to the practical procedure of the master-gunners. The forces propelling the missile were the subject of unceasing conjecture and fantastic combinations but they simply could not be explained.

As well-tried empirical values, which were mostly supported by mathematical and scientific findings at a subsequent date, the art of the gunnery-master took account of the interrelated dependence of the range on the weight of the missile and the charge and on the length and the angle of adjustment of the barrel. Aiming was usually carried out according to tables on sight-positions; for a horizontal point-blank shot, visual judgement was sufficient. This was also the case with the "Göllschuss" which was fired in such a manner that the ball first landed and then rolled into the enemy ranks. For the calculation of the high-angle or "elevation shot", use was made of the quadrant. A 24-pounder cannon, used as a heavy field-gun, had a maximum range of 1,500 metres; its optimum range, when the point of aim coincided with the point of impact, was 600 metres. At this range, a cannon-ball could pierce an oak plank of 80 centimetres in thickness. Fortifications with thick masonry could usually withstand the missiles from such guns and this is why the gates were blown down with petard charges or a gallery driven under the fortress. Pyrotechnics, always closely associated with the artillery for professional reasons, led to the use of missiles carrying explosive or incendiary charges and to the employment of basic rocketry techniques.

In respect of the powder charge for the great variety of guns and hand firearms whose barrels were also cast in alloys of various proportions, the manuals recommended a large number of different mixing-ratios. For heavy weapons, the following proportions were used—more or less: six parts of saltpeter to each two parts of sulphur and charcoal while for lighter weapons the ratio was 75 to 10 to 15. It was known that the finer the granulation of the powder, the higher its power of combustion. Complicated procedures, mostly based on the human senses, were employed to check the quality of the chemical constituents and of the boiled and ground powder-mixture in the finished state.[1]

In view of the increasing numbers of heavy guns used by the artillery, many of the problems of bridge constructions had to be reconsidered since the customary designs in wood could not withstand the strain of exceptional loads. In particular, rapid progress was made in the construction of floating-bridges laid across boats, barrels or rafts which were often built within a few hours by carpenters under the supervision of a "bridge master". Two to ten guns were reckoned for every thousand men, the heaviest field-pieces weighing more than 50 cwt. and needing more than 20 horses to pull them. Heavy battery-guns, which were stationed in siege positions or on the walls of fortresses, weighed twice as much.

The efforts needed for the transportation of such a death-dealing monster and the excitement this caused can easily be imagined and the extent to which the human spirit was tested in the mastery of the new weapons of war, which continued to develop unceasingly and were often of a high artistic level, can likewise be appreciated.

[1] Nowak, T.: Teoretyczna wiedza artylerijska w Polsce w połowie XVII wieku, in: Studia i materiały do historii wojskowości, vol. XII/2, 1966

SCIENCE, POETRY AND ART
IN TIME OF WAR

SCIENCE ON A STONY PATH:
GALILEO,
KEPLER, GUERICKE

If the progress of learning in the Holy Roman Empire were to be measured by the number of new universities founded, the first half of the 17th century may be said to have been an outstanding period. Twelve new universities were established although three of them (Stadthagen, Osnabrück and Kassel) did not survive for very long. Furthermore, when it is considered that the young people of the Empire seeking higher education continued—as had always been the case—to go to the illustrious universities of Italy and the extremely progressive teaching institutions of the Netherlands, especially Leiden (founded 1575), it is difficult to imagine that scholarship was passing through hard times.

Nevertheless, little had survived from its once pre-eminent position in the intellectual life of Europe. During the war, there was a lack of continuity in teaching. Reformed universities such as those at Heidelberg and Marburg, where middle-class Calvinist ideas predominated, were closed for a time and the leading scholars driven away. The increasing uncertainty of life meant that many people decided not to attend a university and some of the students joined the armies so that there was a constant decline in the numbers of students. There is evidence that at most universities there was a deterioration in the arch-evils of German student-life: brawling, endless drinking bouts, shallow foppishness on the aristocratic pattern and the infamous "boarding school" customs (Pennalismus), all of which caused infinite harm to learning attitudes and creativeness.

Quite the opposite was reported from the still young universities in the Netherlands such as Leiden, Groningen and Utrecht where both teaching and learning was a serious business and loose living was despised. Leiden especially was like a magnet for the best brains thirsting for knowledge. Between the year of foundation 1575 and 1600, there was an average annual intake of a hundred new students, about one in ten coming from the Empire. Between 1625 and 1650, an average of about 450 students were immatriculated every year and one in four was German. And they came from all parts of the Empire, apart from those who sought refuge in Königsberg, a Prussian city under Polish sovereignty.[1]

This escape to more peaceful and fertile fields of intellectual life helped to compensate for the loss of the Empire's own contribution in this sphere since outstanding champions of scientific and academic progress who were inspired by the Leiden spirit of genius—such as Martin Opitz, Andreas Gryphius, Otto von Guericke,

Whoever comes from Tübingen without a wife,
From Jena with a healthy body,
From Helmstädt without wounds,
From Leipzig without sores,
From Marburg alive,
Has not studied in all these places.

Saying 1617

[1] Schneppen, H.: Niederländische Universitäten und deutsches Geistesleben. Von der Gründung der Universität Leiden bis ins späte 18. Jahrhundert, Münster, 1960; du Moulin, E.: Geschichte der deutschen Universitäten, Berlin, 1929

Paul Fleming or the jurist David Mevius—returned to their German homeland. The philological-historical schools and circles of the late humanists at Heidelberg, Strasbourg and Hamburg developed in very close contact with Dutch scholars such as Daniel Heinsius, Justus Lipsius and Joseph Justus Scaliger. It was here at Leiden that Hugo Grotius, the great theorist of international law and systematizer of martial law, was active and it was likewise here that the revolutionary doctrine of the omnipotence of reason of René Descartes took root. It was here that the most advanced research in natural science and medicine was established—with a Hortus Botanicus and an observatory—the first at any university; here clinical teaching with a Theatrum Anatonicum was introduced in 1637 and in 1600 an engineering school for military technology and dyke construction was founded. At Middelburg in 1608, the glass-grinders Zacharias Jansen, Hans Lippershey and others invented the telescope which was subsequently copied by Galileo. Kepler enthusiastically called it the "knowledgeable tube, more precious than any sceptre" and supplied a theory for the astronomical telescope which was to henceforth bear his name.

Many hundreds of young students and scholars passed through the Dutch universities in the course of their travels, the *peregrinatio academica*. On their return home to work as teachers, physicians, jurists or men of letters at German universities and grammar schools, they usually came up against the wall of Aristotelian-scholastic book-knowledge and a tangled mass of authoritarian affirmative wisdom without experimental or practical proof. This explains why creative minds found more favourable conditions outside academic teaching—at princely courts and in the great cities as doctors, jurists, advisors or private teachers, although the bread of princely patrons was bitter enough for many of them.[1]

What was the state of medicine, the purpose of which should be to heal the diseases and wounds which afflict people on a greater scale during times of war than on other occasions?[2] Physicians identified symptoms of diseases from the pulse, the temperature of the body and the urine, the latter by means of the observation of the urine or "uromancy". As medicaments, doctors prescribed infusions prepared from medicinal herbs, animal substances such as milk, chicken meat and honey and also crabs' eyes, asses' milk and dirt (even excrements or urine), not forgetting "Theriak", a fraudulent quack-medicine said to heal everything. This "dirt medicine" was especially prevalent during the Thirty Years' War. People put their confidence in magical methods of healing such as the influence of the stars, the "eye" or the "hand" of certain people or magic formulae. Surgeons practised blood-letting on a wide scale and "purged" their patients by applying sorrel, rhubarb and a variety of salves and by administering enemas. The treatment of wounds and the performance of surgical operations was carried out by surgeons, military doctors and barbers of low standing. Among other things, these people couched cataracts, operated on hernias and bladders, amputated limbs and cut out ulcers. The anatomy of the human body was well-known since executions, battle-wounds and the public dissection of bodies provided detailed information. Physiology, on the other hand, lagged far behind and medicine was powerless when confronted with plagues. Lepers were isolated in separate houses and districts and were subject to official supervision. Syphilis, as the *lues ungarica*, was

[1] Reifferscheid, A.: Quellen zur Geschichte des geistigen Lebens in Deutschland während des siebzehnten Jahrhunderts, vol. I: Briefe G. M. Lingelsheims. M. Berneggers und ihrer Freunde, Heilbronn, 1889

[2] Geschichte der Medizin, p. 189ff.

Collegium in Helmstett

brought to Germany at the end of the 16th century by Imperial soldiers and, without
any effective remedy for it, rapidly spread. Bubonic plague, transmitted by contact
with the fleas on rats, was more serious than ever before due to hunger, military movements and the fall in standards of hygiene which prevailed in wartime. According
to a communication of the Medical Faculty at Wittenberg, the official treatment for
it was as follows:[1] The patient was to take pills of random composition, which had no
therapeutic effect and were available from apothecaries in varied price-ranges, was to
stay in bed and sweat for hours on end. It was considered that grated radish, applied
to the soles of the feet, would draw out the heat and poison. It was recommended that
the patient should take plenty of sour food and drink. Rich patients were to swallow
emeralds, sapphires and pearls, prepared with hartshorn but the poor had to be satisfied
with vinegar and sour sorrel-water. For the treatment of the swellings, physicians
prescribed vesicants. The Faculty wrote that some patients also found relief from pul-
verized toads or flies and that it was no mistake, either, to apply young pigeons or hens
until they died. Even whipping the swellings was a treatment which could be used.
To restrict the spread of epidemics, the observance of cleanliness was recommended,
houses were to be smoked out and patients were to be isolated. Slaking of lime was
held to be a disinfectant and vessels filled with water or hot bread were said to draw
out the "poisons". There was little hope for those suffering from a serious disease of
being healed in a hospital since it was the poor who were brought to such places.
Wounded or sick soldiers were usually billeted in private households, who were then
obliged to care for them, or were left to their fate. First-aid was given by army surgeons
or the womenfolk of the soldiers. Trained medical personnel were a rarity in the regimental lists, chaplains being a more common phenomenon since the state of the
soul was considered more important than the health of the body. Guzmán's description
of a hospital is probably not far from the truth: Rooms and beds were filthy and the

[1] Kurtzer Bericht und Ordnung: Wie Män-
niglich in Pestilentz Zeiten sich verhalten
solle ..., durch das Collegium Medicum zu
Wittenberg in Druck gegeben, Wittenberg 1626,
copy in Municipal Archives Stralsund

189

food was often rotten and unhygienically served; the attendants and the superintendent had the reputation of being rapacious, heartless and brutal.[1] However, parallel with this state of affairs, there was a popular medicine which was practised by women and was not ineffective, being based on the healing effect of fresh air and a healthy way of life and on vegetable and animal substances. Books about medicinal herbs were printed and there were a few trained physicians, such as Hippolytus Guarinonius in Hall/Tyrol, who, in their practices and in publications, attacked the superstitions and quackery which were so prevalent in wartime and among the soldiery. This popular physician wrote that not only strict cleanliness and fresh air promoted the health and well-being of human beings but also the traditional games and processions, merriment, storytelling and edifying legends.[2]

In this fashion and in many other ways, the spark of realistic human knowledge continued to glow although the social conditions and the misery of war which affected many areas were less conducive to pioneering achievements of learning than in the Netherlands, England, France or Italy. Nevertheless, the influential and enduring traditions of a greater age, such as the works of Paracelsus or Georgius Agricola, still lived on. New findings were made and recorded, such as those by the physician and chemist Johann Rudolf Glauber, known as the "Master of the Art of Distillation", who died in Amsterdam, concerning the manufacture of saltpeter, a vital war material, and glass and wood-vinegar. In addition to several metallic compounds of chlorine, he discovered sodium sulphate, popularly known as "Glauber's salt".[3]

German scholars were noted for their great zeal in collecting information and in recording descriptions and this was not least reflected in an increasing number of publications in the fields of astronomy, geography, botany, zoology and anatomy. Intellects with universal interests such as Mathias Bernegger in Strasbourg, Lingelsheim and Janus Gruter (or Jan de Gruytere) at Heidelberg continued the humanist tradition of classical philology along Dutch lines or, like Kepler's teacher Michael Maestlin and Wilhelm Schickhard in Tübingen and the Jesuit Christoph Scheiner, turned to mathematics, physics and astronomy. At the same time, through a series of original designs, they improved the technical instruments for the observation and measurement of Nature.

It was the merit of this circle of scholars that they made their contribution to the struggle for the acceptance of the Copernican concept of the world. This struggle, which passed through a bitter and dramatic phase during the period immediately before and at the beginning of the "Great War", was fought without scientific martyrdom in Germany, with the exception of Kepler's harsh fate.[4]

For his open support for Copernicus in 1616, the great Galileo received a warning from the Roman Inquisition. The theological report which formed the basis for this measure also led to the passing of a decree on 5 March of the same year condemning "that false Pythagorean doctrine (of Copernicus) of the movement of the Earth and the fixed nature of the Sun which practically contradicts the Holy Scriptures". This exerted extreme moral pressure on all of those who subscribed to this theory and even exposed them to mortal danger. The decree was published at numerous universities and was a nightmare for science and learning.[5]

[1] Der Landstörtzer Gusman von Alfarache oder Picaro genannt ... First German edition by Aegidius Albertinus 1613, 2nd edition 1631, p. 147f., ibid.

[2] Schreiber, G. W.: Hippolytus Guarinonius. Ein Vorkämpfer moderner Hygiene und seine Beziehungen zum Spitalwesen des 17. Jahrhunderts, Thesis. Munich, 1946

[3] Glauber, J. R.: Furni novi philosophici/ Oder Beschreibung einer New-erfundenen Destillir-Kunst ..., Amsterdam, 1650, copy in Municipal Archives Stralsund; Gugel, K. F.: Johann Rudolf Glauber 1604—1670. Leben und Werk, Mainfränkische Hefte 22/1955

[4] Przypkowski, T.: Dzieje myśli kopernikowskiej, Warsaw, 1972

[5] Schmutzer, E./Schütz, W.: Galileo Galilei, 2nd edition, Leipzig, 1976; Hemleben, J.: Galilei, Hamburg, 1970

The first part of Kepler's *Epitomes astronomiae copernicanae* (Outline of Copernican Astronomy) in seven volumes was also placed on the index of forbidden books immediately after its publication (1618). At the same time as Kepler was working on his popular manual, Galileo was also working on his *Dialogo*, a work which was intended to propagate the doctrine of Copernicus among the educated circles of Italy. In 1632, a Papal instruction ordered the publishers at Florence to stop selling the book, which was printed there, but most of the copies had already been distributed. After the Sanctum Officium had decided in September 1632 to arraign Galileo before the Tribunal, the seventy-year old scholar, who was in ill-health, set out on the fatiguing journey to Rome in the winter of 1633 and recanted, on his knees before ten judges in cardinals' robes, on 22 June 1634—at the same spot where Giordano Bruno heard his death-sentence in 1600. The pope changed the sentence of imprisonment to one of banishment and the *Dialogo* was placed on the index. Nevertheless, from his place of exile near Florence, Galileo succeeded in sending a copy in secret to a friend in Paris.

The translation of the *Dialogo* from Italian into Latin, the international language of science, was undertaken by members of that same circle of scholars at Strasbourg, Heidelberg and Tübingen to which reference has already been made: Bernegger, Lingelsheim and Schickhard. The book was published in 1635 by the famous publishing house of Elzevier at Leiden. In this manner, the work of Galileo was saved for the world and the revolutionary doctrine of Copernicus was propagated without further delay. Scholars in Germany were spared such profound humiliation as that inflicted on the aged Galileo; the arm of the Roman Officium did not reach so far as this and certainly not into the Protestant territories. Nevertheless, the condemnation of the Florentine scholar was a severe shock and all the opponents of the heliocentric planetary system, whatever their religious persuasion, were encouraged in their struggle against truth and scientific knowledge.

The greatest witness to the fact that official scholastic activities at the universities of the Empire suffered under the burdensome influence of theology which, in turn, was split by abstruse quibbles, quarrelsomeness aggravated by the state of war and by violent tirades (known as "ringing the sow-bell"), is Johannes Kepler, a man whose scientific achievements equalled those of Galileo[1]. Just as the latter was exposed to merciless moral pressure and to the punitive justice of the Catholic Church in particular, Kepler suffered from the castigations of feudal society and of the war waged in Germany for religious pretexts: expulsion and enmity for religious motives, material hardship and social uncertainty, royal service reluctantly rendered, infant mortality, the witch-hunting of his mother; plundering by the soldiery and the pest were the only things which he escaped. In contrast to Galileo, who made the Copernican planetary system a subject for discussion, Kepler regarded this view of the world as a definite fact. A drawing produced by him when he was twenty-two years of age (1593) is evidence that he fully subscribed to Copernican theory during the time he was at Tübingen.

In 1594, Kepler accepted a post at the well-equipped Evangelical university at Graz, the intellectual centre of Styrian Protestantism, where, for the most part, he

159 Galileo Galilei, physicist, mathematician and astronomer. Engraving by Francesco Allegrini from a drawing by Giuseppe Zocchi.

[1] Hoppe, J.: Johannes Kepler, Leipzig, 1975; Caspar, M.: Kopernikus und Kepler, Munich/Berlin, 1943; Gerlach, W.: Kepler und die "Kopernikanische Wende", in: Kepler-Festschrift, Regensburg, 1971; List, M.: Kepler und die Gegenreformation, in: ibid; numerous aspects of Kepler's life and views are evident in his letters in: Johannes Kepler. Gesammelte Werke, vol. XVIII: letters 1620—1630, ed. by M. Caspar, Munich, 1959

instructed the sons of the nobility in opposition to the ruler of the country. He taught there as "Mathematum Professor" until Archduke Ferdinand eliminated Protestantism by a forcible re-Catholicization. "Heretical" books were brought to Graz town-hall by the cartload and burnt, the schools were closed and the teachers and preachers expelled.

Kepler was already well-known from an original work dealing with the solar system in a speculative form. This publication had been favourably received not only by Galileo but also by the Danish nobleman Tycho Brahe, the greatest authority on astronomy of the time. The latter invited him to Prague to carry out his extensive programme of observations with the aid of what was probably a unique collection of astronomical instruments. However, this promising collaboration lasted only a few months since Brahe died on 24 October 1601. Kepler received an appointment as "Imperial mathematician" with an annual salary of 500 florins from Rudolf II who took an interest in many subjects, including astrology. He administered the inestimable legacy of observation records left by Brahe, evaluating them with inexhaustible scientific zeal and arriving at great new findings. Although Kepler noted "a manifold dissonance in human matters", he was not hindered by religious intolerance in his work on optics and on the *Astronomia Nova*, even though the Imperial chamber of accounts paid very irregularly. The book was published in 1609 by Vögelin at Heidelberg, substantiated the concept of a uniform physical system for the Earth and the Heavens, for the investigation of which only mathematical methods had been regarded as valid up till that time, and set out the "celestial mechanics" which led to Isaac Newton's discoveries. The book contains the first two laws of motion of the planets, the formulation of which in the words and in mathematical symbols is still valid today. The third law followed in the *Harmonices mundi* or *World harmonies* which was completed at the end of May 1618. It was printed at Linz where Kepler had settled in May 1612 as regional mathematician of the Estates of Upper Austria.

In the book *Mysterium cosmographicum*, which he wrote while still a young man, and the *Harmonices mundi*, Kepler develops an imaginative picture of an ordered and logically arranged universe: a *musica coelestis*, which is accessible not only for the ear but also for the spirit. Since, like all his contemporaries, he had no insight into the laws of motion of human society and because he abhorred any unjust and bloody power, he sought the harmony he longed for in the cosmos which he understood better than the happenings on Earth. Kepler dedicated his "Harmonices" to King James I of England who, he hoped, would re-unite the hostile religions and establish peace. However, reality was far removed from such pious aspirations. Kepler had witnessed the excesses of the "Passauer Kriegsvolk" in Prague resulting from the "Brothers' Quarrel" between the Hapsburgs and he noted with increasing distress the gathering of the clouds of war in the heart of Central Europe.

His years at Linz (1612—1626) were far busier than those spent in Prague. His working conditions were not unfavourable: there were well-equipped libraries, the markets at Linz offered a good range of books and, with Imperial assistance, the printer Hans Planck of Erfurt was persuaded to settle there. Kepler worked unceasingly on

the works already mentioned and on the *Ephemerides* (the calculation of the future positions of the celestial bodies), produced calendars and predictions to support his numerous family, continued the "Rudolphine tables" of Brahe and drew up logarithmic tables based on the work of the Scotsman John Neper and his friend Jobst Bürgi, an instrument-maker and mathematician of Kassel. However, while he toiled at his calculations, often until far into the night, and carried out an almost incredible amount of work, he received serious setbacks. Narrow-minded and fanatical theologians from his Swabian homeland excluded him from Communion in 1612. For Kepler, who had an open mind in religious matters, this meant social degradation and isolation under the conditions of the time, especially for his wife and children. In 1616, he received the news that his mother had been accused of witchcraft. By the time that Kepler, as an Imperial official, finally succeeded in his hard struggle to free his seventy-four year old mother from the claws of the judges, jailers and torturers, she was at the end of her strength and died in 1622.

It was during these years that the Kepler family in Linz was directly affected by the horror of the war in its initial stages. The mercenaries of the Duke of Bavaria moved into the town in July 1620 and persecuted its Protestant inhabitants. Kepler took his wife and children to safety in Regensburg. It must have been with profound sorrow that he heard the news, in the summer of 1621, of the execution of the "rebels" in Prague since he knew and esteemed some of them. Since the Imperial Treasury had great difficulty in financing the pomp and circumstance of the court and the costly war, there was nothing left for the emperor's mathematician and his work. The salary he was owed had already risen to 6,000 florins when he was instructed to approach the treasuries of some of the Free Cities of the Empire and he himself travelled to Vienna, Nuremberg and some of the Swabian cities in 1624/25. At least, he was given 2,000 florins in Kempten and Memmingen since at that time the war had not yet reached that far.

In the meantime, Bavarian military rule in the "Land ob der Enns" had become intolerable. Following the decree on religion of October 1625, schools and churches were closed, the priests expelled and all Protestants threatened with a similar fate. For the time being, Kepler was protected by his official status and his work on the "Rudolphine tables". At the end of June 1626, there then began the fourteen-week siege of the town by the rebellious peasants of Upper Austria. A fire in Planck's printing-house destroyed the "tables" which had been set up for printing. When the victorious Imperial troops forced back the peasants and relieved Linz, the persecution of all non-Catholics became worse. For Kepler, the town had become an alien and uncertain place. In 1626, he moved to Regensburg and travelled to Ulm where he had the "Rudolphine tables" printed under his personal supervision and at his own expense. Kepler took a completed copy with him to Prague where his subsequent destiny was to be determined. Ferdinand II graciously accepted the "tables" and arranged for the payment of a gratuity of 2,000 florins and the reimbursement of the printing costs.

Kepler was instructed to apply to Wallenstein for the payment of the salary-backlog still outstanding but the immensely rich and all-powerful general and prince of the Empire did not meet his obligation. The latter, in the interests of his reputation and

160 Title-plate of Kepler's "Rudolphine Tables". It symbolizes the fact that the "Tables" are based on the work of Copernicus and Tycho de Brahe as well as on the knowledge of scholars of Antiquity. Forschungsbibliothek Gotha

since he had a craze for astrology, offered the scholar, whose name was known throughout Europe, a home and research facilities in his residence of Sagan and arranged for him to be given a professorship at Rostock University in Mecklenburg. Kepler, however, stubbornly insisted on the payment of the salary he was still owed and resolved—what a mistake!—to urge the electors assembled at Regensburg to recognize his claims. He set out on the long and difficult journey in October but he was not allowed to enter and speak since he was in the service of Wallenstein, who was out of favour. In his disillusioned and exhausted state and weak as he already was, a feverish chill meant the end for Kepler, this restless spirit. He died on 15 November 1630: "While the vultures of the Reichstag at Regensburg quarrelled over their prey, a king died of a broken heart in the midst of them, unnoticed."[1] A great number of princes and dignitaries followed his coffin since they were unable to deny this dauntless and honest man, this great scholar, the formal token of respect since they were dwarfed by his immortal achievements.

As it was, enmity and war demonstrated their superiority even in respect of the mortal remains of Kepler: his body could be buried only outside the walls of the town since it was under Catholic jurisdiction and the cemetery there was devastated by Swedish mercenaries in 1633. His tombstone and grave could not be identified afterwards. By a circuitous route, Kepler's scientific papers passed via his son Ludwig, the astronomer Jan Hevelius of Danzig and the well-known German mathematician Leonhard Euler into the possession of the Academy of Sciences at St. Petersburg. The manuscripts are now among the most precious treasures at the Observatory of Pulkovo.[2]

A second great achievement in the field of the exact sciences was the work of Otto Guericke, the son of a Magdeburg patrician, who was raised to the nobility in 1666 as Otto von Guericke. Despite the established assertions that space was finite and filled with matter, Guericke was able to prove experimentally and conclude philosophically that the cosmos was infinite and void and that time and place are "not at all real as such" but dependent on matter. In his *Experimenta Nova (ut vocantur) Magdeburgica de vacuo spatio* which he completed in 1663 and which was published by Janssonius at Amsterdam in 1672, he aggressively confirmed his advocacy of the heliocentric astronomical system. After years of amateur experimentation, he invented the air-pump (1650) and succeeded in demonstrating not only a vacuum but also the pressure of the air. He had to share other inventions, such as the barometer, manometer and the electric machine, with the Italian Evangelista Torricelli and the Englishman Robert Boyle.[3]

News about his activities in his house at Magdeburg and the brilliantly successful large-scale demonstration with the "Magdeburg hemispheres" before the princes who had assembled in Regensburg for the Reichstag in 1654 prove that Guericke had enthusiastically continued his experiments even in the last years of the war. Up to this time, his career—like that of Kepler—reflected the hardships and problems of the time and the stoney nature of the path that led to scientific progress. After law studies in Leipzig, Helmstedt and Jena, he went to Leiden—by reason of the war— to acquire knowledge of fortifications and civil engineering and to study the natural

[1] Huch, R.: Der Dreissigjährige Krieg II, p. 342

[2] Seidemann, A.: Johannes Hevelius, Zittau, 1864

[3] Kauffeld, A.: Otto von Guericke, Jena/ Leipzig, 1954; Schiebold, E.: Otto von Guericke als Ingenieur und Physiker, in: Festschrift zum 10jährigen Bestehen der Technischen Hochschule "Otto von Guericke" Magdeburg, Magdeburg, 1963; Guericke, Otto von: Philosophisches über den leeren Raum, ed. by A. Kauffeld, Berlin, 1968

sciences. An educational journey to France and England extended the intellectual horizon of the young man and the foundations were laid for the discoveries which he made a quarter of a century later. In the meantime, however, Guericke, as a citizen of the mighty and populous city on the Elbe known as the "eye of Germany", had to concern himself with the urgent problems of practical politics since in the mid-1620's the war was already affecting daily life there to a noticeable extent. Imperial regiments operated within the economic area supplying or served by the city, disrupted the supply of provisions and the corn trade and demanded war-taxes.

In the city, the urgency of the situation in 1630 aggravated the contradiction between the patrician council on the one hand and the townsfolk, led by the merchants and guildsmen, on the other. The old council was removed and a new one of which Guericke was also a member—put in its place. At the same time, the townsfolk established a body with a hundred members to give themselves a say in the running of the city and set up a college of 18 men to control the council. The anger of the unsettled citizens again reached a climax when it became evident in 1631 that the council was prepared to negotiate with Tilly, the general of the Imperial troops and the League, who was besieging the city with his troops and shelling it. The majority of the townsfolk was determined to fight for life and liberty, especially since the King of Sweden had sent an experienced city-commandant, Colonel Falkenberg, and promised to send rapid and certain relief. This did not materialize and the soldiery, demoralized by the long siege and the prospect of rich booty, stormed the city on the 10th of May and supplied the horrified world with what was probably the best-known example of that time of inhuman vengeance. Otto von Guericke experienced all this at first hand and was one of the few citizens who, by resolute action, escaped with his life. Some 20,000 inhabitants lost their lives, either at the hands of the enraged mercenaries or in the fire-storm which turned the city into a smouldering heap of ruins in which the only buildings still standing were the cathedral and a few other stone structures.

The counsellor Guericke fled to Schönebeck on the Elbe, entered Swedish service as the chief engineer of Erfurt and, after the victorious campaign of the Swedes, returned to his home-town in 1632. Constructional experts were urgently needed and Guericke drafted a bold plan to turn the area of rubble into a quite new city of modern architectural design and layout. The bridge across the Elbe was certainly rebuilt under the personal supervision of the young engineer but money for the other projects was not to be had within the hard-hit city nor was it available from the Swedes or the Saxon occupation-authorities (after 1635). The city consequently re-emerged house by house on the basis of its own resources; at the same time, the payments demanded by the military had to be met. One who provided hope and good advice was the tireless Guericke who was therefore given municipal positions and performed diplomatic missions. In 1646, he travelled to Osnabrück for the peace negotiations to fight for a hopeless cause—as he subsequently did before the Reichstag and the emperor. This cause was the sovereignty of Magdeburg as a city-state. The city had no chance of achieving this status since it was encircled by land-hungry potentates searching for an opportunity of acquiring the bishopric and the city. It ultimately went to Brandenburg.

With the cruel May night of 1631 still vividly in his mind's eye, Guericke at Erfurt wrote a manuscript in the same year about the siege and destruction of Magdeburg. It is one of the most informative sources about the war since the author not only communicates to the reader his horror at the inhumanity of the city's tormentors and his profound sympathy for the unfortunates (which is amply confirmed by other sources, too) but also, with his scientifically trained mind and eye, conveys a realistic analysis of the socio-economic side of this sinister event so that conclusions can be drawn for the plundering of every other city.[1]

We learn that poor artisans, day-labourers, servants, journeymen and "boys" (apprentices) and mercenaries that had been in the service of the Swedes or the city were obliged to carry the booty for the plundering victors or joined their ranks— since the poor people had no assets and no prosperous bails from whom money could be extorted by violence, threats or torture. Defenceless unmarried women were raped by the brutal soldiers and many—especially the town whores—were kept in the camp as concubines and servants. It was admittedly a "wondrous" thing for Guericke that there were "honourable" and "honest" soldiers who freed the women who had been captured but he only mentions them for the sake of truth.

Guericke also reports that the Imperial artillery general Baron von Schönberg had "all the frying pans, bells and other copper vessels" collected from houses and burnt-out buildings and guarded as his personal booty. The soldiers, in turn, zealously sought iron stoves, jugs, basins and lamps of brass, pewter vessels or melted-down pieces of these metals so that they could use them for trading. Guericke states that this trade was carried out by inhabitants of Magdeburg, Elbe boatmen and merchants. The metal articles acquired or cheaply purchased by soldiers was surreptitiously brought to Hamburg where they were disposed of at a low price. In the opinion of Guericke, many "became much richer from this than before". Easily handled plunder such as jewels, ornaments and luxury tableware, fine clothes, blankets, lace of gold and silver thread, linen and all sorts of small domestic articles were bought up cheaply by sutlers who hurried to the scene and subsequently sold their goods to customers throughout the bishopric of Magdeburg and in the districts of Anhalt and Brunswick.

There is no trace of religious prejudice in Guericke's report nor is there any word suggesting that Tilly or Falkenberg deliberately had the city set on fire. His cool eye for that which was within reach and real marks him as a middle-class type who did not scorn the advantages of princely favour either. The wealthy patrician ran a brewery, leased agricultural land, argued with the council about the pecuniary remuneration for his diplomatic missions. Finally, when peace in the Empire was near, he energetically endeavoured to promote it in his function as a diplomat but devoted himself more and more frequently to his technical and scientific experimentation which, to begin with, seemed to be little more than an amusement. To pass the time and for convenience, princely gentlemen took with them on their journeys all sorts of unnecessary things, including astrological apparatus. In Guericke's luggage, there were always a few well-packed experimental devices and vessels of metal or glass. This alert and far-seeing man obviously obtained a great deal of pleasure from handling these familiar and ingenious objects and they helped him forget the unpleasant feeling that

[1] Guericke, O. von: Die Belagerung, Eroberung und Zerstörung Magdeburgs, ed. by F. W. Hoffmann, Magdeburg, 1860; Geschichte der Stadt Magdeburg, ed. by a team of authors (headed by G. Asmus), Magdeburg, 1975

he, in the midst of the discouraging and confusing conditions in the Empire, was unable to make a significant and useful contribution, despite his never-ending efforts. The question remains as to whether the war and the hopeless Imperial policy diverted him from his research activities or whether Guericke, already nearly fifty years old, pursued these activities even more zealously as a distraction from the war.

Despite the magnitude of Kepler's and Guericke's contribution to the understanding of natural science and to the eclipse of the narrow Aristotelian concept of the universe with the Earth at the centre, the boldest philosophical conclusions were drawn by scholars from the countries of Europe which led in the socio-historical sphere: Bruno, Descartes and finally Spinoza, that ignored and ostracized thinker who equated Nature with God ("deus sive natura") and asserted that the world had no external cause but was a "causa sui"—the cause of itself.[1]

THE WAR,
THE HOMELAND
AND THE ART
OF POETRY

Within the German-speaking area, the efforts of a number of poets, who—like the *Sprachgesellschaften* (language societies) —advocated the creation of a German national literature which was mature in all its genres—were directed towards the development and shaping of the speech of the ordinary people as a literary language. They became aware of the socially stimulating force which inspired poetry in a national language in the course of their travels and studies and in reading the great works of the national literature of Holland, Spain, France, Italy, England and Poland. The political side of the struggle for an equivalent literature in Germany, too was always furthered by the circumstance that the class-language of the feudal upper class with its courtly traditions was French while that of the scholars was Latin—which was often alien to the ordinary people. The young generation of poets of the first half of the 17th century, who were remarkably unanimous in their views, also had to fight for social recognition since the powerful patrons required verses of a panegyric and rapturous style from rhymesters with the status of servants, not from self-assured literary personalities conscious of their dignity and independent in their ideas.

The new bourgeois class with its capitalist economy had not developed to the same extent in Germany as in the Netherlands and in England and thus the seeking and inquiring poets were lacking the social base which could support them. Most of them certainly came from the background of the urban middle class but it was at princely courts that they earned their living as teachers or clerics. Their poetry was concerned with such subjects as war and peace and their native land, it sought refuge in religion

[1] Istorija filosofii, Moscow, 1957, German: Geschichte der Philosophie, vol. I, Berlin, 1959, Vth chapter

The Poets

*Even the lightest
cannot jump over his own shadow.
But poets
can jump over their death.*

Friedrich von Logau

[1] Geschichte der deutschen Literatur 5; team of authors (headed by W. Schmidt): Geschichte der deutschen Sprache, Berlin, 1969; Żygulski, Z./Szyrocki, M.: Geschichte der deutschen Literatur, 2nd vol., 2nd edition, Warsaw/Wrocław, 1972

[2] Szyrocki, M./Żygulski, Z.: Silesiaca. Wybór z dzieł pisarzy śląsko-niemieckich XVII wieku, Warsaw, 1957; Szyrocki, M.: Martin Opitz, Berlin, 1956; "Aristarch" in: Martin Opitz. Gesammelte Werke. Kritische Ausgabe, ed. by G. Schulze-Behrend, vol. I, Stuttgart, 1968

and introspection, stressed the frailty and vanity of human existence—and could still not escape the restlessness, the doubt and the painful quest for a positive answer to the fundamental questions of their time. The poets did not pass every test with brilliance and only a few of their works survived for more than a century. It would seem that the zealously inquiring poets of only average talent who took antique and foreign works as their models represented a transitional period in the history of German literature which was conditioned by their period and by the war.[1]

The most celebrated poet of this time, Martin Opitz, came from a prosperous bourgeois family in the little Silesian town of Bunzlau. In the schools at Breslau and Beuthen attended by Opitz, there circulated the heady ideas of the Arians active in Poland which kept the minds of the young sons of the bourgeoisie open to all kinds of explosive influences. The writings of Daniel Heinsius, who wrote in Dutch and called the language of his people the "princess of all languages", was well-known to the educated circles of the Silesian towns. This can be the only explanation of how Opitz at the age of twenty, in the little town of Beuthen far removed from the cultural centres, came to compose that text which contained a revolutionary programme for German-language literature—the *Aristarchus sive de contemptu linguae Teutonicae* ("Aristarchus or the contempt of the German language"). The young man, who also composed verses himself, passionately appealed to his readers to cultivate the "delightful", "fine" and "honourable" German language so that they could pass on to following generations "the correct way of speaking which your parents handed down to you". Seven years later, Opitz wrote in only five days a theoretical treatise on the art of writing German poetry—the *Buch von der deutschen Poeterey* ("Book on how to write German Poetry") (1624) which for more than a century represented a guideline to poetry-writing in the German-language area.[2]

The whole of his subsequent life was full of unrest and Opitz dedicated his labour to the task he had set himself although he was unable to find social security. He lived in a continuous state of tension—not unusual for a literary innovator. Nevertheless, his unrest is largely the wandering of a man under pressure, under attack, who was obliged time and again to accept the constraints of an oppressive and restrictive order of society which furthermore, during Opitz's lifetime, was passing through a period shaken by war.

In 1619, the young poet stayed at Heidelberg, the capital of the Calvinist Elector of the Palatinate and actual King of Bohemia. The climate there was explosive and highly political since the Elector Frederick was regarded as a rebel against the emperor and the Empire and was expelled by force of arms. Opitz, who had openly spoken out against the Spanish Imperial intervention, departed from Heidelberg in 1620 and moved to Leiden, the stronghold of progressive thinking in the Europe of the time. However, in that same year he travelled via Friesland to Denmark where he was patronized for some time by the son of the king. It was here—still under the impact of his experiences in the Palatinate—that he wrote in the winter of 1620/21 in Jutland his greatest epic poem—the *Trostgedichte In Widerwertigkeit Dess Krieges* ("Poem of Consolation in the Adversity of the War"). In Alexandrine metre, Opitz describes the misery and horror which characterized the Thirty Years' War even in its initial phase:

"The trees stand no more/the gardens are desolate;
The sickle and the plough are now a cold sharp blade."

The war in its religious disguise seemed senseless to the young poet since "force makes no-one pious, makes not a single Christian".[1]

But he does not condemn every war and he even draws attention to the example of the Netherlands, where the struggle for freedom produced a flourishing country, as one worth following. On account of its anti-Imperial tenor, it was only in 1633 that the author dared to publish the *Trostgedicht* but it remained horrifyingly topical.

In 1622, Opitz accepted a position at the classical grammar school in Gyula-Fehérvár, which had been founded by the Reformist Prince Béthlén Gábor. In addition to his teaching work, the Silesian poet worked on an historical book and the merry poem "Zlatna" (named after a mine), a semi-didactic, semi-descriptive poem, the first in the German language to portray the habits and customs of the Rumanian people. It is almost like a confession when Opitz writes: "There is many a drop of noble blood in small peasant-cottages . . ."

The untiring advocate for the renewal of German poetry, for the reconciliation of the religious adversaries, could not stay away from his Silesian homeland and the German theatre of war for very long. In 1626, as a Protestant, Opitz entered the service of the president of the Chamber of Silesia, the Catholic Burgrave Karl Hannibal von Dohna, who ruled the territory in the name of the emperor and gradually restored Catholicism. Imperial dragoons also marched into Opitz's birthplace, causing his father to leave Bunzlau and seek refuge in nearby Poland. Although honoured with the poet laureate title by the emperor and raised to the nobility, Opitz did not remain in the Imperial camp after the death of Dohna but sought political and diplomatic employment at the court of the liberal Piast dukes of Liegnitz and Brieg where he was ultimately entrusted with a variety of commissions as an informer and negotiator with the Swedes on behalf of the Polish king Władysław IV. The latter made Opitz his court historiographer and secretary. In Poland, the poet did indeed find a calmer place to work and many patrons and friends. In 1636, at Torun, he completed the translation of *Antigone* by Sophocles, once again creating a model for dramatic poetry in the German language. At the same time, the celebrated poet maintained close contacts with influential Polish personalities and with groups from Bohemia who had sought refuge in Poland for religious reasons. The latter included Comenius who had found shelter at Leszno. Opitz met with an enthusiastic reception on visiting Königsberg (1638) and Simon Dach and Heinrich Albert dedicated a solemn cantata to him, this being performed with the assistance of students from the university. In 1639, the tireless Opitz died from the pest in Danzig, where bourgeois poetry had found a home-stead.

As with many of his contemporaries who helped to hew a path for the edifying cause of moral and intellectual progress, national or even provincial narrowness of mind was something which was alien to Opitz. To promote the development of German poetry and of German as a literary language, he concerned himself with the literature of many countries of Europe and of Antiquity as well. It is the merit of Opitz that in

161 Martin Opitz. Copperplate engraving by a contemporary. Biblioteka Gdańska

[1] Opitz: Gesammelte Werke I, p. 187ff.

199

an age of urgency he represented the driving force and central pole of a revolutionary literary programme. There is much in the work and life of Opitz which indicates that he favoured the idea of a centrally governed state in which religion played no part in political affairs—a reaction to the endless religious quarrels in Germany whose future seemed threatened in every respect by the long-drawn-out war. The shadow which appears unexpectedly in many of his lyric poems with a bright and merry content is evidence of a more profound aspect, as in the "Abendlied" by Opitz:[1]

> "Schöne glänzt der Mondenschein
> Und die güldnen Sternelein,
> Froh ist alles weit und breit,
> Ich nur bin in Traurigkeit."

("Moonlight bright and beautiful, And the little golden stars, Everyone is happy, far and wide, I alone am sad.")

This gloomy view of the future and the feeling of insecurity was increasingly reflected in the works of the young contemporaries of Opitz by constantly recurring complaints about vanity and a longing for death since their lives and experience were dominated by war and senseless violence. An oppressive feeling of futility is evident in these lines by Andreas Gryphius:

> "Was sind wir Menschen doch?
> Ein Wohnhaus grimmer Schmerzen,
> Ein Ball des falschen Glücks, ein Irrlicht dieser Zeit,
> Ein Schauplatz herber Angst und Widerwärtigkeit,
> Ein bald verschmelzter Schnee und abgebrannte Kerzen."[2]

("But we human beings, what are we? A house of grim pain, A ball of false happiness, A will-o'-the-wisp of this age, A scene of rude fear and adversity, Snow which soon melts and candles which rapidly burn down.")

Gryphius was also the author of moving words of lament about the war which only devastates the countryside and strikes no breach for progress. The "Trauerklage des verwüsteten Deutschland" ("Lament of Germany laid waste"), subsequently called "Tränen des Vaterlandes" ("Tears of the Fatherland"), is full of pain at the deaths of thousands but the poet feels that the loss of the "treasure of the soul" by violated conscience is "grimmer than the pest, fire or famine". He writes that the free space of intellectual self-determination had been the almost impregnable bastion in which pride and creativeness could develop. Gryphius was one of those who saw noble renunciation and manly readiness to accept suffering as the contemporary guide-lines of life and many of the heroes of his dramas incorporate this ideal of Christian-Stoic virtue.

Inspired by the plays of Shakespeare, Gryphius sought great subjects for his works and found them in Byzantine history in the person of the usurper Leo Arminius who, in his own turn, ended as the victim of a conspiracy. Gryphius wrote the play of the same name in German during his stay at Strasbourg (1646) and he certainly also had

[1] Tränen des Vaterlandes, p. 41

[2] Gryphius: Works in one volume, selected and with introduction by M. Szyrocki, 3rd edition, Berlin/Weimar, 1969, p. 6

Ob Ich gleich Wütent Gott, zeig hir mein Wehr vnd Waffn,
So kan doch auch zugleich, die Kunst viel nüzn schaffn.

16 42

163 Portrait of Johannes Kepler. Copperplate engraving by Jacob van der Heyden, who is principally known for his engravings of generals of the Thirty Years' War.

164 The "Kepler Kettle"—designed by the illustrious astronomer and mathematician as a gesture of gratitude to the Free City—is an artistically decorated casting which carries various calibration data for measuring volume and weight. Municipal Archives, Ulm

preceding page:
162 The war was also regarded as a stimulating force for science and art by scholars and technicians in particular. Copperplate engraving by Christian Richter (1642). Staatliche Graphische Sammlung, Munich

165 Otto von Guericke was not only one of
the most famous scientists of his time, due to his
investigations in the field of the vacuum and
atmospheric pressure, the invention of the air-
pump and the construction of the first electrical
machine. In the city of Magdeburg he was
active as a highly efficient town counsellor and
mayor.

166 The hemispheres of Magdeburg—shown
here not as the full-scale experiment performed
in Regensburg before Emperor Ferdinand III
and numerous princes but in an open field with
few spectators. Guericke can be seen in the
background, talking respectfully to a princely
personage. Print from an engraving by an
unknown artist.

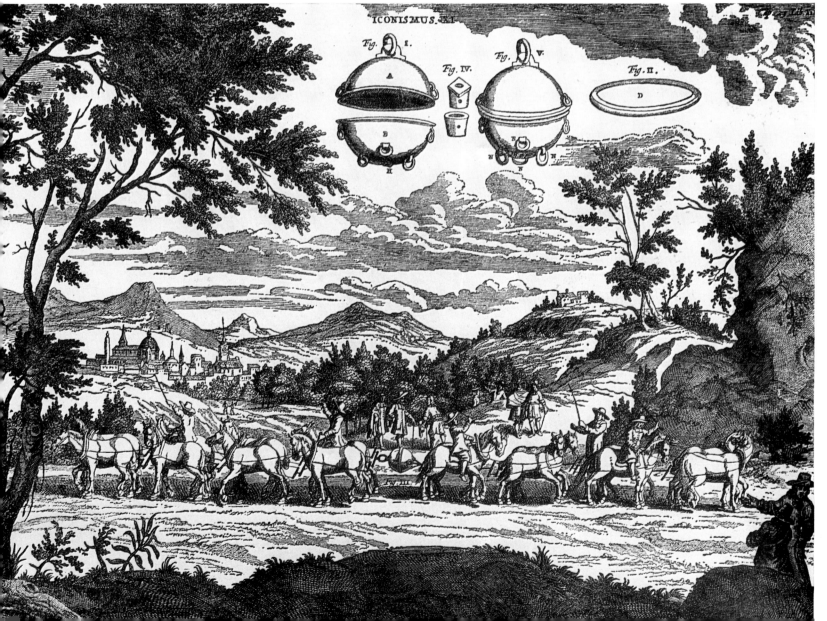

Anno 1620 Als ich Elias Holl.

168 The new Town Hall at Nuremberg, completed in 1621. The lines of its facade are strong and clear and its portals are ornamented with Baroque statues by Lorenz Strauch. Copperplate engraving by Hans Troschel (1621). Staatliche Museen zu Berlin, Cabinet of Copperplate Engravings and Drawing Collection

169/170 The principal buildings of Elias Holl: the Perlach Tower and the Town Hall. Copperplate engraving, Güstrow Museum; to the left the wooden model of the Perlach Tower with scaffolding in position shows the scaffolding technique which remained fundamentally unchanged for centuries. Städtische Kunstsammlungen, Augsburg

171 The splendid Arsenal at Augsburg by E. Holl. Copperplate engraving by Wolfgang Kilian (1659). From: Schulz, *Bilderatlas zur deutschen Geschichte.*

167 In the handwritten *Architekturbuch* by Elias Holl—with his portrait engraved by Lucas Kilian—the celebrated architect declares on the first page that, after the completion of the Town Hall in 1620, he had used the (forced) period of leisure to write this theoretical work. This was not to enhance his reputation, he says, but to pass on his great experience so that it could bear fruit in better times.

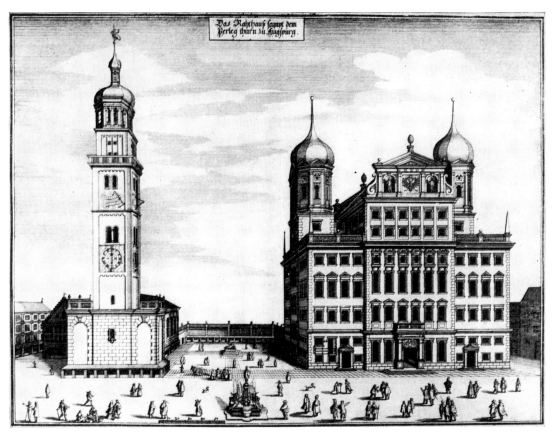

Das Rahthaus samt dem Perleg thurn zu Augspurg.

ARMAMENTARIVM AVGVSTANVM.   Zeighaus der Statt Augspurg.

Elias Holl construxit   Emanuel Wrgien delineauit
Joannes Peguez formauit   Wolffg Kilian sculpsit et
sculp.   excudit
A.° 1619

LABOR IMPROBVS OMNIA VINCIT

WOLFGANGVS KILIANVS CIVIS ET GLIPTES AVGVSTANVS

172 This view of an engraver's and printer's workshop shows how a copperplate engraving is produced: the engraving of the subject with a burin on a polished copperplate; removal with a tampon of the printer's ink applied to the plate so that the ink only remains in the engraved depressions; impression on paper in the rotary press. The drying-process is omitted. The motto in the surround underlines the social significance of the art of copperplate engraving: diligent work conquers everything. The corners outside the oval symbolize areas which need the art of the engraver or from which this art benefits: agriculture, economy, science, music and the pictorial arts. Copperplate engraving by Wolfgang Kilian. Národní Gallery, Prague

173 The portrait of Georg Kilian, one of the later members of the artist family of Augsburg, provides information about the early days of the famous studio. Copperplate engraving by Georg Christoph Kilian. Staatliche Museen zu Berlin, Cabinet of Copperplate Engravings and Drawing Collection

174 Adam Elsheimer, who is lauded in the review of his career in the text as one of the greatest German painters of the Renaissance. Etching by Wenzel Hollar. Moravská Gallery, Brno

175 Stefano della Bella. Etching by Wenzel Hollar with a text referring to the former's great artistic achievements, the equal of those of Jacques Callot of Lorraine. Moravská Gallery, Brno

176 Johann Wilhelm Baur. Etching by an unknown artist. Národní Gallery, Prague

177 Portrait of Heinrich Schütz. Oil painting by an unknown artist. Deutsche Staatsbibliothek, Berlin, Music Department

178 The organ in the Cathedral of Ulm, built by Caspar Sturm, was one of the most admired works of art of the period. From: Mathäus Merian, *Topographia Germaniae*

179 The principal instruments of military march-music: fife and drum; the latter was also used for giving signals. Etching by Rudolph Meyer. Art Collections Veste Coburg

180 A group making music with lute, violin and keyboard instrument. With his back turned to them, a cavalier pursues another form of amusement—the drinking of tobacco. Etching, 17th century. Germanisches Nationalmuseum, Nuremberg

181 Autumn concert in the open air. Detail of a painting on the lid of a spinet by Lukas von Valkenborch, 16th/17th century. Germanisches Nationalmuseum, Nuremberg

182 In the "Concert in the Picture Gallery" by Johann Heinrich Schönfeld—also attributed to Jan Onghers under the title "Musical Amusement at Table"—there are three people singing, one of whom is acting as a conductor with a sheet of music. The middle and high notes are provided by the flute and the viola da braccio, the bass notes by the lute and the viola da gamba and volume is contributed by the lady at the keyboard. The group of performing musicians brings life to the lofty room with its many pictures. It represents the amalgam of three art forms. Staatliche Kunstsammlungen, Dresden, Gallery of Paintings

VANITAS ET

JH Schönfeldt Fecit 1654

183 One of the numerous "vanity" etchings which, with their subject and symbolic figures, express the ephemeral nature and futility of human existence and activities. By Johann Heinrich Schönfeld. Staatliche Museen zu Berlin, Cabinet of Copperplate Engravings and Drawing Collection

184 A group of ruins in the "vanity" style with a half-obliterated inscription referring to the revolutionary concept of Copernicus. Etching by Jonas Zacharias Umbach. Národní Gallery, Prague

185 Soft light illuminates the place where
Jupiter and Mercury meet Philomen and
Baucis, the legendary aged couple of classical
Antiquity. In this highly individual masterpiece
by an outstanding artist, the scene is set in a
farmhouse-room of his own period. Painting by
Adam Elsheimer. Staatliche Kunstsammlungen,
Dresden, Gallery of Paintings

186 A young general in splendid armour with
gold decoration topped by a delicate lace collar.
The bare head, inclined to the side, displays
a self-assured and thoughtful face. Painting by
Anthonis van Dyck. Kunsthistorisches Museum,
Vienna

187 Even in Leiden books on theology and jurisprudence made up half of the book stocks. The volumes were protected against theft by chains. Engraving by J. C. Woudanus (1610).

188 The anatomy demonstration theatre of the Dutch university of Leiden, founded in 1575, was the most modern of its time. A selection of surgical instruments and a collection of animal and human skeletons in a dramatic presentation can be seen in the picture. Copperplate engraving. Güstrow Museum

THEATRUM ANATOMICUM.
Leydense

in mind the fate of the "swindled swindler" Wallenstein and many others who had come to the fore by luck and military adventure and had discovered that "offt nur eine Nacht sey zwischen fall und höh" ("there is often only a single night between ascendancy and fall").

Ten years after the end of the war, there appeared the "Absurda Comica", the first comedy from Gryphius. The Pyramus and Thisbe theme, masterfully exploited by Shakespeare in "Midsummer Night's Dream", had become known in Germany from English players and Gryphius used it for an effective parody of the decline in the tradition of the master-singers and of the primitive play-acting of master artisans. The poet used a sharp pen and his satire was aimed at the snobbery associated with education and the well-established cringing of the bourgeoisie at the princely courts.

It was only in 1663 that Gryphius returned to the subject of war with the comedy "Horribilicribifax"—which indicates that the horror of war was beginning to be forgotten. The action was situated in the last year of the war and its two principal heroes are of the type of Plautus's *miles gloriosus*, the cowardly and vain pseudo-soldier and braggart, as portrayed by Shakespeare, too, in Falstaff. The satire derives its German character not least from the fact that the loquacious soldiers use a language which is a wonderful mixture of German and a rich scattering of foreign expressions (some of which are distorted into a Germanized form). The characters also include fallen aristocrats, a "corrupt" schoolmaster, an old procuress, a Jew and impudent servants who deceive their masters—mostly social flotsam of late feudal society under the scourge of war.[1]

The intellectual and moral development of Gryphius was influenced by his early education and his painful experiences in Silesia and Poland, which were severely stricken by the war, and by the years he spent in the study of literature, the natural sciences and medicine at Leiden (1638—1644). He travelled a great deal within the territory of the Empire, to France and Italy and had the reputation of a learned man whose services were eagerly sought by cities, universities and princes. He nevertheless did not become a courtier but retained an eye and an inclination for the troubles and pleasures of the ordinary people, for simple everyday life, and also considered this worthy of being depicted in literature.

The unshakeable faith in the healthy strength of the peasants who had to bear the main burden of the war is expressed in the poetic works of many others and especially in the fine epigrams of Friedrich von Logau, the clear-sighted and fearless critic of feudal rule and its practices.[2] The same is true of such Silesian poets as Wenzel Scherffer von Scherfferstein and Daniel Czepko, the socio-critical content of whose works has not yet received the attention it deserves. How clearly Czepko exposes the nature of the Thirty Years' War in Germany![3]

189 Andreas Gryphius. Oil painting by an unknown artist. From: *Geschichte der deutschen Literatur in Bildern.*

[1] Szyrocki, M.: Andreas Gryphius, Tübingen, 1964; Clark, R. T.: Gryphius and the Night of Time, Wächter und Hüter 1957; Andreas Gryphius. Lustspiele, ed. by H. Palm, Stuttgart, 1878

[2] Logau, Friedrich von: Sinngedichte. Eine Auswahl, Berlin 1967, with Preface by U. Berger

[3] Silesiaca, p. 62

"Fürsten mögen Kriege führen,
Ich wil, ob sie Drommeln rühren,
Meine Haut doch nicht verkauffen:
Dieses Tichters Handvoll Blut
Darff sich umb des andern Gut

190 Adam Olearius was one of the first scholars of Western Europe who disseminated knowledge of the Tartar alphabet and language. From: *Orientalische Reise*. Książnica miejska, Toruń.

Nicht biss in die Grube rauffen . . .
Ob die Kriege grausam seyn,
Treffen sie doch die allein,
Welche nichts darzu getragen:
Unterthanen sind es bloss,
Diese fället Plitz und Schloss (die Kugel),
Wenn sich grosse Herren schlagen . . .”

("Princes may like to wage wars, But I will not sell my skin when they beat the drums, This poet's handful of blood should not fight unto the grave, For the property of another . . . Though wars may be cruel, They still only affect those, Who did nothing to cause them, It is only the subjects Who are felled by lightning and balls, When great lords do battle . . .”)

The most impressive and poetically realistic picture of the time was created by Johann Jakob Christoffel von Grimmelshausen, who likewise drew on his own experience and whose narrative works, especially *Der Abenteuerliche Simplizissimus*, have become a part of the German literary heritage and have also found a place in world literature.[1] From his fascinating and colourful description which is in the tradition of the Spanish picaresque novel, it has been concluded that the boy, who was born in Gelnhausen in 1621 or 1622, was captured by soldiers during an attack (1635) and taken away from the town to share their restless life in camp and in the field. There is reliable evidence of Grimmelshausen's military service only in 1639 when he became the regimental clerk to the commander of the small fortified Free City of Offenburg in Baden. In 1650, he left the army and earned a living by alternately working as an official and as a small rural entrepreneur in the northern part of the Black Forest. As the agent of the "Ulenburg" estate with its vineyards and orchards, the property of a learned physician of Strasbourg, Grimmelshausen had access to works of literature and contemporary writings and began to write himself. The result was astonishing: between 1666 and 1673, one book followed another in rapid succession. The most significant of these deal with the war and, two decades after its end, found a ready sale. Even today, they are fascinating reading.

As regards the authenticity of Grimmelshausen's works, it must be remembered that his own experiences were not the only source of his knowledge of the world and the progress of the war. He also used contemporary accounts and documents to support and update his own knowledge while it was twenty years after the end of the war that he gave all this a literary shape which was intended to entertain, to delight and to instruct.

The masterpieces of this storyteller, especially his "Simplicissimus-type" writings ("Simplizissimus", "Courasche", "Springinsfeld", and "Vogelnest") on the one hand are a "cultural picture" from the time of the Thirty Years' War while on the other they trace at the same time the career of personalities from the ordinary people. They show what relations were possible between man and society. The message for the reader is that life is eventful and contains much which is hostile to human beings. However,

[1] Grimmelshausen: Works in 4 vols., selected and with introduction by S. Streller, Weimar, 1960; Collected Works in single editions, ed. by R. Tarot, Tübingen, 1967ff.; Streller, S.: Grimmelshausens Simplicianische Schriften, Berlin, 1958; Weydt, G.: Hans Jakob Christoffel von Grimmelshausen, Stuttgart, 1971

nobody should give up because they are weary or get involved in mischief; one should always be prepared to make a fresh start and follow the path taken by Simplex— between his good friend Herzbruder on the right and the wicked companion Olivier on the left. What a contrast there is between this maxim and the prevalent "vanity" outlook! This is why Grimmelshausen's work is testimony of an optimistic attitude towards the solving of the problems left by the war.

Grimmelshausen's confidence, which not only survived the war and the post-war period but was consolidated by it, derives from his unshakeable affection for the ordinary people and permits an understanding but sharp criticism of mistakes and weakness. For him, too, it is the peasant—the class which forms the basis for the whole structure of the feudal class including the accoutrements of war—who merits the highest prize as the substrate which constantly nourishes every human expression of culture:[1]

> "Du sehr verachter Bauernstand,
> Bist doch der best in dem Land,
> Kein Mann dich gnugsam preisen kann,
> Wann er dich nur recht siehet an.
> Die Erde wär ganz wild durchaus,
> Wann du auf ihr nicht hieltest Haus,
> Ganz traurig auf der Welt es stünd,
> Wann man kein Bauersmann mehr fünd."

("You peasantry, so much despised, You are still the best in the land, No man can praise you enough, If only he sees you correctly. The whole of the Earth would be quite wild, If you didn't keep it in order, It would be a sad day indeed for the world, If there were no longer any peasants.")

For the working people, the war between their masters could not be a matter of honour and glory, material acquisition or power and this is why Grimmelshausen questions the value of something which is stained with the innocent blood of so many human beings. With biting satire, Grimmelshausen advises the princes to start an "unnecessary and unjust war" without hesitation if the pace of ruination is too slow for them. He writes that the real purpose of such a war is that it should produce "some profit" for those with an interest in it.[2] However, Grimmelshausen saw no practical alternative to the society of his time with its glaring injustice and serious defects and fled into the realm of dreams. "Nichts denn Wind mit vollen Händen" ("Nothing but handfuls of wind") was how Paul Fleming, probably the most talented lyric poet of the time, described his work in his war-torn homeland.[3] The son of a vicar of Hartenstein on the Zwickau Mulde, he successfully completed the course of studies at the St. Thomas School in Leipzig before going on to study medicine at the university. His medical training was prematurely ended in 1633 when the tide of war swept across Saxony. The spirit of his friends in Leipzig was dominated by the universally admired Opitz but Fleming's verses are marked by the freshness of youth. He wanted to sing "an unheard of song", not of war and weapons but a song "das Himmel hätt' und etwas

191 Title plate of the first edition of Paul Fleming's *Teutsche Poemata*. From: *Geschichte der deutschen Literatur in Bildern*.

[1] Simplicissimus I/3, verses 1 and 6

[2] Grimmelshausen: Rathstübel Plutonis, Works 12, ed. by W. Bender

[3] Geschichte der deutschen Literatur 5; Travuškin, N. S.: Paul Fleming v Rossii, in: Učenye zapiski VIII, Astrakhan, 1959

To everybody what pleases him

I see blood and dust before me,
And a thousand armed men.
I see how so many gilded banners
fly for victory and robbery:
Yet I am burning. Let those
who cannot burn
begin an illustrious existence.

From: Die geharnischte Venus
Venus in armour or love songs composed in war
(1660) by Caspar Stieler (Verse 3)

solches fühlte, das nach der Gottheit schmeck' und rege Muth und Blut" ("which had a heaven and felt like something tasting of divinity and inspiring courage and blood"). But political developments, the defeats of the Protestant camp and "Mars in general", "the monster of all art", spoiled his homeland for this young man who sought a life with a worthwhile content. He consequently joined a delegation which was setting out for Persia. This delegation was financed by Duke Friedrich III of Holstein-Gottorp and it was he who drafted its instructions. Nevertheless, this costly enterprise was intended to serve the war-plans of the Imperial court and Spain which planned to harm the interests of the Netherlands and Sweden by opening a trade-route via Russia to Persia and its silk production. The expedition, which lasted from 1635 to 1639, did not achieve this aim but the literary and scientific fruits of it were immense. This mission, which experienced many adventures and dangers, was headed by Adam Olearius who was born in Aschersleben and received a fine education at Leipzig. In 1647, he published a book with the title *Neue Orientalische Reise* ("New Oriental Journey") which attracted a great deal of attention and remained an authoritative work on Russia and the Orient for Western Europe for more than a century. Olearius' richly illustrated book contained poems by Fleming, some of which are full of praise for the beauty of Russia, as exemplified by these verses about the capital:

"Du edle Kaiserin der Städte der Ruthenen,
gross, herrlich, schöne, reich, seh ich auf dich dorthin
auf dein vergüldtes Haupt, so kömmt mir in den Sinn
was Güldners noch als Gold, nach dem ich mich muss sehnen."[1]

("Thou noble empress of the cities of the Ruthenians, great, splendid, beautiful, rich, when I look at you there, at your gilded head, it seems to me it is more gold than gold for which I must long.")

These are the first poetic thoughts about Moscow in the German language. At the end of the expedition, the poet Fleming settled in Reval to work there as a physician following the completion of his medical studies at Leiden. It was on the return journey from there that he died in Hamburg from a brief but fatal illness.

The poet Georg Rudolf Weckherlin, who was Swabian by birth and whose intellectual horizons had been moulded by many journeys, also had a notable career outside Germany. He rose to a position of confidence at the court of King Charles I of England where he became secretary for foreign affairs in the Parliamentary "Committee of Both Kingdoms" in 1643. Following the trial and execution of the king, Weckherlin's position was taken over by the great bard John Milton but he entered the employment of the Republic already in 1652. It is a remarkable fact that this German poet lived and worked for more than thirty years, from 1620 onwards, in revolutionary England but never lost his lively interest in and his affection for his native land in which a court-caste of restricted vision disregarded the interests of the people in its pursuit of wealth and power and where the flames of war were blazing. Weckherlin was perfectly familiar with the moral countenance of court society and denounced it for what it was. This

[1] Olearius, Adam: Neue Orientalische Reise, Schleswig, 1647, p. 220, copy in Książnica miejska Toruń

militant Protestant attacked the growing power of the Hapsburgs and their papal ally with the sonnet "An das Teutschland" ("To Germany"), in 1641:

"Zerbrich das schwere Joch, darunter du gebunden,
O Teutschland, wach doch auff, fass wider einen muth . . ."[1]

("Break the heavy yoke which binds thee, O Germany, awake, take courage again . . .")

An impressive attempt to arouse a national consciousness by quoting the early history of Germany are the satirical works of Hans Michael Moscherosch. In his book *Wunderliche und warhafftige Gesichte Philanders von Sittewald* ("Wondrous and True Dreams of Philander of Sittewald") (in two parts, 1640, 1642), he takes up the "Sueños" (dreams) of the Spanish writer Quevedo and observes the events taking place in the land as "dreams". These are filled with satire attacking the weaknesses, vices and perversities of his time. In the last dream, entitled "A Soldier's Life", the hero Philander falls among soldiers of the wildest kind, accompanies them across the country on their raids as a forerunner of Simplex.

Moscherosch came from the Baden-Alsace area where the heritage of the Peasants' War was still alive. His period in the service of princes did not obscure his critical, middle-class view of court life and the dangerous war-mania since he had personal experience of the terrors resulting from the bloody quarrels of the upper classes in the Empire. In October 1640, he wrote: "I am like one who is tossed on the stormy seas of war, between the rocks and the tumultuous waves of the sinking Fatherland, whose family and himself does not receive bread and accommodation from the generosity of a prince or through a sinecure or a sure remuneration, I must seek my bread myself behind the plough . . ."[2]

In the rich diversity with which poets and artists faced the harsh conditions in Germany and endeavoured to come to terms with them in a creative sense, there are not only political and patriotic, critical and resigned voices but also two other quite different reactions. On the one hand, there was the emergence of a deeply felt and simple religiousness, of a sensitive introspection and a lyrical poetry concerned with Nature, as exemplified by Friedrich Spee, Paul Gerhard and the songs of the "Königsberg Circle" with Simon Dach and Heinrich Albert. The second kind of reaction was that which was characteristic as a leitmotif of the average mercenary—the enjoyment of life in an unrestrained, carnal manner in a brief and dangerous age as symbolized by the "freedom in the field". This is directly reflected in the poems of Georg Greflinger and Kaspar Stieler. Both men were widely travelled soldiers and Greflinger's career was strikingly similar to that of Grimmelshausen's Simplex. He had been looking after the sheep when his father and family were killed "in the ravages of war". He was taken along by the soldiers and sang, drank and fought with them, ultimately becoming a military clerk. Like so many others, Greflinger tried to earn money and a respected position in bourgeois society with his poetry but met with little success. He returned to a military life in the 1640's to achieve "with the sword" that which "through pen and kisses" was out of reach. Aided by friends and patrons, he ultimately found a peaceful occupation in Danzig in 1644 and in Hamburg (1647).

[1] Geschichte der deutschen Literatur 5, p. 68ff.

[2] Ibid, p. 266

Greflinger was also responsible for the first German translation of Corneille's *Le Cid*, which was still being read in the 18th century, and for a comprehensive and didactic history of the Thirty Years' War. Even after he had settled down as a respectable citizen, he retained the restlessness and strange energy which he had acquired during the eventful days of his youth and military service. At times, it was this which aroused the concern of the council of the Hanseatic city which attached great importance to serious and solemn behaviour. Greflinger gives the following description of himself in time of war:

> "Ich raaste, buhlte, tobte,
> Was ich am besten lobte,
> War Sünde ...
> Gemeine Diernen suchen,
> Gassaten gehen, fluchen,
> Versaufen Geld und Blut
> War alles köstlich gut."[1]

("I roared, loved and romped, And what I lauded most was sin ..., seeking common whores, vagabonding, picking quarrels, cursing, Drinking away money and blood, Everything was splendidly good.")

MUSIC
ABOUT AND DURING
THE WAR

A brief look at the musical scene also reveals how tangible were the needs and distress of society in time of war and how they gave art an often painful direction. Germany was not poor in folksongs, hymns and temporal music and the activity of organists and conductors created a profusion of vocal and instrumental works. The climate of a general preparation for war provided a stimulus and a need for fresh, lively and heroic music which had long flourished in Italy as *musica battaglia* (battle-music). This proved popular in the German cities and at the princely courts and the Strasbourg composer Vinzenz Jelič of Rieka even wrote a motette with the title "Parnassia militans" (1626).[2]

Stirring music and flying flags were part of the military scene. The rhythm of drums, the shrill sound of the pipes and a vigorous melody helped keep an orderly and lively marching-step and strengthened esprit de corps and morale. It was not without reason that military musicians enjoyed privileges not extended to the common soldiery. The following song recalls the siege of Magdeburg in 1631:[3]

[1] Oettingen, W. von: Über Georg Greflinger von Regensburg als Dichter, Historiker und Übersetzer, Hamburg, 1882

[2] Moser, H. J.: Geschichte der deutschen Musik, vol. 2, 2nd/3rd edition, Stuttgart/Berlin, 1923; Ibid: Deutsche Tonkunst in alter und neuer Kriegszeit, in: Preussische Jahrbücher 3/184, 1921

[3] Tränen des Vaterlandes, p. 280

"Zu Magdeburg auf der Brücken
da liegen zwei Hündlein klein,
die bellen alle Morgen
und lassen keinen Spanier ein."

("At Magdeburg on the bridge, There lie two little dogs, They bark all the morning, And allow no Spaniards in.")

The verses below summoned the soldiers to battle from their camp:

"Frisch auf, ins Feld zu rucken,
die Trommel hört man lärmen schon,
wol mit Kartaunen und Stucken
dem Feind das Hütlein rucken,
auf der Drometenton."

("Wake up and march on to the battlefield, The drums have been sounding long since, Knock the enemy's hat off, With guns and cannon-royal, At the sound of the trumpet.")

Spanish regiments sang their "Viva la guerra por mar y tierra" on German battle-fields.

As in the past, acoustic signals and music were used to control the line of battle and the course of events. Cries of fear and the fearful din raised by the enemy had to be drowned by the beat of drums, the blare of trumpets and the penetrating sound of the pipes. Through fortunate circumstances, some of this mighty volume of field music has survived, as for instance a series of Swedish cavalry signals which were blown sometime during the first few days of November 1632 at the orders of a quick-thinking Swedish officer from the town-tower of Delitzsch. The episode was related by the wife of one of the town-councillors: A group of Imperial soldiers, whose task was to force the townsfolk to surrender, fled without loss of time when they heard the familiar sound of the trumpets since they could assume that the town was full of Swedish troops. The score reveals the increasing urgency of the demanding, appealing call:[1]

Soldiers' song

*How the drum sounds,
how the fife sings,
How the shawm,
the trumpet and the drum
ring out,
See how bravely the flag is
fluttering,
That the heart throbs with
merriment!*

Johannes Grob

[1] Bitthorn: Geschichte der "Schwedischen Reitersignale", 4th edition, Berlin, 1910

Zwey schöne neue Lieder.

Das Erste:

Warumb sollen wir denn trau-
ren/vnd weinen überal/rc.

Das Ander:

Kein Soldat soll nicht trau-
ren/vnd weinen überal/rc.

In voriger Meloden:

Gedruckt/Im Jahr 1632.

192 Title-page of a four-leaved print containing two soldier's songs (1632). The frequently used woodcut depicts an army drummer.

[1] Schein, J. H.: Sämtliche Werke, ed. by A. Prüfer, 3rd vol., Leipzig, 1907, p. 143

[2] Petzold, R.: Heinrich Schütz und seine Zeit in Bildern, Leipzig, 1972

It is true that religious music—psalms, vocal arrangements, concerts and dirges, passions and so on — developed to a more marked extent during the war than temporal music but the carefree song, full of *joie de vivre*, never disappeared entirely. This is demonstrated, as representative of many of its kind, by the "Studentenschmaus" ("Students' Feast") of Johann Hermann Schein, the son of a preacher of Meissen and organist of St. Thomas' in Leipzig from 1616 onwards. A satirical verse of the Reformation period attacking the drinking habits of the monks and which also survived as a children's rhyme:[1]

"Trink aus das gute, frische Bier
In Hals hinein nach Hofsmanier (!)
　　Der Abt der reit:
Er holt uns allen Indulgenz,
Wir han noch Zeit zur Poenitenz,
Sa, sa, sa, sa, trinkt aus, ihr Brüder,
Er kommt wedr heut noch morgen wieder."

("Drain the good, fresh beer, Down your throat in the manner of the Court (!), The Abbot's out riding, He's fetching an indulgence for us all, We've still got time for penitence, Sa, sa, sa, sa, drink up, my brothers, He will return neither today nor tomorrow.")

However, music was also able to convey most effectively those feelings which were strangely characteristic of the misery of war: anger and excitement, passionate appeals to Heaven, pain, grief and silent resignation, the longing for a blessed end but also for peace on Earth. Samuel Scheidt, an organist of Magdeburg, set to music Luther's German version of the 130th Psalm "Aus tiefster Not schrei ich zu dir, Herr Gott, erhör mein Rufen", and many others did the same with other psalms.

The war influenced the destinies of innumerable musicians. Andreas Hammerschmidt, who came from Brüx in Bohemia, had to leave his native land with all its musical traditions in about 1626. In 1644, the organist Andreas Herbst gloomily wrote to the city-council of Nuremberg that when the calf's skin thunders, David's harps must be silent. The life and work of Heinrich Schütz, the outstanding German musician of that time, were especially marked by the specific features and hardships of the cultural development of Germany.[2] He grew up in a respected middle-class milieu at Köstritz-on-the-Elster and at Weissenfels. After completing his studies and with the assistance of Maurice, Landgrave of Hesse, who patronized the arts, he went to Italy, the homeland of European music. In Kassel, he worked as a court-musician until his patron yielded to the insistent demands of the Elector of Saxony who wanted to lend brilliance to his court at Dresden by the presence of this young musician of such ability. Schütz remained in the service of the elector for 55 years but subsequently confessed that he bitterly regretted having stayed so long.

As a retainer who, like other personnel, had to satisfy the requirements of an idle court-society, he composed table-music, religious works and solemn music, the latter for state occasions such as princely baptisms, marriages and funerals, visits and the signing of treaties. One of these pieces of "wedding music" was the opera "Dafne" which was based on a libretto by the Italian Rinuccini and was performed for the first time at Torgau in 1627. Since he set Opitz' German translation to music, Schütz has a place in the broad intellectual stream of nationally orientated progress.

In the electoral train with two coaches and an armourer's waggon in which the instruments were stowed, the Dresden court-musicians travelled to Mühlhausen in the same year for the Collegiate Meeting of the electors. Schütz again produced pioneering music which was designed to make an impact. In "Da pacem Domine in diebus nostris", there is a blend and confrontation of temporal and religious music: while one choir greets the princely "bringer of peace" with cries of "Vivat!", the other ardently prays for peace. Another choral piece with the title "Teutoniam dudum belli atra pericula molestant" ("Germany is oppressed long since with terrible martial dangers") treats the problem of war and peace even more urgently; for what occasion Schütz wrote it is not known.[1]

In the period up to the early 1630's when he produced much that won acclaim, he made another fruitful journey to Italy (1628/29) but then war and the military dominated the scene in the Electorate of Saxony. Already by 1630, the electoral treasury owed 500 florins to the Master of the Music; without regard to the fate of the suffering musicians, the elector allowed the court orchestra to break up. Many turned their backs on Dresden and moved to more peaceful areas, to Poland and Prussia. Of the 36 musicians, only ten were still there in 1639—too few for the performance of works requiring a powerful volume of sound. In 1641, Schütz, who knew the music scene and the musicians of Germany like no other, wrote that the art of music, in the "desolate state of our beloved Fatherland", had almost disappeared"; a memorandum by Schütz of 1645 sadly records that the "electoral court music" had completely ceased to exist—a fate shared by other bodies of court music. That at Stuttgart had disintegrated already in 1634.[2]

This upright man and great artist was not the sort of person to follow the "wrong martial direction"—as he wrote to King Christian IV of Denmark in 1647—without complaint and without doing something. His immortal works are not primarily marked by lamentation but generate comfort and the strength to withstand adversity. To be sure, Schütz accepted the hospitality of the Danish court at Copenhagen and travelled there three times, seeking asylum from the "wickedness" of "times inimical to the free arts" (1633, 1637 and 1642), but he remained steadfastly obstinate in his struggle for the survival of musical life in Germany and especially in Dresden. He submitted petitions to the authorities time and again, sometimes with an angry, aggressive tone, requesting but never servile. He advanced money from his own pocket to help needy musicians. In 1651, he told the elector's confidential secretary in plain words of the plight of the court-musicians, stating that it was neither Christian nor laudable that such a rich country could not maintain twenty musicians.

This tireless personality also devoted his attention to the coming generation and, at his insistence, the "Chorkapellen-Institut", a school for young musicians, was finally established in Dresden. His "Geistliche Chormusik" (1648), comprising 29 motets, was written for the St. Thomas' Choir of Leipzig which had survived even the

O thou Orpheus of our times,
Thalia taught thee,
Even Phebus hears thy song and
golden pages
With pleasure,
To what purpose then this lament?
Can fear drive away death?

From: An H. Heinrich Schützen/
auff seiner liebsten Frawen Abschiedt,
Martin Opitz an Heinrich Schütz, 1629

[1] Schütz, H.: Sämtliche Werke, ed. by Ph. Spitta, vol. 15, Leipzig, 1893; Schütz, H.: Neue Ausgabe sämtlicher Werke, vol. 5, Kassel/Basle, 1955, No. 4

[2] Schütz, Heinrich: Gesammelte Briefe und Schriften, ed. by E. H. Müller, Regensburg, 1931, p. 141

225

worst days of that city. Since works for a large number of performers were popular neither with musicians nor with publishers, Schütz in the late 1630's wrote his "Kleine geistliche Konzerte" in which simplicity and restrained vocal scoring achieved a rare transparency and depth. The Leipzig music publisher Grosse produced plain editions of these works, obviously assuming that they would not be very successful.

With the end of the war, there was only a gradual improvement in conditions for music and musicians. For some years, there was an urgent demand for festival music to be played at celebrations of peace which, following this period in which there was little joy, were even on an extravagant scale in many places. Schütz did not find the peace and quiet for which he longed. The elector forced him to continue as the master of the court music, an exhausting position. It seems miraculous that his creative ability was still maintained. Innumerable musicians and pupils received instruction from this man whose character and presence were synonymous with mild authority and dignity which inspired confidence. It was in their works in particular that the genius and style of this "musicus excellentissimus", as he is described in the inscription on his tombstone, survived, since fires in the 18th century destroyed most of his remaining temporal works.

HARD TIMES FOR ARCHITECTS AND SCULPTORS, A GREAT AGE FOR ENGRAVERS

Architecture, as the most costly of the arts, was the hardest-hit by the lack of princely or middle-class "patrons" with the financial resources to take advantage of their services. The building of the archiepiscopal castle at Aschaffenburg, the first example of the residential type with official and prestige functions, was completed in 1614. There then followed a noticeable decline in the building fever which had been evident in many places and hardly any structure worth mentioning was subsequently erected. The busy activity on the scaffolding gradually ceased, building artisans found work in the construction of fortifications, had to put their skills at the disposal of the army or, on account of the non-payment of their wages, joined the anonymity of the armed forces themselves. Uncompleted structures such as Wallenstein's palaces were often left in the unfinished state. There was a vigorous building activity in the areas on the edge of the warlike events, as in Salzburg and other Austrian areas where the Catholic Church and the Jesuits, following Italian models, demonstrated their gains in landed property in the counter-reformation by prestige edifices of a high architectural standard.[1]

[1] Stamm, R.: Die Kunstformen des Barockzeitalters, Berne, 1956; Tapié, L. V.: Baroque et classicisme, Paris, 1957; Deutsche Kunstgeschichte, 5 vols., Munich, 1942, 1949ff.; Matějček, A.: Die Geschichte der Kunst. Umrisse und Brennpunkte, Prague, 1961; Alpatow, W.: Geschichte der Kunst, vol. II, Dresden, 1964; Allgemeine Geschichte der Kunst, vol. V, Leipzig, 1966 (Russian edition 1963); Hubala, E.: Die Kunst des 17. Jahrhunderts, Propyläen Kunstgeschichte 9, Frankfort on the Main/Berlin (West)/Vienna, 1970; biographical details in Thieme/Becker: Allgemeines Lexikon der bildenden Künstler, Leipzig, 1907ff.

As early as the beginning of the 17th c., German architects had initiated the change in style from the Renaissance to the Baroque period. The most outstanding of these architects was Elias Holl with his new city-hall and arsenal in Augsburg in which the traditional simplicity and well-balanced proportions of the facade are combined with the extravagant magnificence of the vast "Golden Hall". However, in this time of war, no further developments followed the first few steps in this new direction which was preceded by the controversial period of "mannerism" with its *linea serpentinata*. It was only in the decades after the war that the exciting and intoxicating Baroque style, the expression of new and complicated mechanisms of authority, began its triumphal progress. The castle of Gotha with its magnificent spatial dimensions was built between the middle and end of the 1640's. It was given the name of "Friedenstein" ("Stone of Peace") and was a pointer to the new epoch in style.

As is evident from Furttenbach's works, hesitant experiments were made by German architects in the flourishing spheres of festival and stage scenery and in theatre architecture, areas which had been marked by true masterpieces in Italy. Although such costly extravagances were still rare in Germany, artists nevertheless tried their hand at facade decorations, gates of honour with elaborate banderols and firework programmes for tournaments, weddings, martial processions, masquerades, state occasions and funerals of magnificent solemnity. The princely rulers were not prepared to sacrifice such pomp and circumstance even when the privations of war were at their worst.

Long after the war had begun, famous sculptors worked on ecclesiastical, princely and municipal commissions and created not only works of great size but also increasing numbers of small statuettes of wood, ivory and metal since the time-consuming casting of bronze objects became more and more seldom. Military applications also restricted the practise of the noble art of bell-founding, something for which Germany was celebrated. Numerous works of sculpture came from the studio of Hans Krumper in Munich. He was responsible for the monumental tomb of Ludwig, the Imperial ancestor of the Wittelsbach family, with the bearded figures of soldiers standing guard at the corners in the Frauenkirche. He also created one of the most beautiful staircases of the late Renaissance at the Imperial court in Munich (1616). The erection of St. Mary's column (Mariensäule) in 1638 marked the end for some time of the upswing in sculpture and architecture at the Bavarian capital. It commemorated the victory at the White Hill near Prague and was also a warning for all "heretics".[1]

Between 1603 and 1606, Hans Reichle crowned the portal of the arsenal at Augsburg with a bronze group featuring the Archangel Michael in victorious struggle with Lucifer as the incarnation of Evil writhing on the ground. The flaming sword of the victor, held up high, and the dynamic arrangement of the group with its expression of energy indicate the powerful expression of which German sculpture was capable. It is significant, however, that Reichle left his homeland and in 1619/20 created the Neptune Fountain in front of the Artus court building in Danzig. He died as the court architect of the bishop of Brixen.

In Saxony, Sebastian Walther created the burial scene for the tomb of Lucas Cranach the Younger in the Castle Church at Wittenberg. Jörg Zürn carved the Baroque group "Adoration of the Shepherds" at the altar of Überlingen Cathedral but

193 Johannes von Aachen, who worked as a painter at the court of Emperor Rudolf II in Prague. Etching by Georg Christoph Kilian. Staatliche Museen zu Berlin, Cabinet of Copperplate Engravings and Drawing Collection

[1] Weltstädte der Kunst: Munich, Leipzig, 1967

194 Peter Isselburg. Copperplate engraving by Georg Christoph Kilian. Staatliche Museen zu Berlin, Cabinet of Copperplate Engravings and Drawing Collection

his brothers were forced by the war to move to the Inn area where they worked on a series of altar pictures. In addition to sensuous sculptures of a merry character, Georg Petel also produced the bronze figure of "Mary Magdalene at the Cross" in the Niedermünster at Regensburg while the "Fountain of Virtue" at St. Lorenz-Kirche in Nuremberg was the work of the founder Johann Wurzelbauer. Leonhard Kern's great achievement were the chiselled decorations around the portal of the Town Hall there. The goldsmith and wax-modeller Hans von der Pütt, the son of an immigrant from Dordrecht, and the sculptor and wood-carver Georg Schweigger portrayed the figure of the victorious Gustavus Adolphus in a variety of forms. After the war, Schweigger worked on the casting of a monumental fountain in commemoration of the Peace of Westphalia of 1648 but this work was not erected in Nuremberg. Its individual parts were stored for a long period and it was only in 1797, after they had been purchased by the czar, that they were brought out again and set up in front of Peterhof Castle.[1] In the urban cultural centres of the Empire with their great traditions, the art of carving continued to develop, although this was in a small format in the innumerable workshops of the medal-coiners who produced exhibition and commemorative medals for prosperous clients, including many generals. The armourers, engravers, chasers and stamp-cutters, who catered for the prestige and routine needs of the military and the state administration, experienced an upswing rather than a decline.

The great works of sculpture of the first decades of the 17th century are not characterized at all by the idea of vanity and flight from the world which was so current in literature. Most of them are full of life and in touch with the world, with a content and form worthy of the great Renaissance tradition and constituting a link with the age of the great masters Fischer von Erlach and Andreas Schlüter which began again only at the end of the century. It was the same with the art of sculpture as with music: decades passed after the end of the war before a new selection of creative spirits emerged who were able to master the demands of the new epoch in style.

Village craftsmanship, which had ancient roots in the Southwest of Germany and was primarily evident in the building of churches, survived intact or reappeared and passed on its traditional skills. Construction gangs from Vorarlberg, organized on a co-operative basis, appeared on the building sites when summer came. Stucco-workers from Bavarian villages and especially from the area around Wessobrunn in the years after 1630, supplied the decoration for walls and ceilings which was becoming increasingly more popular at this time. In the Alpine regions, which had scarcely been affected by the war, and in the Northwest of the Empire, the art of wood-carving for the embellishment of village houses continued to flourish. Joachim von Sandrart mentions glass-painting of a high artistic standard in the Nuremberg area and also a new etching-technique which is said to have been invented by Heinrich Wessler. Although interrupted repeatedly by the tide of war, the art of glass-painting developed steadily, especially in the wooded upper regions of the Erzgebirge to which miners retreated on account of the decline in ore-mining. The "jug-kiln" in the village of Creussen in Upper Franconia, which had flourished as early as the 16th century, continued in operation even while the war was in progress. It was the Vest family who was largely responsible for the shape and decorative styling of the products.

[1] Barock in Nürnberg, Nuremberg, 1962

The appearance of an increasing number of individual states within the Empire, a phenomenon which was reinforced by religious differences and a continuing separate economic development, was a serious obstacle to the emergence of a "national school" of painting such as those that characterized Spain, the Netherlands, Flanders or France. Many promising artists, for lack of resources and well-equipped studios or to flee the privations of war, went to these countries or, attracted by the outstanding masters and schools of Italy, went to Rome, Venice, Naples or Florence. The only artist who founded a school and influenced many great painters of Europe was Adam Elsheimer who spent the last decade of his life in Italy and died in Rome. The North and West of the Empire were dominated by the great Flemish and Dutch schools. Hamburg, as an international trade-centre and with its self-assured and conservative patricians, was regarded as the eastern outpost of Dutch painting—also because a number of Dutch artists found refuge and work here.[1]

Almost all of the more outstanding German painters who experienced the war sought their own path, their own artistic expression, without much contact with the work of others. They all came from the middle class and undertook commissions for merchants or wealthy intellectuals and also to a large extent for the Church and princely patrons, too. The travels of Joachim von Sandrart, who was born in Frankfort on the Main of a middle-class family, took him to many of the important cultural centres of Western Europe: Prague, Utrecht, London, Venice, Rome, Bologna and Naples. He sought refuge and rest in Amsterdam but moved to Germany again where he was directly affected by the vicissitudes of war on several occasions. The estate of Stockau near Ingolstadt, which he had inherited, was devastated. In his home-town, he painted a portrait of the councillor Johann Maximilian zum Jungen, who took an interest in art, and also princes and emperors. His stay at Nuremberg in 1649 was devoted to the preparations for what is certainly his best-known picture, the "Peace Banquet" with fifty generals and diplomats. This picture is remarkable for the totally individual portraits of the participants and also for the portrait that Sandrart painted of himself. He is depicted at work in a free and sovereign pose in the foreground—stressing his social equality with those who argued about power, land and wealth. In the decades after the war, Sandrart wrote a theoretical work about the history of art, the first systematic presentation of world art. This was the *Teutsche Academie der edlen Bau-, Bild- und Malerey-Künste* (1675, 1679, two volumes).[2] This was a pioneer achievement, especially on account of the wide range of interests of its author, who was unable to develop a characteristic style of his own in his paintings.

In addition to their marked inclination for subjects of an official and universal nature, German artists also developed a fine touch for intimate and everyday affairs in which resignation is expressed just as much as the keen artistic interest for the entirely personal and characteristic aspects of life. Georg Flegel, a native of Olmütz, was influenced by the artistic climate of Frankfort on the Main which was dominated by Dutch painters. He painted softly-lit still-lifes which convey an atmosphere of gentle melancholy.[3] The paintings of Johann Heinrich Schönfeld, who was influenced by the Neapolitans and by Nicolas Poussin, the leader of the classical French school of painters, often combine realism with profound feeling and imagination or unexpectedly

195 Hans Ulrich Franck at the age of 60 years. Self-portrait, engraved by Georg Christoph Kilian (laterally reversed). Staatliche Museen zu Berlin, Cabinet of Copperplate Engravings and Drawing Collection

[1] Izergina, A. N.: Nemeckaja živopis' XVII veka, Leningrad/Moscow, 1960; Portret niemiecki 1500—1800, Catalogue, Warsaw, 1961

[2] New edition by A. R. Peltzer, Munich, 1925

[3] Kunst und Altertum in Frankfurt a. M., Munich, 1955

196 Raphael Custos. Copperplate engraving by Georg Christoph Kilian. Staatliche Museen zu Berlin, Cabinet of Copperplate Engravings and Drawing Collection

reveal a romantic touch, as exemplified by the "Concert in the Art Gallery". The predominant themes of death, transitoriness, futility and so on show that he attempted to come to terms with the enduring socio-psychic effects of the war in the drawings he produced between 1653 and 1663. His etchings appear to have a casual style but they are imbued with spiritual agony of exceptional magnitude. They are no less harassing than the vanity poems of Gryphius and many others. Death as a great subject of art—this is a clear sign of the creative exhaustion of not a few painters.

The theme of war in its many variations was chosen by numerous Dutch and Flemish painters including Anthonis van Dyck, a pupil of Rubens, who painted portraits of generals in his vast studio, Sebastian Vrancx, the founder of the Flemish school that specialized in the painting of battles, Philips Wouwerman of Haarlem and the many artists who depicted soldiers and camp scenes. The highly significant act of the signing of the January Peace of Münster in 1648 was painted by Gerard Terborch, a master of the genre who worked mainly in Deventer, in an impressive group-picture. It gives no indication at all of the wounds left by the war. In this respect and also as regards the basic idea and artistic execution, there is a picture by the great Spanish painter Diego Velázquez which is on quite a different level from the mass of the pictures of the war. This is "The Surrender of Breda", known as "Las Lanzas" in Spanish. It depicts one of the memorable happenings in the historic contest between two epochs and states. Against the sombre background of a land smoking with the conflagrations of war, a meeting is taking place between two groups, the first of which embodies Spanish feudal power, bristling with lances and with the self-assurance of centuries as a world-power while the other consists of relaxed, natural but strong figures from the ordinary people—the incarnation of the first bourgeois state in the world which was born from the struggle for liberation.

The most profound and detailed impressions of the war, military life and the joys and sorrows of the people come from graphic art and especially from copper-plate engravings and etchings, woodcuts being of practically no importance. The works of the greatest engravers of that time such as Jacques Callot, Wenzel Hollar—a native of Bohemia, the Florentine Stefano della Bella or Mathäus Merian the Elder have been well documented. [1] However, the thousands of sheets which they produced were only a fraction of the total quantity which included the products of less well-known engravers and draughtsmen of only average ability whose work was epigonic such as the Custos and Kilian families, Jonas Umbach, Wilhelm Baur, Hans Ulrich Franck, Christian Richter of whom often only the name or a few sheets have survived.

The triumphal progress of the copper-plate engraving, which began already in the 16th century, inspired by Albrecht Dürer's work, is based on its function as a product of "mass art". In contrast to painted figures, of which copies were seldom made and then only a few, innumerable prints could be obtained from long-lasting copper-plates, some of which survived for centuries. This technique enables even tiny details to be shown and even transitions from light to dark areas. For the production, drying, storage and distribution of the sheets, production facilities of considerable size, paid labour and business acumen were needed. The entrepreneurs had to be daring, unscrupulous and quick-witted since every fairly large printed product was subject to

[1] Dostál, E.: Václav Hollar, Prague, 1924; Hollar, W.: Handzeichnungen, ed. by F. Sprinzels, Vienna/Leipzig/Prague, 1938; Angerhausen, P.: Wenzel Hollar. 1607—1677, Krefeld, 1957; Richter, S.: Václav Hollar. Umělec a jeho doba 1607—1677, Prague, 1977; Callot, J.: Das gesamte Werk. Handzeichnungen, introduction by A. Dohmann, 2 volumes, Berlin, 1972

the alert censorship of the authorities and the Church, among others to an Imperial book commission. To slip through their nets or to circumvent them was difficult.

There were close personal and artistic contacts in the production of copper-plate engravings and the guild traditions survived here, too so that artist-dynasties and family enterprises frequently emerged. The engravers of the Sadeler family came from Brussels, perfected their skills in Italy and moved on to Leiden, Venice, Munich and Prague. In the capital of Bavaria, the two Raphaels, father and son, specialized in the requirements of the Catholic renewal and from their workshop they supplied engravings for the Jesuit "Bavaria pia et sancta" movement—("pious and holy Bavaria") (1618). The talented Egidius, who preferred delicate and clear tones, recorded many aspects of the beauty of Prague where he worked for the Imperial court. He made engravings of a number of paintings and produced portraits of a long series of high-ranking personages. The Custos and Kilian families joined forces in Augsburg. Most of the Kilians spent some time in Italy and France to learn the art of copying and engraving before returning to Augsburg. Wolfgang and Lukas ran their own art publishing-houses there and passed them on to their descendants. Although Lukas, the most outstanding artist of the family, became a member of the Evangelical city council in 1632 as a result of the victorious Swedish campaign, he did a great deal of work for Catholic clients, including Emperor Ferdinand II and produced portraits of numerous rulers, generals, scholars and artists of his time. The series of illustrations he produced include a rare one with the title "Newes Soldaten-Büchlein" ("New Soldiers' Booklet") containing scenes and pictures of military life on sixteen separate sheets. Below these pictures are explanatory verses of no great literary pretensions.[1]

Most fame and a field of activity which covered nearly the whole of Europe was achieved by the de Bry-Merian family in Liège and Frankfort on the Main.[2]

197 The publisher's seal of Mathäus Merian with the Calvinist slogan: Pious diligence wins. From: Mathäus Merian, *Theatrum Europaeum*

Theodor de Bry
(b. 1528 Liège,—1570—1588 Strasbourg, then book and art trade in Frankfort on the Main, d. 1598)
|
Johann Theodor
(1561 Liège—1623, in the service of the sultan, from 1593/94 active in his father's studio)
|
daughter *Maria Magdalena* ∞ *Mathäus Merian the Elder*
(1593 Basle—1650, engraver, heir of de Bry)

Joachim	*Mathäus the Younger*	*Caspar*	*Maria Sibylla*
municipal	(1621 Basle—1687)	(1627—after 1700)	(1647—1717)
physician	Pupil of van Dyck	worked in	Active in Germany,
at Frankfort	carried on and	father's studio	the Netherlands,
on the Main	inherited		Surinam (South
	publishing-house		America), naturalist,
			painted flowers
	Johann Mathäus		and insects
	(?—1716)		
	last owner		

[1] Hämmerle, A.: Die Augsburger Künstlerfamilie Kilian, Augsburg, 1922

[2] Burckhardt-Werthemann, D.: Mathäus Merian. 1593—1650, Basle, 1951; Wüthrich, L. H.: Das druckgraphische Werk von Mathäus Merian a. Ae., 2 vols., Basle, 1966

Although the vast artistic and business activities of the family and the studio was the result of close collaboration so that the authorship of many sheets is not clear, the contribution made by Mathäus the Elder was nevertheless outstanding. Born in the Free City of Basle with its great traditions, he was the son of a city councillor. He completed his apprenticeship in Zurich, worked as a journeyman in Strasbourg, Nancy, Châlons and Paris, returned to Basle and then went on to Augsburg, Stuttgart and Nuremberg. He avoided Italy on account of an outbreak of the pest there and he never travelled to the Netherlands. However, he subsequently visited Frankenthal where a colony of Dutch painters had established themselves. In Basle, Merian engraved a map of his home-town which in accuracy and social importance has few rivals—with the exception of the map of Frankfort which he produced at a later date.

At the turn of the century in 1616/17, Merian came to Oppenheim where de Bry owned a studio. He was employed here to produce fresh illustrations for reprints of books. He achieved the status of a master-craftsman and in 1617 married the daughter of Johann Theodor de Bry and moved to Heidelberg where he ran his own studio. This was not for very long since the scourge of war in the shape of Spanish troops forced him to flee from the Palatinate since he was a Reformist by religion. He sought refuge in Basle, his birthplace, where there was still peace. It seems to have been a period of happy activity for it was during this time that he produced his finest travel, village and rural scenes with their characteristic atmosphere. However, on the death of his father-in-law, he had to move northwards again in 1623 since he was the joint-heir and he took over the celebrated art-studio. From his early Frankfort period, there exists a statement in the introduction to the sequence of pictures for the Fifth Book of Moses in his illustrated Bible—also known as the "Merian Bible"—highly esteemed even by Goethe—which throws a revealing light on his view of the world. Merian wrote in 1625 that the arts were fatally ill on account of the "new barbarisms" of the war which he describes as a "Gothic and Hunnish thing". He speaks angrily of the "princely paunches" who "will not be remembered at all one day". This is the language of a self-assured artist who regards his own achievements as far superior to those which depict the hollow pathos of war.

On assuming the management of the publishing-house, he evidently devoted less and less of his energy to creative artistic work and more to the prosperity of the business which had to survive many unexpected dangers and demands resulting from the changes in the political and military situation. He did this with such success that the enterprise went from strength to strength as the war proceeded. At almost every fair, there appeared new publications from Merian's art publishing-house: travel-books, which were becoming more and more popular everywhere, books on medicine and midwifery, philosophy, the haute école of horsemanship and military treatises such as Maurice of Orange's *Treatise on Weapons*, Wallhausen's *Soldiers' ABC* (1631) and the Swedish *Art of Warfare* by Troupitz. The publications offered also included histories, chronicles, botanical works, books on mechanics and geography as well as light reading and the widely read *Piazza Universale*.

However, his success in business did not change Merian's basic attitude to the war of the princes and rulers. He published anonymous leaflets, including texts by the theologian Joachim Betke of Brandenburg. The latter was an outspoken critic of the religious dispute which he regarded as the source of the senseless war. He sought a true and humane Christianity and a better world of a visionary nature. Merian was also certainly familiar with the writings or views of Valentin Weigel and Kaspar Schwenckfeld and had personal contacts with the "silent enthusiasts" of Nuremberg. The fact that he engraved emblems for the members of the "Fruchtbringende Gesellschaft" ("Fruitful Society") is also evidence of his open mind.

In the preface to one of his most memorable works, the *Topographia Germaniae*, Merian's firm conviction of the victory of life over death, his noble wish to improve people, is again clearly apparent: he wrote that the atlas was not intended for use in bloody war but was to convey the picture of the Fatherland's great and peaceful past to the rising generation. The numerous pictures and the geographical and historical explanations were to provide inspiration for rebuilding the past in an even more beautiful form. Merian began the atlas in 1642 and pursued his task with energy. It was continued even after his death until 1688 and comprises thirty volumes containing valuable information about the past of Europe, especially the maps and 2,500 views of cities, monasteries, castles, villages, great houses, much-admired production centres and noble edifices. The uncertainties of postal and other communications obliged Merian to visit fairs and markets, art studios and dealers himself and he travelled to many cities—including Prague, Dresden and Nancy—to procure engravers and plates and to select engravings and take them back in his luggage. He sent out the draughtsmen of his studio to make copies and collect engravings. As a result, it was a work of greatly varying quality and did not reach the standard of such outstanding publications as the maps, atlases and globes of the Blaeu printing-office in Amsterdam. Nevertheless, and despite the shortcomings caused by the war, it remains a unique source of vivid, pictorial information about human life and construction before the transformations of the absolutist era.

There are also many pictures in the second great publication from Merian's publishing-house—the *Theatrum Europaeum*. It was initially planned as the continuation and final volume of the *Weltchronik* ("World Chronicle") by the Offenbach vicar Johann Ludwig Gottfried. It dealt with history up to 1618 and appeared in illustrated form in eight quarto volumes between 1629 and 1634. The "Continuation" for the events of 1629—1632 was already available by the time of the Lent Fair of 1633. It was the work of the "Magister Artium" Johann Philipp Abelinus or Abele of Strasbourg who had the reputation of being lazy and superficial. This cannot be confirmed, in view of the mass of the literature which he had compiled and classified. In actual fact, a flood of topical news did indeed pour into Frankfort and needed an energetic and ordering hand if it were to be included as a manuscript or printed product in the copy for the *Theatrum Europaeum*. Taking his own judgement and the profit expected by his employer as his criterion, Abele and his successors selected those items of information which were demanded by the readers and which were likely to arouse their interest. However, the basic material came mainly from those categories which then appeared in the printed volumes: political and military events, largely from the viewpoint of the ruling class, notes about princely families and regents, all kinds of deeds by noble persons and sensational news of every type copied from leaflets. Lengthy descriptions are given of the sufferings of the ordinary people during the war, but their many demands and petitions are mentioned less often, mostly in a regretful tone, and are presented as being of no purpose.

Merian the Elder was still in charge up to the fifth of the total of 21 folio volumes of this news magazine which record contemporary history in the style indicated above and ended a century (1718) after its first appearance.[1]

The illustrations were made by various engravers, including Merian himself with the grim scene of the nocturnal murder of Wallenstein at Eger. Many panorama views of battles were included and the general view of Prague by the greatest Bohemian painter in the Baroque style, Karel Škreta. The battle pictures, often of a noticeably uniform composition, did not omit idyllic landscapes and genre-scenes.

A strange and rapidly produced publication of the Frankfort printing and publishing world was the *Thesaurus philopoliticus* ("Political Thesaurus"), a joint work by the Bohemian poet Daniel Meissner and the publisher and engraver Eberhard Kieser. It was printed by the latter on the basis of an idea by Meissner.[2] The "Thesaurus" was published between 1623 and 1631 in two volumes, each consisting of eight parts which were ready in time for almost every Fair. They provided a growing number of readers who wanted to know something about the world with 830 engravings (mostly copies and not originals from master-studios) of towns, fortresses, castles and monasteries which carried *Emblemata* sive *moralia politica* (verses of a politico-moral content). Paul Fürst, the resourceful "picture-man" of Nuremberg, acquired the valuable plates and in 1637/38 brought out a new edition with the title *Sciographica cosmica*. The material was used again in 1700 for the *Statistische Städte-Buch* ("Statistical Book of Cities") which was likewise published in illustrated form. As a result, numerous old engravings have survived which would otherwise have been lost. The four-line verses in German and Latin convey not only a profusion of moral platitudes for everyday guidance but also contain very specific criticisms of princely arbitrariness and war-policy while peace and labour are the subject of high praise. The pictures of the cities, and many of the verses in this popular work may be regarded, perhaps, as the manifestation of the self-assertion of the busy bourgeoisie.

[1] Bingel, H.: Das Theatrum Europaeum — ein Beitrag zur Publizistik des 17. und 18. Jahrhunderts, Munich, 1909

[2] Daniel Meissners Thesaurus philopoliticus (Politisches Schatzkästlein), new edition by F. Herrmann and L. Kraft, 2 vols., Heidelberg, 1927

NEWSPAPERS, WAR OF THE PENS, THE VOICE OF THE PEOPLE

POSTAL COMMUNICATIONS AND THE PRESS

The evident increase in the need for reliable informations about events within and outside Europe became even more apparent in the first half of the 17th century as the war began to affect more and more people. Merchants, diplomats and governments (as demonstrated by the Venetian and papal correspondence in particular) had long since been able to meet their requirements in this respect with the aid of letters, handwritten news-sheets, couriers and special agents and reporters dispatched to courts and theatres of war for the purpose. Government and business interests wanted regular information which was as accurate as possible and largely free from political prejudice and bias.

"News-merchants" had sold news-sheets as early as the 16th century at busy spots in the cities and towns, often announcing the content of their wares with loud voice and urgent gesticulations. At the time, these news-sheets were commonly known by the collective term "Newe Zeitung" (new newspaper). They were bought by fairly large numbers of the ordinary people in particular and they were accordingly already characterized by topicality and publicity in no small measure. Less topical but more regular were the reports contained in the "Relationes Semestrales"—six-monthly publications which had been sold at every fair in Frankfort on the Main since the 1580's like other books. However, the six-monthly interval was too long in those "quick-moving times" and the publicity of the "Fair Relations" was too limited to satisfy the need for the latest news which was being felt by more and more people. The decisive stimulus to bring regularity into the numerous printed news-sheets which fluttered throughout the countryside was provided by the link with the postal communications system. Even contemporaries recognized that the origin of newspapers was intimately associated with the post-houses.[1]

The "Newe Post-Ordnung"—the timetable and price-list for the conveyance of packets and letters of the Frankfort on the Main postmaster Johann von den Birghden of 1634 covered eighty destinations in the Reich, France, Italy, Spain and Sweden. Postal traffic was on a more comprehensive scale during the Fair periods and in the summertime. The Nuremberg "Meilenzeiger" quotes the distances of some 500 post-stations in the area mentioned above and names 50 places which were linked with Nuremberg by postal vehicles and regular courier services. The arrival of the post was always a principal event of the day. When the sound of the post-horn was heard from afar, a crowd of people streamed to the post-building to find out the latest news.

[1] Opel, J. O.: Anfänge der deutschen Zeitungspresse. 1609—1623, Leipzig, 1879; Freytag, R.: Post und Zeitung. Ein Streifzug durch die Geschichte des Post- und Zeitungswesens bis zum Beginn des 19. Jahrhunderts, Munich, 1928, 1930; Laurin, A.: Všeobecné dějiny periodického tisku, Prague, 1932; Weil, G.: Le journal. Origines, évolution et rôle de la presse périodique, Paris, 1934; Schoene, W.: Die deutsche Zeitung des siebzehnten Jahrhunderts in Abbildungen, Leipzig, 1940; Die deutschen Zeitungen des 17. Jahrhunderts. A list with historical and bibliographical details compiled by E. Bogel and E. Blühm, Bremen, 1971

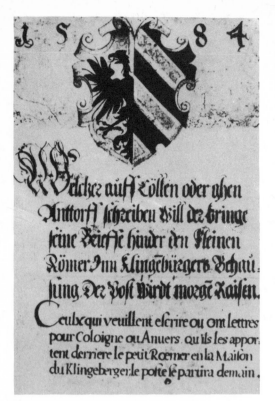

198 A printed notice for public display (1584) from Frankfort on the Main announces the regular conveyance of letters to Cologne and Antwerp—an indication of the close links with the Netherlands at war. From: Steinhausen, *Deutsche Kultur*

The quick succession of events and the changing situation led to a kind of "news fever" and led to that phenomenon which was known at the time as *fama* (rumour) and is now described by the modern expression "public opinion".[1] The above circumstances explain why the first printed weekly newspaper appeared in the Empire (Reich). This was the "Relation": "Aller Fürnemmen und gedenkwürdigen Historien/so sich hin und wider ... Inn diesem 1609. Jahr verlauffen und zutragen möchte", which certainly dates back to 1609 but probably existed before this. It appeared in 52 numbers and contained news from the whole of Europe and from Turkey, which extended far into Asia. It was published by Johann Carolus of Strasbourg. Following the appearance of this first publication, others were produced in many other places and by the end of the war there were at least a couple of dozen, demonstrating the political disintegration of the Empire and a transformation in the history of the Press. A New Year's leaflet of 1632 provides an impression of a newspaper office employing no less than ten persons: news-classifier, couriers, writer, compositor, engraver, printer, newspaper-boy and vendor. It was not long before the first daily newspaper appeared, this being at Leipzig in 1660. By the end of the century, this was already producing an annual lease of 13,000 thalers.

The printed newspaper, which consisted of only a few pages, was similar in appearance to the news-sheet or the page of a book, octo and quarto being preferred for the format. To begin with, the title still alternated but vignettes distinguished it from its competitors. Winged Mercuries, coats of arms, couriers on foot or horseback were used for the decoration of the title-page. The modern Press was also emerging in its presentation.

Even in its early stages, the periodic newspaper was utilized as a medium for forming the opinion of its readers in a systematic manner and directing it. Of the many weekly newspapers which soon became current throughout Europe, this is demonstrated by the celebrated "La Gazette" (Paris, 1631), an official publication produced jointly by the omnipotent Cardinal Richelieu and the amazingly active publicist and respected parish-physician Théophrast Renaudot. Even King Louis XIII drafted reports for the paper.

In this connection, the development of the Press in the territory of the Empire was rather different. It was largely spontaneous in its emergence, without plan or order, and had its origin in middle-class circles. It had not yet developed as a vehicle for political controversy and printed a succession of news items which were presented as impartially as possible. The manipulation of the reader's opinion was left to the vast quantity of pamphlets and news-sheets in single- and multi-page form.

[1] Bauer, W.: Die öffentliche Meinung in der Weltgeschichte, Wildpark-Potsdam, 1930

THE FLOOD OF
PAMPHLETS
AND LEAFLETS

Among the multitude of printers in numerous villages and towns where leaflets were produced, the art-dealer Paul Fürst occupies an outstanding position. From the mid-1630's onwards, he devoted his energies to this fast-selling market-commodity and printed hundreds of leaflets with illustrations, verses and songs. The "picture-man of Nuremberg" was always an eagerly awaited arrival at the Leipzig Fairs where he carried on business in Auerbachs Hof.

Although an incident which took place at Nuremberg in September 1631 was set off by a "newspaper" from Leipzig, it was characteristic of the entire wide-ranging sphere of small-format literature which endeavoured to mould public opinion. The supervisor of the municipal messenger service had received a printed "news-letter" from Leipzig about the Swedish victory at Breitenfeld. This news-letter came into the hands of the printer Caspar Fuld, who carried on his trade in Nuremberg between 1615 and 1631 and, at his request, the Town Council gave him permission to reprint it, two reams of paper being made available for the purpose. The first edition of 1,000 sheets was rapidly sold by merchants and booksellers and subsequent runs were offered for sale in churches and on squares where servants and children were also present. At the same time, it was reported that there were many "base scribes"—officially authorized and undesirable—in Nuremberg who recorded news of all kinds.[1] Without doubt, this was also a reference to the much-discussed "lampooners" who kept an observant eye on the upper classes and town-beadles since they were quarrelsome and opinionated and had a sharp pen and an irritating style.

There is a report from Lüneburg of 1630 that "political books"—a reference to pamphlets intended for readers with a higher standard of education—were snatched from the hands of booksellers by their customers. It was said that the turnover of such publications led to many, who were less diligent and active than others, obtaining honour and wealth. From the end of the 16th century, the Frankfort Fair Catalogue noted a steadily rising number of brochures with a quarrelsome and insulting content whereas there was a decline in the range of books offered. In 1617, or thereabouts, a "simple layman" complained that all the power of the spirit was devoted to the "war of the pens" which was waged with much bitterness and maliciousness.[2]

What were the subjects which made the news-sheets and pamphlets so attractive? Apart from the familiar Biblical matters and religious questions, moralizing warnings, prophecies, admonitions to repent and return to a life of modesty acceptable to God, they dealt with subjects which had their origin in the realm of worldly experience: death and ruination, violence, power, gluttony, avarice, deceit in coinage and weights, litigous dispositions, crime, miracles, the quarrelsome nature of women, the annoyance of matrimony, social injustice, wealth and poverty, fortune and ill-luck, the latest fashions, the decline in moral and linguistic standards, state events—and especially

[1] Soden: Kriegs- und Sittengeschichte der Reichsstadt Nürnberg, vol. 3, p. 196f.

[2] Kirchhoff, A.: Lesefrüchte aus den Acten der kurfürstlichen Bücher-Commission zu Leipzig, in: Archiv für Geschichte des deutschen Buchhandels VIII/1883

the persons, parties, events and the vicissitudes of the war, such as the guilty and the victims, those really and supposedly responsible, news ("relations") from the theatres of war, of negotiations and treaties. The flood of single-sheet pamphlets increased in volume for the first time at the beginning of the war and in the years of the debasing of the coinage and again when the shining, tragic figure of the King of Sweden and that of the sombre Wallenstein caught the public imagination.[1] The glory of the Imperial-Spanish arms at Nördlingen was spread throughout the whole of Europe by 54 (known) pamphlets and leaflets in various languages. Up to this time, the mischief of war had a certain aura of splendor associated with it but in the second half of the war there was less evidence of fantasy on the part of the authors of these publications.[2]

The profusion of single-page leaflets and news-sheets must be carefully examined if an idea is to be obtained of the mood of the people and of their general attitude to these happenings. There are hundreds of them which, in terse prose or verse form, relate and comment on, *post factum*, events of a historico-political or sensational character. The sequence of verses, sometimes running into dozens, usually ends with a serious and significant warning. No standard term has been found for this kind of journalism in verse form which referred to specific events and was primarily intended for the ordinary people or was produced by them. The names used for this include "political", "historical", "event" or "newspaper" songs. It is considered that their authors came from members of the intelligentsia who were in close touch with the people—students, teachers, preachers and scribes—and that the pedlars of their products (newspaper vendors, intinerant merchants, newspaper "chanters", wandering students, priests and preachers impoverished by the war, etc.) became an itinerant vocational group which grew vigorously in numbers in many countries of Europe and not least in the Empire.

The greatest impression on listeners and readers was probably made by those songs in which the text was accompanied by a picture or set of pictures. "Was Gelehrte durch die Schrift verstahn, das lehrt das Gmähl den gemeinen Mann" ("What scholars understand from writing, this is communicated to the ordinary man by pictures")—as one sheet put it.[3] Many made use of the popular echo or conversational form. Very many of the songs indicate a melody of an already known song which fits the text and begin with imperative brevity, addressing the "dear worthy or Christian people" or "brothers" with "Listen", or "Come here", "Wake up" or "See here". An appropriate reference here is the "Newspaper Chanter" in an etching by Jan Georg van Vliet: "I sing a song, I don't know how …". From a raised position, an obviously ragged man reads vigorous verses from a sheet of paper to a group of passersby at a market, some of whom listen while others walk past, while his companion, with a slightly sardonic expression, sells copies of the sheet. A dandy in the foreground listens with rapt attention while a pickpocket, exploiting the situation, "inspects" the breeches of the young man—a masterly depiction which exposes like no other the limits of leaflet propaganda.

At the beginning of the war, the miserably disintegrating Union and its leader, the defeated King Frederick of Bohemia, offered a welcome target for taunts of a partly vitriolic, partly sympathetic nature. An illustrated leaflet puts it this way: Frederick

[1] d'Ester, K.: Flugblatt und Flugschrift, Handbuch der Zeitungswissenschaft, ed. by W. Heide, vol. I, Leipzig, 1940; Beller, E. A.: Propaganda in Germany during the Thirty Years War, Princeton, 1940; Wäscher: Das deutsche illustrierte Flugblatt I; Brednich, R. W.: Die Liedpublizistik im Flugblatt des 15. bis 17. Jahrhunderts, vol. 1, Baden-Baden, 1974

[2] Rystad, G.: Kriegsnachrichten und Propaganda während des Dreissigjährigen Krieges, Lund, 1960; Tham, W.: Den svenska utrikes politikens historia, vol. I/2, Stockholm, 1960

[3] Coupe, W. A.: The German illustrated broadsheet in the seventeenth century, 2 vols., Baden-Baden, 1966

mounts a wheel of fortune, sits on top and finally falls into the water from which he is pulled by Dutch fishermen with their nets. In falling, he loses not only his crown and sceptre but also the English Order of the Garter, which is intended to imply the loss of the assistance of the English king. Other engravings show the elector and king without a country, as a beggar with his wife and three children or depict him as a sleeping lion (the lion figures on the coat-of-arms of Bohemia). Others show him toiling for his hosts, the wealthy States-General, who permit him to keep a miniature court at The Hague. He is to be seen building a house on sand, weighing and selling cheese, digging a grave for himself and so on.

Soon after this, the fate of many other potentates and generals caught the public attention: Ernst von Mansfeld, Holck, Tilly, Christian of Brunswick, Wallenstein. "Allen ein Stein" (a play on words with "Wallenstein", meaning a "tombstone for them all") was the mocking contempt of a leaflet about the overthrown and the dead. In a conversational song on a copper-plate engraving, there is a picture of the unscrupulous Mansfeld having a steambath prepared in which all the estates of the Empire have to sweat money; instead of blood, coins flow from the cupping-glasses applied to them. The "Bauersmann" (peasant) speaks the following words:

> "None must bathe so hot as we,
> The bloody sweat flows from many
> Our misery is not be expressed,
> How these baths afflict us."[1]

A "Leipzig Student Poem" entitled "In Memoriam & obitum Holckij" (1633) deals with the misdeeds of the Imperial commander committed in Saxony. He caught the pest, so it is said, because he ate too much "Leipziger Confect". The leaflet shows the dying man lamenting on his death-bed; the soul escaping from his mouth still clutches the stolen treasures in chains.

Tilly, who was so often the victor but was fatally wounded at the Lech, is depicted lying lifeless on a stretcher in another leaflet: "Mr. Till, so still/like the work, so the wage."[2] Tilly's warlord, the Bavarian Elector Maximilian is said in a news-sheet to suffer from the mysterious "Bavarian" complaint. His body is swollen like the "great belly of a Hungarian ox", he has gorged himself on the (ermine) lining of the Palatine's hat and he is as sick as a pig from drinking too much Palatinate wine. Melancholy, however, comes from the robbery of the "Calvinist Library". The court jester of Maximilian dreams that his master will feel better when he vomits the contents of his stomach: Palatine cities and a large pile of books.[3]

These leaflets are merciless in the explicitness of their attacks, despite the allegorical trimmings. His Princely Highness, gorged with the lands and cultural property he has stolen, lies sick on the ground, exposed to the taunts of the public! Only the emperor is spared the full causticity of these scourging attacks. The criticism of the "Hansischer Wecker" leaflet (1629), written at Swedish instigation, is mild and sympathetic: Ferdinand II, "the pious emperor", probably does not intend to be so wicked. He is warned not to pay too much attention to the evil Spanish and Jesuit advisors and he

[1] Scheible: Die Fliegenden Blätter, No. 79

[2] Copy in the Museum für Geschichte der Stadt Leipzig

[3] Bayerischer Mercurius: Anzeygende Bayerische Kranckheit ..., 1632, copy in University Library Greifswald

is even urged to turn away from them.[1] The emperor is mercilessly criticized only in those leaflets which are characterized by the right of Calvinist resistance against tyrannical authorities. In the publication "Quod defensio sit ex lege naturali. Von der Defension und Gegenwehr" (1632) of Regius Selinus, it is asserted that the Hapsburg emperor was "a Captain of the Roman beast and whore" who had forgotten his duty to protect his subjects and that this was why the latter were no longer bound to obey him.[2] But these radical words were not addressed to the peasants who did not read such learned discussions. Sharp words continued to be the weapons used since one had to rely on God and not on the sword and violence.

Although the satire in these leaflets, by reason of vague hopes and traditional respect for the sacredness of the person of the emperor, avoided direct attacks on him, taunts, bitter criticism and anger were directed at his counsellors, at Cardinal Khlesl and the emperor's confessor, Father Lamormain and especially at the Jesuits. The latter, who stubbornly, unscrupulously and successfully carried on intrigues in the ruling circles and at the same time made great sacrifices in caring for the sick and devoted much effort to education and art, were just the right persons to attract the suspicion and hatred of large numbers of people. As the socio-psychic "scapegoats", the Jews disappeared from the limelight and the satirical "penny literature" paid no attention to witches. Belief in the Devil and witchcraft was a self-evident part of the Christian view of the world and it was nothing new or exceptional.

The following is quoted from the wealth of the anti-Jesuit texts to convey an idea of their peculiar form. The tone of the words of abuse in it may still be regarded as relatively tame.

I	hr	st
E	hrlosen	in
S	chalck	aw
V	erleckte	erwüst
I	ns	n
T	euffels	eutschland
A	rschloch	lles

(approximate rendering, left-hand column: You dishonest rogues, ... in the Devil's a**hole; right-hand column: everything is in a mess in Germany.)

At that time, vigorous and direct expression was customary even in scholarly circles. Now, however, although brawls did not occur, language began to be noticeably coarse and objectionable. The heritage of the powerful language used by Luther and Fischart took a turn in the opposite direction. The symbols of the written word can claim more interest than the rude flood of words.

A news-sheet of 1620 shows a "Spanish spinning-room" where "unholy yarn"— dangerous weapons and money for the Imperial war—is being busily spun. The military intervention of the world power Spain was indeed so effective that the German Hapsburgs emerged as victors from the numerous uprisings by the Estates and the people in the early years of the war. The Spanish envoy at the Imperial court had a

[1] Grünbaum, M.: Über die Publicistik des dreissigjährigen Krieges von 1626—1629, Halle, 1880

[2] Copy in University Library Greifswald

weighty word to say since it was backed up by silver. The broad masses in Germany rightly feared that the expansive ambitions of Spain would impose a heavy burden on them, too. It is not difficult to identify an incipient feeling of nationalism in the anti-Spanish propaganda literature and satire. This is indicated by the titles of news-sheets and leaflets: "Spanish Wolf's Gut" (1625), "Spanish Fish-Hook" (1630), "Spanish enormous Thirst" (1632) or "Spanish Soporific" (1620).

The anti-papist texts, directed against the Jesuits and Spain, echo the spirit of the great Reformist movement among the people and in scholarly circles but without its radical and progressive tone. With the triumphal progress of Calvinism, a new adversary appeared for the followers of the "Augsburg Confession"—Lutherism—organized by the authorities. But even Calvinism, the "Reformed" faith, had been harnessed by the beginning of the 17th century for the exercise of princely authority and the interests of foreign policy. Thus there were not only two different religious camps within Protestantism but also two groups of rulers: the Electorate of Saxony was regarded as the stronghold of orthodox Lutherism while the Palatinate was the bastion of restless, rebellious Calvinism. The scribes of the two camps—much to the satisfaction of the Catholic powers—missed no opportunity of waging a war of words with each other.

Mathias Hoë von Hoënegg, the all-powerful court-chaplain of the Electorate of Saxony, who normally indulged in violent tirades against the "papists" and Jesuits, was no less active in his attacks on the "Calvinist arch-lies" and thundered—in complete harmony with his lord and master at Dresden—against the "Calvino-Turkish" rebellion in Bohemia. There were Lutheran theologians who said that with two or three hundred reasons they could easily prove that the doctrine of Calvin was worse than that of the Devil. Many Lutherans believed that to be buried in the same consecrated earth as Calvinists was blasphemy.[1]

Such invective, filled with hatred, was repaid in kind by Reformed theologians and preachers who were said to have a particularly accurate knowledge of the Bible. It was asserted that the Lutherans "spawned" with the papists and that they were ruthless "smiths of peace", strong in drinking and weak in faith. In general, however, the supporters of the Reformed Church were apparently less malicious and readier for reconciliation than the disciples of the Augsburg Confession.

The authors of Catholic texts did indeed wage this war of the pens with increasing bitterness but they were mainly on the defensive—a position into which they were forced by the unrelenting attacks of the Protestant scribes. Their forte was that they could call on a power which was of weighty slow pace—tradition. Time had a consecrating effect, especially as the old faith assumed a new guise. The defenders of the increased claim to power of the Catholic Church showed that they were equal to the malevolent torrent of words produced by their opponents. In 1617, a Franconian vicar distributed a pamphlet entitled "Evangelical Pot-Cheese", depicting Lutheran preachers licking from a pot of this rotten, stinking cheese, crawling with maggots. This "harbour-cheese" was said to be a real "Contrafactur"—an image—of the Augsburg Confession. Two counter-pamphlets immediately appeared with the title "Catholic Pot-Cheese".[2]

199 The title-page of the "Aviso", a weekly newspaper with a wide circulation, covered a large area, as is evident from the place-names. The vignette (woodcut) is a vivid representation of the "newsboy" with his lance and horn. From: Schoene, *Die Deutsche Zeitung*

[1] Much information on this in Janssen, J. J.: Geschichte des deutschen Volkes, vol. 5

[2] Ibid, p. 453ff.

The temporal rulers were somewhat dismayed at this furious polemic which was difficult to restrain. They attempted to control it by bans on speeches and publications but wihout apparent success. It must be assumed that the paper-mills, despite the destruction of war, were still able to produce sufficient writing material for such texts and that it was not such a bad time for the printers. For their part, the feuding princes and their paid scribes developed a spectacular war of revelations. The words of the Swiss satirist Johannes Grob, who still had close links with the humanist and reformist poetic tradition, might well be used for them, too:

> "Die Feder und das Schwert verrichten grosse Sachen,
> Sie können beide Krieg und wiedrum Friede machen:
> Die Feder gehet zwar dem Degen vor;
> Doch bringt das Schwert den Mann zu Zeiten mehr empor."[1]

("The pen and the sword can do great things, They can both make war and peace again, It is true that the pen precedes the sword, But sometimes progress is quicker with the sword.")

In the early years of the war, model examples of the *bellum chartaceum*—diplomatic propaganda-warfare—again caught the attention of large numbers of the educated public of Europe. These were revelation pamphlets which became known under the shortened title of "Anhaltische Kanzlei" (1621) and "Spanische Kanzlei" (1622), appearing in numerous editions and reprints. They both had an eventful history.[2]

Following the two-hour battle of the White Hill near Prague, there was no longer any time in the confusion of the hasty and shameful flight of the "Winter King" to take away or destroy the correspondence of the Government. It was hard enough to save one's own skin, jewels and clothes. Waggons packed full with files and other chancellery papers fell into the hands of the Bavarian-Imperial victors. Two of Duke Maximilian of Bavaria's counsellors and jurists, Jocher and Leucker, of proven obedience and skill in writing, made an expert selection of numerous letters of Prince Christian of Anhalt for the purposes of publication. Prince Christian had maintained a chancellery which, with its vigorous correspondence, reflected the efforts which were made to forge a European coalition against Spain and the Hapsburgs. It was now obvious that treasonable plots had been prepared at Prague against the Head of the Empire. It was asserted that a "Turkish Dominion" had intended to establish a "Calvinist spirit" in the Empire. The possession of the original documents, so it was said, was worth more than a battle won. They came at just the right time to justify before the world the Imperial ban against King and Elector Frederick and the loss of his lands and the electoral status. It were these two aspects which Frederick's cousin, Duke Maximilian of Bavaria, had his eye on.

But Frederick was still the son-in-law of the King of England whose goodwill was considered important by the Spanish Government, the emperor's salvation and support Madrid and Brussels were worried that James I of England might intervene in the war which had begun again against the liberated provinces of the Northern Netherlands. With papal support, Emperor Ferdinand wanted to persuade the Spanish Govern-

[1] Deutsche Gedichte des 16. und 17. Jahrhunderts, ed. by W. Milch, Heidelberg, 1954, p. 110

[2] Koser, R.: Der Kanzleienstreit, Halle, 1874

ments to agree to the transfer of the Palatine Electorate to Bavaria. The emperor wrote the letters in his own hand, sealed them and showed them to no-one. The courier set out at all speed for Brussels, the residence of the Spanish governor but he never arrived there. Soldiers of Ernst von Mansfeld, who was an advocate of the cause of King Frederick, intercepted him. The precious booty was examined and utilized for a number of pamphlets which, for the sake of simplicity, will be referred to as the "Cancellaria Hispanica". The author of these pamphlets was Ludwig Camerarius, the political counsellor of King Frederick and the grandson of the celebrated humanist Joachim Camerarius. With the aid of the letters, he presented a picture of the grim and lethal fabric of Hispano-Imperial intrigue against the Protestant world and France.

SWEDISH PROPAGANDA

Everything which had been written in the way of polemic and politico-religious propaganda in the course of the war reached a climax—at least as far as volume is concerned—when it became apparent that Sweden was about to intervene—and actually did—in the "German war". Two streams flowed together in the vast flood of paper: leaflets of German-Protestant origin and those commissioned and produced by the Swedish side. There were sufficient printers and publishers in the Empire for mounting a propaganda campaign.[1]

In Sweden, it became increasingly more apparent during the 1620's that the Royal Government and the clergy were concentrating their political and clerical influence on one aim. This was to convince the largely peasant population, which had been hard-hit by the continuing recruitment of troops, of the urgency of the struggle against the "papal yoke" which was coming dangerously closer. The intentions of the king and the aristocracy in Germany were presented as a just cause and were intended to strengthen the readiness for sacrifice and the steadfastness of the young peasant generation. Not only were a growing number of "White-Books", "Relations" and "Newspapers" distributed among the ordinary people, but the country vicars, who were loyal to the king, also propagated the religious aid for the German Protestants.

Gustavus Adolphus also demonstrated his divine plan for liberation in a spectacular manner: at the end of August 1628, the "Vasa", a three-masted warship of exceptional size (1400 T) intended for the "German war" set out from Stockholm on her maiden voyage. The head of a lion, one metre high, decorated her bows— the heraldic beast of the Vasa family. Those contemporaries familiar with Biblical history recognized the carved image of Roman warriors and the Jewish hero Gideon in bright colours on the stern of the ship which was as high as a house. The King of Sweden was often compared to him. Unfortunately, the vessel heeled over and sank.

[1] Böttcher, D.: Die schwedische Propaganda im protestantischen Deutschland. 1628—1634, Thesis. Jena, 1951, or: Archiv für Reformationsgeschichte 44—45/1953—1954

The loss of the truly royal ship did not hinder the dispatch of the military expedition and the fleet set sail two years later from Älfsnabben.

Scarcely had Gustavus Adolphus set foot on Usedom than he had the famous "War Manifesto" printed in German. Twenty reprints followed in 1630 alone and 23 different editions are known. The author of the leaflet was the diplomat and Royal Secretary Johan Adler Salvius and its content was evident from the title—like many others of its kind: "Ursachen, Dahero Herr Gustavus Adolphus ... endlich gleichfalls gezwungen worden, mit dem Kriegsvolck in Deutschland Überzusetzen und zu verrucken ..." ("The Reasons why King Gustavus Adolphus was also finally compelled to come to Germany with his army ...") The "Reasons" listed here and in numerous other pamphlets and apologies are of a diverse nature. It was asserted that the House of Austria wanted to establish a "new and complete monarchy" in the entire world; that it was restricting the "liberty" of the princes and Free Cities of the Holy Roman Empire; that the armies and men-of-war of the emperor which had moved up to the Baltic coast were intent on "dominion at sea". Formulated as "special causes", there are demagogic catchwords in the pamphlets such as the "security" of Baltic trade and "protection" for peaceful "commerces". The task of making the religious and liberating mission of the Swedish army as convincing as possible was undertaken for the most part by eloquent theologians and preachers of fervent faith such as Jakob Fabricius, court chaplain of the King of Sweden for many years. This author dealt with no less than 35 "questions of war" in his leaflet and postulated that the war in Germany, which had not been undertaken lightly, was a profoundly Christian enterprise.[1]

Although the landing and deployment of the small Swedish army, which was expanded with mercenaries recruited from the area conquered, took place successfully and the Imperial troops, much hated by the population, were unable to offer any major resistance some noteworthy events occurred in the German theatre of war in 1630/31 which put the Swedish liberation enterprise in a dubious light. Like many of the people of North Germany, the citizens of the town of Pasewalk had also breathed with relief at the news of the approach of the Swedish army and had joyfully greeted the first Swedish contingents. However, Imperial troops recaptured the town and set fire to it. The premature jubilation was followed by a cruel vengeance. "A Sad Song of Complaint", the Laniena Pasewalcensis", was immediately composed in commemoration of this fearful 7th of September 1630. It had two dozen verses and was sung to the melody of "Come here to me, saith the Son of God".[2]

As the second great torch proclaiming the resistance and hope inspired by the presence of the Swedish troops and their widely announced claim of imminent liberation, Magdeburg went up in flames in May 1631. Doubt and fearful questions made the rounds. Could not the "people of Midnight" who were called to punish Babylon (Rome and its adherents), could not the "Gothic expedition" and its King Gustavus Adolphus, who was compared with Alaric, prevent such horrifying mischief? At the same time with a wave of protest against the inhuman Imperial soldiery and Tilly, pamphlets of Swedish origin were distributed throughout the countryside, listing a series of political and military reasons to explain why the Swedes were unable to come to

[1] Copy in Municipal Archives Stralsund
[2] Ibid.

the rescue of the city on the Elbe in its hour of greatest danger. Was this not already evidence of the questionable and reckless traits of the "Royal Swedish war waged in Germany"?[1]

For the time being, however, the Swedish army, which had gone from victory to victory since the Battle of Breitenfeld, was able to advance on a great wave of sympathy. Nor did the king directly force Catholics to become converted, contenting himself with fleecing the beneficiaries of rich Catholic sinecures. In Erfurt, the king invited the city council and representatives from the guilds and the townsfolk to his headquarters and, in a speech of half an hour, explained to his "kinsmen and brothers in religion" that all those of the Evangelical faith were in the same boat in a wild and violent sea. It was his, the king's, "Divine vocation" to guide this "suffering ship of religion and freedom" to a safe harbour. He stated that Erfurt would become a "Free Republic" again but that the city would have to accept a garrison and not be afraid of labour and expense in making its contribution to the great work of liberation.[2]

In Frankfort, it was a similar story and he expressly protected the activities of the Fair by a strict decree against plundering soldiers and even prolonged the Autumn Fair of 1631 by one week so that trading losses were not too excessive on account of the war. "Wake up, wake up, all you people who are not yet Swedish" was the call made by a leaflet of this period entitled "Swedish Alarm-Clock". The picture shows a mechanism made up of all kinds of military equipment, this wondrous timepiece illustrating the predilection for mechanical toys which was evidently well-developed at that time.[3]

It was not long—and especially after the death of Gustavus Adolphus at Lützen—that the enthusiasm for the Swedes began to ebb, disenchantment and disillusionment became widespread and criticism was heard. The pamphlet "Rossomalza/Das ist: Der Schwedische Vielfrass . . ." ("The Swedish Glutton" . . .) (1644) contains words pregnant with meaning such as "Teutschland" and "German Fatherland" and mercilessly attacks the "appetite" of the Swedish politicians and generals. It is monstrous, so it reads, that they—together with German princes—greedily swallow whole provinces and cities, that they devour every day more than an entire duchy for the maintenance of their court. In the pamphlet, the Swedish Chancellor Axel Oxenstierna is unflatteringly named "ox" or "wolf's face".[4]

[1] Lahne, W.: Magdeburgs Zerstörung in der zeitgenössischen Publizistik, Gedenkschrift des Magdeburger Geschichtsvereins, Magdeburg, 1931

[2] Chemnitz: Königl. schwedischer Krieg I, p. 3ff.

[3] Scheible: Die Fliegenden Blätter, No. 31

[4] Copy in Germanisches Nationalmuseum, Nuremberg

THE VOICE
OF THE PEOPLE

There is a simple but very moving child's
ditty which was sung even in places to which the Swedish soldiers did not come and
which describes the shame of the ruination of the land:

> "Bet, Kinnl bet!
> oitza kinnt da Schwed,
> oitza kinnt da Oxensterna,
> wiard ma Kinnl betn lerna.
> Bet, Kinnl, bet!"

("Pray, child, pray! The Swede is coming now, Oxenstierna is coming, My child
will learn to pray, Pray, child, pray!")

Even at the beginning of our century, phrases such as the following were in common
use in the Vogtland: "Kinner bet't, die Schweden kummn!" ("Children, pray, the
Swedes are coming") or "die schwedische Not kriegen" ("to suffer Swedish misery").[1]

The example of the openly pro-Swedish propaganda reveals the limit of the deliberately encouraged but spontaneous expressions of public opinion. From the confusion of rumours, pamphlets and leaflets and the urgent words of preachers and "newspaper chanters", the truth which has stood the test of daily life emerges. This truth,
which took account of the basic deeds of the social and state orders, had to be of a
partisan nature. It was precisely the war which provoked numerous complaints and
protests about intolerable conditions. Most of these "democratic" songs or "folksongs
of a democratic character" were not written down and have been lost. Those of these
songs which have survived and which clearly express the social and political interests
of the oppressed people are mainly concerned with the great class-struggles of the
peasants during the war.[2]

Unlike the Great Peasants' War of 1525/26, songs of the militant peasants of the
Peasants' War in Upper Austria of 1626 have survived in manuscripts, prints or leaflets and especially the lines already mentioned which the peasants carried with them
on black flags:

> "Von Bayerns Joch und Tyrannei
> Und seiner grossen Schinderei
> Mach uns, o lieber Herr Gott, frei!
> Dieweil es nun gilt Seel und Gut,
> so soll's auch gelten Leib und Blut!
> O Herr, verleih uns Heldenmut!
> Es muss sein!"

[1] Sahr, J.: Das deutsche Volkslied, vol. I,
Leipzig, 1912, No. 10

[2] Steinitz, W.: Deutsche Volkslieder demokratischen Charakters aus sechs Jahrhunderten,
vol. I, Berlin, 1954; Hüttel, W. O.: Zur Geschichte des deutschen Volksliedes im 17. Jahrhundert, Thesis. Berlin, 1957

246

("From Bavaria's yoke and tyranny, And its harsh oppression, Make us free, Dear God, Since it is now a matter of soul and possessions, Let it also include body and blood! O Lord, give us courage! It has to be!")

A verse by the "Student Casparus"—an historically elusive preacher from Bohemia—names the social causes of the uprising even more clearly. The verse was sent to the enemy town-commandant of Gmunden. It refers to the "tyranny" and "thieving" of the senior officials and the "financial tricks" (cheating and usury) of the minor ones and to the "religious intolerance" and "conditions".

A prayer has also survived which was sung by the peasants four times daily and before they went into battle, kneeling on the ground with hands raised and head uncovered: "We therefore move in Thy name against those who oppress us". In the same year as the rebellion, there appeared a "Warhafftige Relation und Gründlicher Bericht" ("A True Relation and Thorough Report"—a title much in use at that time) which was printed in Ulm. Danube boatmen, who had supported the peasants, brought detailed news of the event home with them to the Free City—and a ten-stanza song was composed in commemoration of it. Another newspaper song of 20 verses, which has survived in a leaflet and was sung to the tune of "Wie man den Grafen von Serin singt", reveals that it was intended as a song for a "newspaper chanter" in verse five with the following words:

"Höret in kurzer Summen,
ich muss euch zeigen an,
die ihr da steht herummen,
ihr Frauen und auch Mann."

("I have to tell to all of you standing around, you women and men.") The peasant uprisings in Sundgau (1633) and Zillertal (1645) were also celebrated and commented on in terse song-form.

The numerous "peasant lays" from different parts of the Empire achieve a very moving effect with their vividness and detailed realism.[1] A pamphlet with the title "Newe Bauern-Klag" (1643) was illustrated by the art-dealer and engraver Peter Aubry with a picture depicting a soldier—the "merciless peasant-rider"—riding on the back of a peasant. At the end of the song, mercenaries are threatened outright with the vengeance of death by weapons and "well-known (peasant) instruments". Another publication parodies the boastful rise and humiliating fall of the "peasant-flayer Hansen" (1636) in a series of illustrations reminiscent of a film-strip. In the background, grim instruments of torture and retribution are ready for the felonious soldiers. Lamentations extending over many verses were also printed in such leaflets as the "Peasants' Our Father" which has survived in several different versions (1610, c. 1620) or the "Lay and Prayer of the Poor" on the constant troop movements along the upper Rhine. Words from one of the most popular hymns of the time, the "Da pacem Domine in diebus nostris" are interposed between the twelve verses. At the end, there are the optimistic but warning words from the psalm "Zerstöre die Völcker/die

[1] Strobach, H.: Bauernklagen. Untersuchungen zum sozialkritischen deutschen Volkslied, Berlin, 1964; Wäscher: Das deutsche illustrierte Flugblatt, pp. 55 and 58

lust haben zu Kriegen/etc. Dann ihre Werck sind Werck der Bossheit ..."[1] ("Destroy the nations who lust for war, etc. For their works are the works of Evil ...")

The working people continued to raise their voices in complaint and accusation and also in ridicule, even though their words were usually penned by amateur and unpractised poets, against coin-clippers, war-profiteers, greedy lawyers and usurers, language corrupters, idle fops and dandies, boasters and braggarts. To quote a simile from a many-versed pamphlet: although threatened by fierce dogs and a rough sea, the "old fiddle of truth" is still played "with a new E-string" even in hard times.[2]

In addition to the text and meaning, the pictures in the pamphlets, as a means of influencing the broad masses of the people, presented a great variety of all that which an imaginative tradition had preserved and was able to create in human, animal, objective and scenic symbolism: mythical animals, monsters, weapons, the dance of death, allegories from medicine (military surgeons, blood-letting, gangrene, tooth-drawers), from daily life and work such as the general store, the spinning-room, fishing and bird-catching, knife-sharpening, the mill, ships, wheel of fortune, bells, drums, fiddles, alarm-clocks, ladders, wanderers and pilgrims, dancing, banquets, cap of invisibility and so on.

In the face of the growing and humiliating pressure of the numerous lords and despite the arrogance of the newly emergent court nobility and the miseries of war, the working people retained their self-respect and were not just a patient beast of burden which had been largely demoralized by the war. The "Bauern-Preis" song, known since 1646, proclaims:

> "Ob mein Stand gleich ist eben schlecht,
> So acht ich mich doch eben so gut,
> Als einer der am Hoffe thut,
> Traltiralla!
> Ich bin noch mein eigen,
> Darf mich vor keinem bücken noch neigen."

("I am a free peasant, We are in a bad way at present, But I am just as good, As one who is at the court ... I am still my own master, I don't have to bow or scrape to anyone.")

Although this was no longer true of the mass of the dependent peasants at all, the memory of a better time, typical for the thinking of the peasantry of that period, was a source of strength and the expression of an indestructible will to live. In the last verse of the "Bauern-Preis" song, there appears once more—and perhaps for the last time in Germany—the immortal lines from Wat Tyler's Peasants' Rebellion in England (1381):[3]

> "When Adam delved and Eve span,
> who was then the gentleman?"

The determination to survive and the pleasure of living, love and Nature was evident throughout the course of the war. May melodies continued to be sung and

[1] Strobach, H.: Bauernklagen, p. 59

[2] Copy in possession of Veste Coburg

[3] Steinitz: Deutsche Volkslieder, No. 19

201 News-sheet
vendor and singer.
Etching by Jan
Georg van Vliet.
Art Collections
Veste Coburg

Alte Geige der Warheit / mit einer newen Quinte.

Lucas Schn: sculp:

INSIGNIA IESVITARVM.
das ist
Aller Jesuitten oder Esauitten rechtes / eigentliches vnd Natürliches / mit Schildt vnd Helm geziertes Wapen / welches sie auff alle ihre Blutdürstige Consilia vnd Rathschläge / so sie täglichs practiciren vnd treiben / an statt eines Sigills oder Prieschafft / auffrucken vnd auffhencken pflegen.

Sie haben eine Gruben gegraben vnd außgeführet / vnd seind in die Grabengefallen / die sie gemacht haben. Ihr vnglück wird sie auff ihren Kopff kommen / vnd ihr Freuel auff ihren Scheittel fallen. Psal. 7. v. 15. 16.

Publication des Friedens
Zwischen Ihro. K. M. von Hispanien, vnd der vereinigte Niederlanden, geschehen zu Antorff dens Juny A°, 1648.
Publicatio Pacis, conclusæ inter Regem Hispaniarum Catholicum, et confœderati Belgii Ordines exhibita Antverpiæ 5. Junÿ. Anno 1648.

202 Pamphlet propaganda for Sweden's intervention in the internal "civil war" of the Empire: the well-founded house of the Evangelical faith is threatened by a manyheaded dragon, the papal church. However, a ship with the Swedish flag brings succour; the aggressive "Lion from Midnight" goes on land to destroy the monster spewing fire and poison. A noteworthy point is the symbolic representation of the sources of material aid for Sweden's "work of liberation": at the mast-top of the ship, there is a cock—the symbol of France—

holding a bag of money (the grants provided since 1631) while the seaman is an armed Dutchman. Copperplate engraving by Lucas Schnitzer. Staatliche Museen zu Berlin, Cabinet of Copperplate Engravings and Drawing Collection

203 Pamphlet with a socio-critical and moralizing tone, complaining of the general restlessness of society and the misery of the people; printed in the 1620's. Copperplate engraving. Art Collections Veste Coburg

204 This anti-Catholic pamphlet shows the militant Roman Church and the Jesuit Order with all the attributes—in the form of an imaginary coat-of-arms—of sinister aggression (1620). Etching. Art Collections Veste Coburg

205 The conclusion of peace on 30 January, 1648 was solemnly proclaimed in Antwerp before a great assembly of the ordinary people and with the ceremony customary at the time. Copperplate engraving. Historisches Museum, Frankfort on the Main

206 A great historical victory was won: on 30 January 1648, the Spanish feudal monarchy and the young Dutch Republic of the merchant bourgeoisie signed a peace treaty after eighty years of hostilities ending the war and recognizing the first bourgeois state of Europe. On the 15th of May of the same year, the conclusion of peace was solemnly ratified in the "Peace Hall" of the Town Hall at Münster. In the centre of the crowded room, Count Peñeranda, the envoy of the King of Spain, his proud face revealing the sorrow which he feels, affirms the treaty by swearing an oath on the Evangelium in his individual capacity. The envoy of the States-General, Barthold van Gent, reads the oath with self-confident dignity from the sheet of paper, his right hand raised. Finally, all the members of the legation, dressed in simple black, join Barthold as he declares "So help ons Godt". The picture, one of the greatest representations of an act of State, is an accurate record of the event. The artist was an eye-witness to this solemn occasion and has portrayed himself as an attentive listener at the left edge of the picture. Painting by Gerard Terborch, who is often described as the "historian among the painters". National Gallery, London

207 Title-plate from the "Bavaria" volume of the *Topographia Germaniae* published by Mathäus Merian (1644). The allegorical Baroque décor is an antithetical representation of war and peace, ruin and prosperity. Municipal Archives, Stralsund

208 Title-plate of the *Thesaurus philopoliticus* (2nd part), filled with moral extracts, mottoes and symbols as customarily found on banners, banderols and door-decoration: endurance, steadfastness, compensation and so on. The sylvan idyll with the animals symbolizes the state of peace. Biblioteka Gdańska

209 This allegorical, satirical pamphlet attacks the restlessness and subservient position of the newspaper and also its abuse. Copperplate engraving by an unknown artist. Art Collections Veste Coburg

following page:
210 Electoral Saxon copy of the Peace Treaty of Münster (section), concluded between the Emperor and the King of France, with the signatures of the Imperial deputies Johann Ludwig Count of Nassau and Doctor Isaak Volmar as well as of the French embassador Comte de Servien. State Archives, Dresden

Güete Zeittung
Glück.

Besse Zeittung.
Vnglück.

Ich arme tochter lauff durch die Welt.
    ein ieder mir mit fleiss nachstellt.
Bin alle tag ein newe braut.
    doch leider mich nie keiner trawt.
Kan nit ein tag bey einem bleiben
    gschwind thut er mich zu andern treibe.
Kom ietzt gen Franckfurt in die mess.
    ob ich da meines leids vergess.
So gehts mir ärger als anderswa.
    iagt mich der ein zum andern da.
Man trägt mich in dem maul herumb.
    schleust mich in brieff vnd macht mich krub.

Verstümelt, verkürtzet, vnd verlänget.
    der Trucker vnder d Press mich pfränget.
Muss lauffen in Vngern, Polen Niderlaut.
    Spanien, Franckreich, vnd zuhand.
Italien, vnd gar in Türckey.
    noch bin ich meines ampts nit frey.
Dem sing ich süess, dem andern saur.
    er sey gleich Edel oder Baur.
Thu einen betrüeben vnd weinen machen
    andern zu zürnen, irnen zu lachen.
Tröst mich allein das nach meiner sag.
    all welt ihr gschäfft ordnet all tag.

qualité de Nostre Ambassadeur Extraordinaire & Plenipotentiaire, tout
ainsy qu'il auroit faict, ou peu faire conjoinctement auec led. S.r Comte d'Auaux
tant en vertu dud. pouuoir du xx Septembre, que des presentes, lesquelles se-
uiront aud. S.r Comte de Seruien pendant le temps qu'il demeurera seul aud.
lieu de Munster, & auquel en tant que besoing est ou sera, Nous auons
de nouueau donné, & donnons pouuoir special de negocier, promettre, ac-
corder, & signer seul tous Traictez & Articles, & faire tout ce qu'il jugera
necessaire pour l'effect de lad. Paix Vniuerselle, tout ainsy & auec la
mesme authorité, que Nous mesmes ferions & pourrions faire, si Nous
y estions presens en personne; jaçoit, que le cas requit mandement plus special, qu'il n'est contenu en cesd. presentes: Promettons en Foy & Parole de Roy
et soubs l'obligation & hypotheque de tous Nos biens presens & aduenir, de
tenir ferme & accomplir ce qui aura esté par led. S.r Comte de Seruien seul
ainsy stipulé, accordé & promis.   En tesmoing de quoy Nous auons
faict mettre Nostre Scel à cesd. presentes. Car tel est Nostre plaisir.
Donné à Paris le xx Jour de Mars, l'an de grace 1648 et de Nostre Regne
le Cinquiesme. Signé, Louis. Et sur le reply, Par le Roy, la Reyne Regente
Sa Mere presente, de Lomenie.   Scau en Cire jaulne &c:

Johannes Ludouicus Comes
de Nassau &c

Isaacq Volmar Doctor

200 The change from the dignified and serious dress of the old period to the courtly, decorative attire now in fashion marks an evident change in attitude as compared with the 16th century and a tendency to the extravagant display characteristic of life at court. The pamphlet regrets this change and thus expresses one of the main directions of the social consciousness of the time—nostalgia for the "old days", the "Old German" ways, instead of confidence in the future. From: Schulz, *Bilderatlas zur deutschen Geschichte*

Simon Dach's and Heinrich Albert's merry words and tunes found a firm place among the ordinary people. Yet it was an eventful period with a thousandfold everyday experience as formulated by the Silesian poet Angelus Silesius in these words:

> "Das grösste Wunderding ist doch der Mensch allein:
> Er kann, (je) nachdem er's macht, Gott oder Teufel sein."[1]

("But the most wonderful thing is man alone, Depending on what he does, he can be God or Devil.")

Devilish behaviour on the part of Man occurred with horrifying frequency and lack of restraint. The working people reacted to it with anger but also with an exceptional degree of sadness in which there is often an element of hopelessness and where the certainty of death seems to be the way out. In the song "Der grimmig Tod mit seinem Pfeil" ("Grim Death with His Arrow"), it is said that "life vanishes like smoke in the wind". Another sings of the "Reaper who is called Death" (1638) and its verses all end with the warning "Take care, beautiful flower"; only the last one reads "be joyful"—in anticipation of the life to come, the "heavenly garden". There is a folksong of 1626 which contains the line "Sag', was hilft alle Welt mit ihrem Gut und Geld?" ("Say what use is all the world with its possessions and money?") Friedrich Spee's poignant lay from his "Trutz-Nachtigall" remained in the memories of the ordinary people for centuries: "In the silent night at the first watch, a voice begins to lament".[2]

Melancholy fills what is probably the best-known song of the war years. It was used in the 1640's by a scholar as an example of rhythm:[3]

> "Es geht eine dunkle Wolken rein/
> Mich deucht es wird ein Regen sein:
> Ein Regen aus der Wolken/
> Auffs Grass und auff die Zäun."

("A dark cloud goes over, It seems to me it will rain, A rain from the clouds, On grass and fence.")

[1] Tränen des Vaterlandes, p. 235

[2] Deutscher Liederhort, ed. by L. Erk, Berlin, 1856

[3] Werlin, Johannes: Rhitmorum varietas. Typi, exempla et modulationes rhythmorum, no place stated, 1646, copy in Bayerische Staatsbibliothek, Munich

PEACE:
ACHIEVED AT LAST, LAUDED, DOUBTED

There existed an urgent longing for peace throughout the war. As soon as even a limited peace was negotiated by the statesmen as in 1629 at Lübeck or in 1635 at Prague, the working people immediately began to make preparations for living in peace and songs and hymns of thanks appeared. Strangely enough, however, the soldiers remained or soon returned, kept in readiness to use coercion on the weaker partner. And the fearful monotony of troop movements, billeting, contributions and new impositions by the local ruler began again.—This may be read in sources of an exceptionally direct nature as in the "writing calendars" (diaries), a long series of which were kept by a citizen of Minden and are still in existence.[1]

The first entry by this sober man dates from 1642: "Hopefully there will be peace throughout the year"—and he noted that repair-work was in progress during the warmer months on public buildings—including dance-floors—and the town-gates. In the following year, the writer recorded an event of rare joy: the casting of a large bell. It is clear, too, that the news rapidly made the rounds that the Swedish envoy Johan Adler Salvius had passed through to take part in the peace negotiations which finally began in July 1643 in Osnabrück. And now, at the beginning of every year, there is a prayer for peace, that it be "good" and "eternal". In the Autumn of 1648, the municipal coaches again carried the Swedish envoy but on this occasion he had a precious document with him: the "Instrumentum Pacis", known as the "Peace of Westphalia" from the towns of Münster and Osnabrück where the negotiations were held. There can have been few occasions in history when a treaty of this kind took longer to negotiate than this.[2]

These two towns, which could hardly be described as large with their 10,000 inhabitants, had to shelter for some years an equal number of guests since 150 official delegations arrived to arrange the ending of the "European war" with a comprehensive peace treaty. The representative of the mighty states came with great pomp and circumstance, past glaring poverty in town and country, together with their numerous families, servants and scribes. All this was necessary since the other side in the protracted negotiations had to be outmanoeuvred by the spreading of rumours, the acquisition of confidential information and bribery. It was also impossible to prevent crowds of beggars streaming into the town; whores made preparations to welcome a numerous clientele; clowns and English and Polish comedians provided entertainment and amusement; painters and engravers set up their studios and the celebrated Dutch

[1] Copy in Municipal Archives Stralsund

[2] Meiern, J. G.: Acta Pacis Westphalicae oder Westfälische Friedensverhandlungen und Geschichte, 6 vols., Hanover, 1734—1736; Bougeant, G. H.: Histoire du traité de Westphalie ..., 6 vols., Paris, 1875; Odhner, C. T.: Sveriges deltagende i Westfaliske fredskongressen, Stockholm, 1875; Sveriges Tractater med främmande magter jemte andra dit hörande handlingar, vol. V/2, Stockholm, 1909; Pax optima rerum. Beiträge zur Geschichte des Westfälischen Friedens 1648, ed. by E. Hövel; Münster, 1948; Braubach, M.: Der Westfälische Friede, Münster, 1948; Dickmann, F.: Der Westfälische Frieden, Münster, 1959

artist Gerard Terborch painted the portraits of the leading delegates, a task which kept him busy for several years.

The envoys at the Peace Congress spent the whole of 1644 arguing about reciprocal modes of address and protocol. Such behaviour might well seem ludicrous but it was motivated by efforts to avoid taking the responsibility for this or that step or measure. To begin with, none of the diplomats was prepared to make certain proposals or name subjects to be discussed since they all wanted to retain a free hand. It has to be remembered that bloody battles were still being fought and campaigns were still sweeping across the Empire. In 1643, Sweden had attacked Denmark and occupied extensive areas along the Baltic coast. At the same time, a Turkish fleet had landed on Crete, marking the beginning of a war lasting 25 years with Venice. Contarini, the conciliating and highly polished representative of Venice urged the delegates to reach agreement without delay since they had to move against the "arch-enemy" with united forces. He also pointed out that in this way it would also be possible to dispose of the armies, which were becoming more and more of a burden with their demands, and their ever more numerous camp-followers.[1] As it was, the questions which had to be settled —the property of the Church, the legal classification of the many Estates of the Empire, the remuneration of the soldiers and the recognition of the Reformed Church —were too involved and the procedure for dealing with them too complicated and long-winded.

A powerful and positive influence on all this was exercised by the conclusion of the separate Peace of Münster between Spain and the liberated Netherlands on 30 January 1648. After the people of Catalonia had risen in rebellion and Portugal had broken away from the Spanish monarchy in 1640 and after the silver fleets from America had fallen victim to the depredations of Dutch privateers and the Crown had had to suspend all payments, the decline of Spain as a once-proud world-power was not to be denied. It received a further blow in Naples and Sicily in 1647 when there was a mass-uprising by the people in protest against the merciless taxation imposed by the Spanish viceroy and the local barons. The people were led by Tommaso Aniello (Masaniello), a fisherman of Naples who called himself "Capitano generale del fidelissimo Popolo". Money and troops in considerable numbers had to be sent to Italy to re-establish the authority of the Government in the Spring of 1648. It was no wonder that the emperor waited in vain for Spanish financial assistance.[2]

With the conclusion of peace between Spain and the Republic of the United Netherlands, there ended one of the longest and most uncompromising conflicts of European history. This peace after an "eighty years' war" marked the appearance of the first bourgeois republic on the European political scene and, at the same time, initiated a more peaceful phase in the "Golden Age" of Dutch-Zealandish mercantile capital. This was not without benefit for the material and intellectual progress of all the nations of Europe but, simultaneously, not without negative consequences either for those regions overseas which were ruthlessly plundered by Dutch businessmen, the wealthy "Mijnheers".[3]

From England, alarming news reached the ears of the kings and their envoys, accustomed to divine power, in Münster and Osnabrück. The troops of Parliament,

[1] Acta Pacis Westphalicae, Series III A (Protocols), vol. 4, 1: Die Beratungen der katholischen Stände 1645—1647, Münster, 1970, No. 28

[2] Villari, R.: La rivolta antispagnola i Napoli. Le Origini, Bari, 1967

[3] Dillen, J. G. van: Van Rijkdom en Regenten. Handboek tot de economische en sociale Geschiedenis van Nederland tijdens de Republik, s'Gravenhage, 1970; Wittman, T.: Das Goldene Zeitalter der Niederlande, Leipzig, 1975 (Hungarian edition 1970)

representing the middle-class and the country nobility, especially the hard-hitting and bold "Ironsides" under the command of Oliver Cromwell, had seized power in England. King Charles was convicted of high treason and was executed in 1649. This event, the subject of many pamphlets and leaflets, was a great shock for the monarchs of the Continent. The well-informed diplomat Salvius, who was not at all of a nervous disposition, wrote that there were uprisings of the people against their rulers everywhere—*seditiones populi contra principes*—even in China and Turkey, in France, Germany and Poland. Radical voices were to be heard from the revolt of the aristocracy and Parliament in France—which was supported on a large scale by the ordinary people—calling for the same fate for the young King Louis XIV as that suffered by Charles I of England. Even in Sweden, there was no end to the unrest among the peasants who had suffered so much from the eternal war and the repeated raising of troops. The young Queen Christina wrote at the beginning of 1647 that if the opportunity was not now taken to conclude peace, a "great upset" could be expected in political affairs. A general compromise had to be decided in Münster and Osnabrück since the voice of the people was taking on a threatening tone. A deaf ear had to be turned not only to the urging of the project-makers with their interest in war but also to the entreaties of the exiles from the Hapsburg countries who were desperate to return to their homeland and regain possession of the estates which had been taken from them.[1]

On the 24th of October, the peace documents were signed by the envoys of the European Powers—with the exception of England, the Ottoman Empire and the pope, who solemnly lodged a protest. This marked the end of the first, unprecedented, All-European Congress, the result of which was said by Schiller to have been the "dear fruit of thirty miserable years of war".[2] Even at the Secular Celebration of 1748, it was asserted that the Peace of Westphalia was the result of state wisdom on the highest level. At the time, millions of people saw it as the long-awaited and redeeming event which put an end to the wild and savage rule of the military. It seemed that the statesmen had at least heard the "powerful thunder and sound of trumpets" which Ludwig Friedrich Gifftheil, a vicar of Württemberg, had directed at them in passionate pamphlets, urging them to end the satanic religious quarrel.[3] In the towns, the bells were rung for hours on end to mark the conclusion of peace. Innumerable Church services and secular celebrations lauded the state of peace to which most people were unaccustomed and which they scarcely knew. Beacons of peace were to be seen burning on the hills along the River Main. Three poets of Nuremberg praised peace in numerous works since "inter arma silent musae" ("the Muses are silent when arms clash"). It seemed that a new "Golden Age" of the Arts was about to begin. Johann Rist wrote the play "Das friedejauchzende Deutschland" ("Germany sighing for peace") (printed in 1653), Sigmund von Birken his drama "Deutschlands Kriegs-Beschluss und Friedens-Kuss" (1650) which was full of allegories and linguistic artifice and Johann Klaj his poem "Geburtstag des Friedens" ("Birthday of Peace"; 1650). "Praise God", wrote Paul Gerhard, "the true word of peace and joy has sounded". Many poets, in the fashion of the age, were tireless in the formulation of similes and imagery: swallows nested in military helmets, ploughs and spades were forged from pikes and swords, pipes were

[1] Šindelář, B.: Vestfálský mír a česká otázka; Poršnev: Francija, anglijskaja revoljucija; idem: Narodnye vosstanija vo Francii pered Frondoj (1623—1648), Moscow/Leningrad, 1948; (German Leipzig, 1954, French Paris, 1963)

[2] Prologue to Schillers' "Wallenstein"

[3] Schleiff, A.: Selbstkritik der lutherischen Kirchen im 17. Jahrhundert, Berlin, 1937, List of Authors No. 54

lit with slow-matches. The cavalry steed hauled a plough and banners served as signs for taverns.[1]

But the war had ravaged too long and the signs and memories of suffering and loss were still too fresh for people to believe that the peace would last. Soldiers were encamped or on the move everywhere. Their commanders had to take determined action to expel them from the land and a separate congress had to be held to implement the military consequences of peace, demobilization and compensation for the restless masses of sodiers. The Execution Congress took place in Nuremberg and, in the course of the proceedings, a "Peace Banquet" was arranged for the generals.[2] Twelve chefs supplied the tables in the splendid Town-Hall with 150 meals of six courses each, not to mention the mountains of cakes and confectionery. The fifth course consisted of garden fruits, some of which were served on dishes and others hanging on little green trees. A pleasant aroma came from the incense concealed in the foliage and four choirs on the corner-galleries of the great room intoned the Te Deum, psalms and hymns of praise in honour of peace in an "artistic and delightful" manner.

Two centre-pieces with ingenious figures and slogans catered for moral uplift. The one, an *Arcus Triumphalis Concordiae* with innumerable inscriptions, was supposed to symbolize the unanimity of the three monarchs of Germany, France and Sweden while the other was decorated with an eagle—the heraldic beast of the emperor— sitting peacefully in its nest, a cock—the symbol of France—crowing from its perch on a helmet and a lion, recumbent on a shield and a sword. Large quantities of bread were distributed to the curious and hungry people in the streets and squares and two oxen, roasted on the spit, supplied an appetizing aroma. The wine to wash this down flowed from the snarling jaws of a hollow lion of wood and cardboard, which held a broken sword in its right paw and a palm-branch in its left.

At a late hour in the evening, one of the diners suggested that they should play soldiers once again. To the accompaniment of much noise, the guests formed closed ranks and Lieutenant-General Piccolomini, the Imperial negotiator, put himself at the head of the parade as "captain" and marched up to the castle by the light of torches. On their arrival there, cannons and muskets were fired while on the way back the individual gentlemen were released from military service "as a jest".

A few months later, on 22 June 1650, another celebration took place in the Free City, this being to commemorate the successful activities of the commissioners who had organized the "Satisfaction" and demobilization of the soldiers. The children made their own contribution to the festivities. Their delight in war games had given pleasure —or cause for concern—to the citizens even in times of peace. On this occasion, a noisy crowd of almost 1,500 boys rode through the streets on hobbyhorses to the residence of Piccolomini. The latter responded to the children's parade with a gesture in grand style: without delay, he had square "peace pennies" of silver minted, bearing a hobbyhorse rider on one side and the Imperial eagle on the other, and had them distributed to the jubilant children.[3]

The entire "programmed" behaviour of the princely organizers was as hollow as the giant figures at such peace celebrations. The lives of the working people continued to be marked by long years of privation. Nevertheless, their genius gradually achieved

[1] Weithase, I.: Die Darstellung von Krieg und Frieden in der deutschen Barockdichtung, Weimar, 1953

[2] Kurtze Beschreibung/Des Schwedischen Friedensmahls/Gehalten zu Nürnberg den 25. Herbst-Monats des Jahres 1649. Copy in Municipal Archives Stralsund

[3] Böhme, F. M.: Deutsches Kinderlied und Kinderspiel, Leipzig, 1897, p. 418

a return to peaceful life and transformed the end of violence and "Germany's destruction" into a new beginning. The number of marriages rose rapidly and the birth figures even more so. The ruling feudal authorities as the representatives of law and order again introduced new obligations. In an "Eclogue or Conversation between Two Herdsmen about War and Peace", one of them remarks:[1]

> "Du alberner Tropf, du bist ja wohl betrogen;
> Hat der Soldat dich nicht gänzlich ausgezogen,
> Der Schlösser Amtmann kommt, der Schreiber und Fiskal,
> Die nehmen Haupt und Haar und bringen neue Qual."

("You poor fool, you've been tricked; As if the soldier had not stripped you entirely, There comes the bailiff from the castle, the scribe and the tax official, They take hair and head and bring new torments.")

Bitter though the lines were which Friedrich von Logau wrote at the end of the war—they were really true: "Der Fried ist ungewiss, Ruchlosigkeit gewisser. Viel Frevler hat es noch, und wenig rechte Büsser."[2] ("Peace is uncertain, wickedness more certain. There are many evil-doers still and few real penitents.") Half a century later, a good judge of intellectual life wrote in retrospect: "As regards the outcome of the war, it is described as very welcome by the majority but on the other hand it is held to be insufficient."[3] The most obstinate sceptics frequently quoted the Latin saying: "Mars gravior sub pace latet"—under peace a worse war is often waiting. To a few far-sighted contemporaries such as Czepko, Scultetus, Logau or Grimmelshausen, it seemed that genuine and lasting peace was only possible on the basis of friendship between people and nations. In their dream of the future, farms would flourish and busy cities be full of diligent people only when resources were in the hands of those who dwelt there and cared for them.

[1] Lamprecht, K.: Deutsche Geschichte, 2nd section, 2nd vol., p. 354

[2] Horn: Die Poesie und Beredsamkeit der Deutschen, p. 213

[3] Arnold, G.: Unparteiische Kirchen- und Ketzerhistorie, selected and edited by R. Riemeck, Leipzig, 1975 (first published 1699/1700)

APPENDIX

CHRONOLOGICAL TABLE

year	Political and military events, principally in Central Europe	Economics, social life, social climate	Science, technology	Art, architecture, literature, music
1600	Repeated attempts by Protestant princes of the Holy Roman Empire to form a Union (to 1608); Peasant rebellion in Salzkammergut (to 1602)	End of the elimination of Calvinism in the Electorate of Saxony; signs of insanity in Emperor Rudolf II	Bruno burnt in Rome	Lorrain and Calderón born
1601		Execution of Krell, the chancellor of the Electorate of Saxony; Dutchmen in Japan	Death of Tycho de Brahe	Moscherosch born; Shakespeare: Hamlet
1602	Completion of the re-catholicization of Central Austria under Archduke Ferdinand, the later emperor	Dutch East India Company	Guericke born; Galileo: laws of gravity	Caravaggio: Burial of Christ (1602—1604); de Key: Haarlem meat market
1603	Death of Elizabeth; Stuarts ascend the English throne (James I)		Althusius: Politica	Academia dei Lincei Florence; Reichle: portal group of the arsenal at Augsburg
1604	Chapter of Paderborn re-catholicized; popular uprising in Hungary/Transylvania against Catholic-Hapsburg expansion (Bocskaj, leader up to 1606)	Most of Siberia conquered by Russia	Kepler: Astronomia pars Optica; F. Bacon: Nova Atlantis (Utopia)	Logau born; Shakespeare: Othello
1605		death of de Bèze (disciple of Calvin); Lübeck stock-exchange founded	Modernization of the fortifications of Ulm	Cervantes: Don Quixote (2nd part 1615)
1606	Emperor concludes peace with Turks (Zsitva-Torok), later extended; peasant rebellion in Russia (Bolotnikov)	rapid growth in depredations of Corsairs in the Mediterranean		Brouwer, Rembrandt, and Sandrart born

year	Political and military events, principally in Central Europe	Economics, social life, social climate	Science, technology	Art, architecture, literature, music
1607	Uprising by Protestant citizens in Donauwörth, occupation of the Free City by Bavaria as blow against the "liberty" of the non-Catholic rulers	1st Spanish state-bankruptcy; Jesuit mission in Paraguay founded		Hollar born; Monteverdi: "Orfeo" opera; Holl: Augsburg arsenal
1608	Founding of "Union" under Palatine leadership; break-up of the Reichstag at Regensburg	Climax of trade between Seville and America	Torricelli born; Lippershey and others: telescope	Milton born
1609	Emperor guarantees religious freedom to Bohemian Estates: Letter of Majesty; founding of the "League" of Catholic princes, truce between Spain and the Republic of the Netherlands (to 1621)	Beginning of the expulsion of the Moriscos from Spain; 1st German weekly newspaper; Amsterdam: "Wisselbank"; great upswing in Dutch marine trade	Kepler: Astronomia Nova; Grotius: Mare liberum	Schönfeld born; Elsheimer: The Flight to Egypt
1610	Dispute over Cleves-Jülich succession; murder of Henry IV of France; Polish troops in Moscow (false Demetrius to 1612)	Tea-drinking introduced in Europe	Scheiner and Galileo observe sunspots (to 1612)	Death of Elsheimer in Rome; Stefano della Bella born; Death of Caravaggio
1611	Revolt by Protestant citizens in Aachen; intervention of Spain and the Netherlands, Imperial ban; Kalmar war between Sweden and Denmark	Devastation by Passau soldiery in Upper Austria and Bohemia (1612)		Quevedo: Sueños; Solari: Salzburg Cathedral (to 1628)
1612	End of the "Brothers' Quarrel" in the House of Hapsburg: overthrow and death of Rudolf II, election of his brother Mathias as emperor	Dismissal of the Passau soldiery	Ratke's programme of educational reform before the Reichstag at Frankfort—unsuccessful	Böhme: Aurora
1613	Alliance between the Union and the Netherlands; major Turkish invasion of Hungary; Mikhail Feodorovich (Romanoff), son of the Metropolitan Pilaret, elected as Tsar	Denmark hampers Hanseatic trade by repressive customs policy		
1614	Catholic restoration in Aachen with aid of Spanish troops; civil revolt in Frankfort on the Main under Fettmilch; Swedish invasion of Russia	Expulsion of Jews from Frankfort on the Main and Worms and protective measures by emperor; Rosicrucian text: "Fama Fraternitas"	Napier (Neper): logarithmic tables	Completion of Aschaffenburg castle; El Greco: Ascension of Mary

year	Political and military events, principally in Central Europe	Economics, social life, social climate	Science, technology	Art, architecture, literature, music
1615	Civil unrest in the Electorate of Brandenburg following the introduction of Calvinism	Gradual spread of the use of tobacco in Western Europe (to c. 1630)	1st microscope University of Frankfort on the Oder reformed	Rubens: The Last Judgment Holl: beginning of Augsburg Town Hall
1616	Alliance between Hanseatic League and Netherlands Republic; execution of Fettmilch and associates	Teachings of Copernicus officially banned; Galileo warned by Inquisition	1st military academy at Siegen (to 1619)	Death of Cervantes and Shakespeare; Gryphius born; Hals: George's archers
1617	Ferdinand of Styria elected King of Bohemia; peace of Stolbovo: Narva and other Russian territories to Sweden; Treaty of Oñate between emperor and Spain			Opitz: Aristarch; Weimar: Fruitful (language) society; Terborch born

THIRTY YEARS' WAR (1618—1648)

1st Period: Bohemian-Palatine War

year	Political and military events, principally in Central Europe	Economics, social life, social climate	Science, technology	Art, architecture, literature, music
1618	23rd May: Defenestration of Prague —beginning of the rebellion of the Bohemian nobility against the Emperor	Great anxiety at appearance of comet; royal copper company in Sweden	Harvey discovers double circulation of the blood (1628: De motu cordis)	Murillo born; Rubens: The Fall of the Damned (to 1620)
1619	Death of Mathias, election of Ferdinand II as emperor, Confederation of the Estates in the Bohemian and Austrian territories; removal of Ferdinand as king and election of Elector Frederick of the Palatinate; Bohemian and Imperial troops clash in Bohemia, Moravia and Austria; another unsuccessful Polish attack on Moscow	Climax of Hanseatic trade; economic crisis in Italy (to 1622); banks founded in Hamburg and Venice, major political crisis in United Netherlands	Burning of the materialist and atheist Vanini; Kepler: Harmonices mundi; University of Rinteln founded	Andreae: Christianopolis Schütz: The Psalms of David
1620	League and Imperial troops destroy Bohemian army in battle of White Hill; collapse of the power of the Estates and flight of King Frederick;	101 Religious emigrants from England and the Netherlands reach America in the "Mayflower";	Bacon: Novum Organum	Opitz: Trostgedicht (published 1633)

year	Political and military events, principally in Central Europe	Economics, social life, social climate	Science, technology	Art, architecture, literature, music
	Gábor King of Hungary; Polish-Turkish War (to 1621)	Bloody excesses against Protestants in Veltlin/Switzerland; arms production increased in metalworking centres		
1621	Execution of 27 Bohemian "rebels" on the Altstädter Ring in Prague; wide-scale confiscation of estates by the emperor in Bohemia and Austria, new aristocracy, first great wave of emigrants; revival of the war between Spain and the Netherlands; Swedes capture Riga	Inflation from coinage speculation and popular insurrections (to 1623); flow of American silver to Spain ends		Grimmelshausen born in 1621 or 1622; La Fontaine born
1622	Spaniards occupy Rhenish Palatinate; League troops and Imperial armies defeat enemy mercenary leaders (Mansfeld, Christian of Brunswick, George Frederick of Baden-Durlach) at Höchst, Wimpfen and Stadtlohn (1623); capture of Heidelberg by Tilly, Peace of Nikolsburg between emperor and Bethlen Gábor, who waives claim to Hungary	Emperor leases right to mint coins to "coin consortium"; propaganda of "Chancellery Dispute"; founding of "Congregatio de Propaganda Fide" for Eastern Europe	Closure of Heidelberg University	Spezza/Pieroni: Wallenstein's Palace at Prague (1622—1624); Molière born; Schütz: Resurrection Oratorium; Robbery of "Palatina" and removal to Rome
1623	Cession of Upper Palatinate and Palatinate Electorate to Bavaria; beginning of Turkish-Persian Wars (to 1639); anti-Hapsburg Pope Urban VIII (to 1644)	Inflation ended by coinage reforms; decline of the 1st great pamphlet wave	Campanella: Civitas solis; Jungius: Societas Ereunetica	Rottenhammer: ceiling painting in Augsburg Town Hall; Merian at Frankfort
1624	Relative lull in war, Tilly's troops in Lower Saxony; Cardinal Richelieu Prime Minister in France; new peace with Gábor	Founding of New Amsterdam (New York)		Opitz: Buch der deutschen Poeterey

year	Political and military events, principally in Central Europe	Economics, social life, social climate	Science, technology	Art, architecture, literature, music
	2nd Period: Lower German-Danish War			
1625	Great anti-Hapsburg Alliance—Hague Convention: Netherlands and England finance and promote invasion of Empire by several armies: Christian IV of Denmark, Johann Ernst of Weimar, Mansfeld, Christian of Brunswick; Courland and Prussia invaded by Swedish troops; Wallenstein Imperial commander-in-chief	Large-scale recruitment of troops in Empire; Hans de Witte finances Wallenstein	Grotius: De jure belli ac pacis	Maderna/Bernini/Borromini/Cortona; Palazzo Barberini Rome (to 1633); Swedes plunder art treasures in Prussia/Poland
1626	Wallenstein and Tilly defeat armies of the "Great Alliance" at Dessau Bridge and Lutter; Spaniards capture Breda; peasant war in Upper Austria	Increase in politico-religious pressure in Hapsburg territories	Death of F. Bacon	Jesuit church of Innsbruck (to 1640)
1627	League and Imperial armies expel enemy forces from Holstein, Mecklenburg and Pomerania; beginning of the conflict with Stralsund (to 1628)	Stock exchange in Bremen; de Geer's arms' production monopoly in Sweden	R. Boyle born; Kepler: Tabulae Rudolphinae	Schütz: "Dafne"—first German opera
1628	Gustavus Adolphus signs treaty of Alliance with Stralsund as bridgehead; French royalist troops take Huguenot fortress of La Rochelle	Campaign plans and propaganda wave in Sweden in preparation for invasion of Empire	Comenius begins "Didactica Magna"	Sinking of the "Vasa"; Bernini: tomb of Urban VIII (to 1647)
1629	Peace of Lübeck: Denmark withdraws from war following defeat; Richelieu arranges truce between Poland and Sweden (Altmark); Swedish Reichstag approves king's plan for invasion	Imperial "Edict of Restitution": recovery of "alienated" property of the Catholic Church; witch-hunting reaches a climax in Empire	C. Huygens born	Bernini in charge of construction of St. Peter's (colonnades)

year	Political and military events, principally in Central Europe	Economics, social life, social climate	Science, technology	Art, architecture, literature, music
	3rd Period: Swedish War			
1630	Swedish army lands on Usedom, conquers Pomerania; electors force emperor to dismiss Wallenstein; decline in numbers of Imperial army under command of Tilly	Swedish propaganda-offensive and shipment of copper coins to Empire; bankruptcy of de Witte	Death of Kepler	Plundering of Mantua and robbery of art treasures on a vast scale by the Imperial army following the war in Mantua between Spain and the emperor on the one hand and France on the other; Ribera: Martyrdom of St. Bartholomew
1631	Treaty on subsidies between France and Sweden; Tilly captures and sacks Magdeburg; after victory at Breitenfeld advance to the Rhine, allied Saxon army in Bohemia	Renaudot: "La Gazette" (Paris); Wallenstein's "model state" in Bohemia (Friedland); Spee: Cautio criminalis	Guericke: History of the Siege of Magdeburg	Swedish plundering of art treasures in the area along the Rhine known as "Priests' Lane"; Zurbarân: The Apotheosis of St. Thomas Aquinas
1632	Recall of Wallenstein, Imperial army forces Saxony to withdraw from Bohemia; Swedish army conquers Bavaria, forced to fight a battle of attrition at Nuremberg; victory at Lützen, death of Gustavus Adolphus; peasant rebellion in Mühlviertel district (Jakob Greimbl); War of Smolensk between Poland and Russia (to 1634)	Stock Exchange at Frankfort on the Main, protection of the privileges of the Fair by Gustavus Adolphus	Galileo: Dialogo; Spinoza born	Callot: Misère de la guerre (1632/33) Brouwer: The Tobacco Smokers
1633	Union of Heilbronn signed by Protestant Estates of the Empire and the Swedish Chancellor Oxenstierna secures supremacy for Sweden in Empire; great peasant rebellion in Bavaria, civil unrest in Sundgau district	Marked increase in the flight from the countryside to the towns in Upper Germany	Galileo recants before the Inquisition	Hals: St. Adriaen's archers Poussin: Rape of the Sabines; Lully born
1634	Imperial army in Bohemian winter-quarters, dismissal and murder of Wallenstein by colonels' plot; catastrophic defeat of Swedes at Nördlingen, after which they plunder and evacuate the whole of Southern Germany; peasant disturbances there	Destruction of Suhl, Swabia and Upper Rhine district plundered; stock exchange in Leipzig		Calderón: Life is a Dream Velázquez: Surrender of Breda (1634/35)

year	Political and military events, principally in Central Europe	Economics, social life, social climate	Science, technology	Art, architecture, literature, music
	4th Period: Franco-Swedish War			
1635	Protestant Estates of the Empire break with Sweden, conclude Peace of Prague with emperor; cancellation of the Edict of Restitution; France begins war with Spain (to 1659) and hires army of Duke Bernhard of Weimar for operations in Empire, alliance with Sweden renewed, Netherlands as allies; peasant rebellion in Styria (Cilli)	"Lutheran Witches' Hammer" of the Leipzig jurist Carpzov; gradual decline in politico-religious pressure	Departure of legation to Russia and Persia with Olearius and Fleming	Death of Lope de Vega
1636	Swedish victory at Wittstock, Imperial armies invade France; wide-scale peasant revolts in Southern France (to 1637); Emperor Ferdinand's son elected as German king	Biggest outbreak of plague during war (to 1638); hostilities spread over greater area	Founding of universities of Utrecht and Harvard	Corneille: Le Cid
1637	Ferdinand III elected emperor; Bernhard active against Imperial forces along Upper Rhine		Descartes: Discours méthode	First permanent public theatre in Venice
1638	Victories of Bernhard at Rheinfelden and Breisach; new treaty concerning subsidies with France at Hamburg	Revival of hopes of peace and national aspirations in person of Bernhard	Galileo: Discorsi	Schütz: Kleine geistliche Konzerte; death of Flegel; Rubens: Consequences of War
1639	Death of Bernhard and rise of his army; Admiral Tromp destroys last great war-fleet of Spain; peasant rebellion in Normandy	Last upswing in production of pamphlets		Death of Opitz; Poussin: Herdsmen in Arcadia
1640	Reichstag at Regensburg suggests peace negotiations (to 1641); hostilities still continue, however; beginning of bourgeois revolution in England; revolts in Catalonia and Portugal (independence) against Spanish Crown			Death of Rubens; Rembrandt: The Night Watch (1640—1642); Moscherosch: Philander (2nd Part 1642); death of Fleming
1641	Renewal of alliance between Sweden and France; preliminary peace between emperor and Sweden at Hamburg			Death of van Dyck; Rembrandt: Saskia

year	Political and military events, principally in Central Europe	Economics, social life, social climate	Science, technology	Art, architecture, literature, music
1642	Sweden again achieves upper hand in Empire; death of Richelieu; beginning of the Civil War in England		Death of Galileo; Pascal: 1st calculating machine	Monteverdi: Coronation of Poppaea; Merian: 1st vol. Topographia Germaniae
1643	Peace negotiations started at Münster; Swedish-Danish War (to 1645); Cardinal Mazarin Prime Minister; revolts in Central France; French army destroys Spanish élite infantry at Rocroi		Toricelli: barometer; Newton born	death of Monteverdi; death of Frescobaldi (organist)
1644	Negotiations between Brandenburg and Sweden (truce)			Milton: Areopagitica— for freedom of conscience
1645	Truce between Saxony and Sweden; French victories under Turenne at Mergentheim and Nördlingen over Imperial forces; "Cretan War" between Venice and Turkey. Cromwell's "New Model Army" defeats king at Naseby			Schütz: Sieben Worte Christi am Kreuz; Calderón: World Theatre; Paul Gerhard: songs
1646	French and Swedish troops devastate Bavaria		Leibniz born	Gryphius: Leo Arminius; Le Nain: Peasant Family; death of Holl
1647	Bavaria arranges truce with France; revolts in Naples (Masaniello) and Sicily against Spanish rule	Major outbreak of plague in Spain; State bankruptcy again	Bayle born; Hevelius: map of the Moon; Gassendi: atomic theory	Rist: Das Friede wünschende Deutschland
1648	Peace treaties of Münster and Osnabrück (Peace of Westphalia); 2nd Civil War in England; anti-monarchist Fronde in Paris; rebellion of the Ukrainian Cossacks against Polish expansion (Chmelnizki, to 1654)	Festivals, church services, plays and songs to celebrate peace		End of the Prague art collection by Sweden; van Campen: Amsterdam Town Hall (1648—1655)
1649	Climax of the English Revolution; execution of Charles I	Russia reaches the Amur	Guericke: piston-type air pump	Sandrart: Friedensmahl; Amati, celebrated violin-maker of Cremona
1650/ 1651	Execution of Peace Congress at Nuremberg; demobilization and paying-off of the armies	Cromwell: navigation Acts against Dutch sea-power (1651)	Death of Descartes (1650) Hobbes: Leviathan	Public Comedy House, Vienna

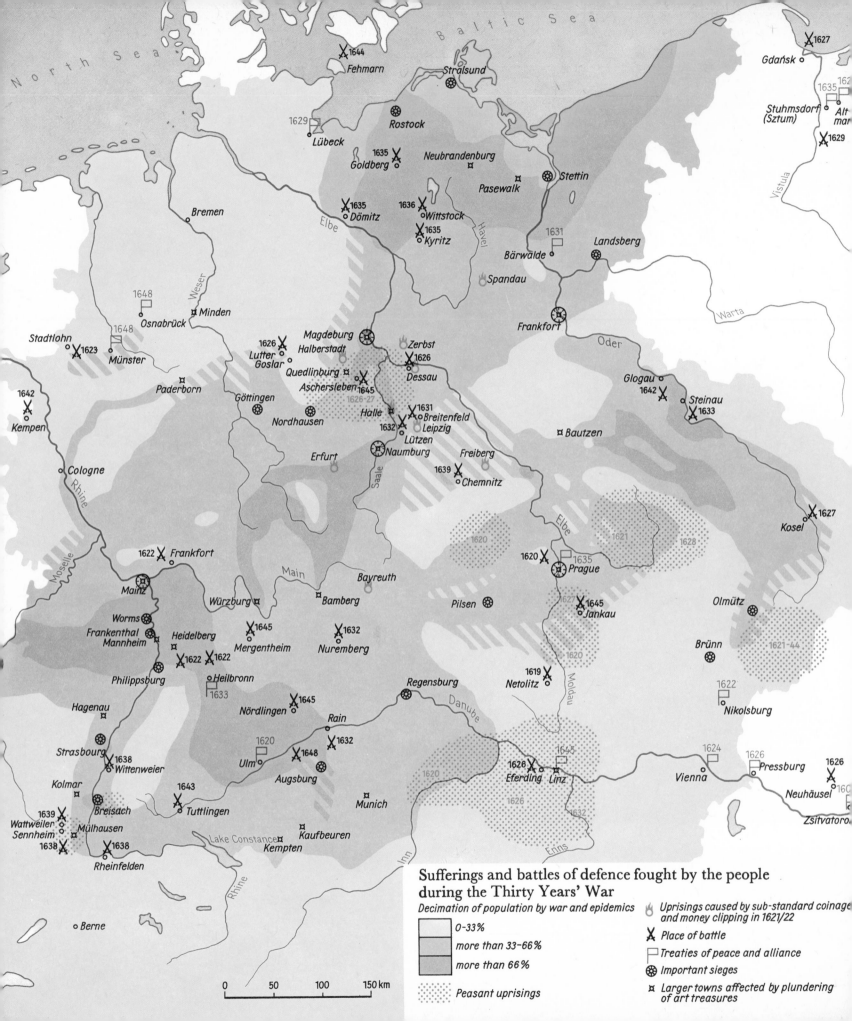

Sufferings and battles of defence fought by the people during the Thirty Years' War

Decimation of population by war and epidemics

- 0–33%
- more than 33–66%
- more than 66%

⬛ Peasant uprisings

🔥 Uprisings caused by sub-standard coinage and money clipping in 1621/22

✗ Place of battle

▢ Treaties of peace and alliance

⊛ Important sieges

⊠ Larger towns affected by plundering of art treasures

North Sea
Baltic Sea

Fehmarn 1644
Stralsund
Gdańsk 1627
Stuhmsdorf (Sztum) 1635
Rostock
Lübeck 1629
Goldberg 1635
Neubrandenburg
Pasewalk
Stettin
1629
Dömitz 1635
Wittstock 1636
Kyritz 1635
Bärwalde 1631
Landsberg
Spandau
Bremen
Minden
Osnabrück 1648
1648
Frankfort
Oder
Warta
Stadtlohn 1623
Münster
Magdeburg
Halberstadt
Zerbst 1626
Glogau
Steinau 1642
1633
Lutter 1626
Goslar
Quedlinburg
Dessau
Paderborn
Aschersleben 1645
1626–27
Göttingen
Halle
Breitenfeld 1631
Bautzen
Kempen 1642
Nordhausen
Leipzig
1632
Lützen
Naumburg
Freiberg
Erfurt
Chemnitz 1639
Cologne
Rhine
Kosel 1627
1620
1621
1628
Frankfort 1622
Main
Bayreuth
Prague 1620
1635
Olmütz
Mainz
Würzburg
Bamberg
Pilsen
1627
Jankau 1645
Worms
Frankenthal
Mannheim
Heidelberg 1645
Mergentheim
Nuremberg 1632
1621–44
1622 1622
Brünn
1620
Philippsburg
Heilbronn
1633
Netolitz 1619
Moldau
Nikolsburg 1622
Hagenau
Nördlingen 1645
Rain
Regensburg
Danube
1624
Strasbourg
Ulm 1620
1632
1645
Pressburg 1626
Wittenweier 1638
Augsburg 1648
Eferding 1626
Linz
Vienna
Neuhäusel 1626
Kolmar
Tuttlingen 1643
1645
Breisach
Munich
1632
Wattweiler 1639
Sennheim
Mülhausen
Kaufbeuren
Zsitvatoro
1638
Rheinfelden 1638
Lake Constance
Kempten
Berne
Rhine
Inn
Enns

0 50 100 150 km

North Sea

Baltic Sea

Gustavus Adolphus

Stralsund
Warnemünde
Greifswald
Wolgast
Rostock
Demmin
Wismar
Stolp
Köslin
Kolberg
Gdańsk
Stettin
Stargard

Stade
Horneburg
Buxtehude
Boizenburg
Dömitz
Gartz
Landsberg
Verden
Werben
Elbe
Weser
Havel
Küstrin
Wallenstein 1633
Warta
Hannover
Spandau
Berlin
Brandenburg
Osnabrück
Minden
Hildes-
heim
Brunswick
Magdeburg
Gustavus Adolphus, 1631
Tilly
Frankfort
Oder
Wolfenbüttel
Halberstadt
Goslar
Quedlinburg
Wittenberg
Dessau
Glogau
Steinau
Paderborn
Göttingen
Münden
Torgau
Breslau
Kassel
Halle
Merseburg
Leipzig
Lützen
Freiberg
Dresden
Pirna
Friedland
Brieg
Erfurt
Altenburg
Saale
Tilly
Chemnitz
Aussig
Oppeln
Cologne
Rhine
Zwickau
Leitmeritz
Glatz
Brüx
Elbe
Koblenz
(French garrison)
Königshofen
Saaz
Coburg
Eger
Wallenstein 1632
Brandeis
Prague
Pardubitz
Frankfort
Hanau
Schwein-
furt
Main
Kulmbach
Moselle
Gustavus Adolphus
1632
Aschaffenbg.
Würzburg
Bamberg
Bayreuth
Pilsen
Bingen
Mainz
Kreuznach
Worms
Tábor
Brünn
Frankenthal
Mannheim
Speyer
Heidelberg
Rothenburg o.T.
Nuremberg
Amberg
Philippsburg
Dinkelsbühl
Duke
Bernhard
1633/34
Regensburg
Budweis
Nikolsburg
Nördlingen
Donauwörth
Rain
Ingolstadt
Danube
Moldau
Strasbourg
Ulm
Passau
Duke of Feria 1633
Augsburg
Landsberg
Munich
Eferding
Linz
Wels
Vienna
Pressburg
Kolmar
Breisach
Memmingen
Vöcklabruck
Freiburg
Tuttlingen
Überlingen
Kaufbeuren
Mülhausen
Lake Constance
Kempten
Inn
Lindau
Bregenz
Rhine

At the climax of the war (1630–1634)

Important garrisons in November 1632

● Swedish garrisons

○ Imperial-League garrisons

← Routes and
✕ battles of great field armies

0   50   100   150 km

INDEX OF PERSONS AND PLACE NAMES

Unitalicized numbers refer to the page in the text,
numbers in *italics* to the illustrations.

INDEX OF PLACE NAMES

NOTES ON LITERATURE

The first masterly description of a social type, although Protestant in character and pessimistic in tone, was that of Gustav Freytag with the Chapter "Aus dem Jahrhundert des grossen Krieges" ("From the Century of the Great War") in *Bilder aus der deutschen Vergangenheit* (1859—1867); use was also made of "Vollständige Ausgabe" (Complete Edition) in two volumes, 1927. Ricarda Huch's *Der grosse Krieg in Deutschland* in two volumes and with a sociocultural orientation was published on the eve of the First World War (1912/14); the publication consulted here was the Leipzig edition of 1957 with the new title of *Der Dreissigjährige Krieg*. Cicely Veronica Wedgwood's *The Thirty Years War* (London, 1938), written in the shadow of the imminent Second World War, still retains its validity; the edition used here was the first German edition of 1967 (Munich) with the title *Der Dreissigjährige Krieg*. Valuable material is also to be found in respect of cultural history in J. Janssen's *Geschichte des deutschen Volkes* from vol. 5, 1886 ff. and K. Lamprecht's *Deutsche Geschichte*, 2. Abt., Neue Zeit, vol. 2; use was made here of the 4th ed. (1920). Of the many historical descriptions published in more recent years, mention may be made of:

Alekseev, V. M.: *Tridcatiletnjaja vojna*, Leningrad, 1961

Aston, T. (ed.): *Crisis in Europe. 1560—1660.* London, 1965

Beller, E. A.: "The Thirty Years War", in: *The New Modern Cambridge History*, vol. 5, Cambridge, 1970

Braudel, F.: *Civilisation matérielle et capitalisme XVᵉ—XVIIIᵉ siècle*, Paris, 1968

Chaunu, P.: *La civilisation de l'Europe classique*, Paris, 1966

Livet, G.: *La guerre de trente ans*, Paris, 1972

Mann, G.: "Das Zeitalter des Dreissigjährigen Krieges", in: *Propyläen Weltgeschichte*, 7th vol., Berlin (West)/Frankfort on the Main/Vienna, 1964

Mehring, F.: "Deutsche Geschichte vom Ausgang des Mittelalters", in: *Gesammelte Schriften*, vol. 8, Berlin, 1967

Mousnier, R.: *Les 16ᵉ et 17ᵉ siècles. Les progrès de la civilisation européenne et le déclin de l'Orient, Histoire générale des civilisations*, vol. 4, Paris, 1954

Pagés, G.: *La guerre de trente ans. 1618—1648.* 2nd edition, Paris, 1949

Polišenský, J.: *Třicetiletá válka a evropské krize 17. století*, Prague, 1970; Engl. edition: *The Thirty Year's War*, London or Berkeley, 1971; Idem: *War and Society in Europe 1618-1648*, Gambridge, 1978

Poršnev, B. F.: *Francija, anglijskaja revoljucija i evropejskaja politika v seredine XVII v.*, Moscow, 1970

Rabb, T. K.: *The Thirty Years' War. Problems of Motive, Extent and Effect, Problems in European Civilization*, Boston, 1964

Schmiedt, R. F.: "Vorgeschichte, Verlauf und Wirkung des Dreissigjährigen Krieges", in: M. Steinmetz: *Deutschland 1476—1648, Lehrbuch der deutschen Geschichte* (Beiträge) 3, Berlin, 1965

Steinberg, S. H.: *The Thirty Year's War and the Conflict for European Hegemony 1600—1660*, London, 1966; Göttingen edition 1967: *Der Dreissigjährige Krieg und der Kampf um die Vorherrschaft in Europa 1600—1660.*

In addition to the specifically relevant book on cultural history by B. Haendtke: *Deutsche Kultur im Zeitalter des 30jährigen Krieges*, Leipzig, 1906, older and newer "cultural histories" provide numerous details about the first half of the 17th century:

Döbler, H.: *Kultur- und Sittengeschichte der Welt*, 10 vols., Munich/Gütersloh/Vienna, 1972

Flemming, W.: "Deutsche Kultur im Zeitalter des Barock", in: *Handbuch der Kulturgeschichte*, ed. by E. Thurnher, Constance, 1960

Friedell, E.: *Kulturgeschichte der Neuzeit*, vol. I, Munich, 1960

Fuchs, E.: *Illustrierte Sittengeschichte vom Mittelalter bis zur Gegenwart*, 1911

Gebauer, C.: *Deutsche Kulturgeschichte der Neuzeit*, 1932

Hirth, G.: *Kulturgeschichtliches Bilderbuch*, 6 vols., 1896ff.

Lüdtke, G./Mackensen, L.: *Deutscher Kulturatlas*, 5 vols., 1928ff.

Much regional information is contained in:

Soden, Fr. L. von: *Kriegs- und Sittengeschichte der Reichsstadt Nürnberg vom Ende des 16. Jahrhunderts bis zur Schlacht bei Breitenfeld*, vols. 1—3, 1860ff.

Steinhausen, G.: *Geschichte der deutschen Kultur*, revised by E. Diesel (1936)

SOURCES OF ILLUSTRATIONS